Manual of Modern Viticulture: Reconstitution with American Vines

Gustave Louis Émile Foëx

Nabu Public Domain Reprints:

You are holding a reproduction of an original work published before 1923 that is in the public domain in the United States of America, and possibly other countries. You may freely copy and distribute this work as no entity (individual or corporate) has a copyright on the body of the work. This book may contain prior copyright references, and library stamps (as most of these works were scanned from library copies). These have been scanned and retained as part of the historical artifact.

This book may have occasional imperfections such as missing or blurred pages, poor pictures, errant marks, etc. that were either part of the original artifact, or were introduced by the scanning process. We believe this work is culturally important, and despite the imperfections, have elected to bring it back into print as part of our continuing commitment to the preservation of printed works worldwide. We appreciate your understanding of the imperfections in the preservation process, and hope you enjoy this valuable book.

DEPARTMENT OF AGRICULTURE.

VITICULTURAL STATION, RUTHERGLEN, VICTORIA.

MANUAL OF MODERN VITICULTURE:

RECONSTITUTION WITH AMERICAN VINES.

BY

G. FOËX,

Inspector-General of Viticulture, France;
Sometime Director of the National School of Agriculture, Montpellier.

Translated from the Sixth French Edition by

RAYMOND DUBOIS, B.Sc.,

Diplomé E.A.M.,
Director of the Viticultural Station, Chief Inspector of Vineyards for Victoria,

AND

W. PERCY WILKINSON,

Government Analyst for Victoria.

By Authority:
ROBT. S. BRAIN, GOVERNMENT PRINTER, MELBOURNE.
1902.

10890.

TRANSLATORS' INTRODUCTION.

Practical viticulture has undergone remarkable changes since the advent of phylloxera in Europe, particularly in regard to the reconstruction of vineyards on a phylloxera-resistant basis, necessitated by the continuous advance of this terrible scourge.

For the same reasons, these radical transformations are now being gradually but surely forced on Victorian vine-growers, and will at no distant time become imperative. The phylloxera has, in spite of repeated assertions to the contrary, gained a permanent footing in Victorian vineyards. It would therefore be absurd to ignore any longer the necessity for vigorous action in regard to the reconstitution of our infected vineyard areas on phylloxera-proof stock; costly annual treatments of infected vineyards with insecticides, on obvious grounds of expense, being simply out of the question in Victoria.

The advance of the phylloxera has proved throughout European, Asiatic, and American vineyards to be irresistible. All attempts to eradicate the insect, or even localize its outbreaks, have been utter failures, notwithstanding enormous public expenditure. It is deliberately courting disaster to disregard the costly experience of all the great wine-growing countries of the world in this matter. Phylloxera eradication and even localization have failed in every country. It would, therefore, be sheer folly to establish new vineyards in Victoria in or near infected areas except on phylloxera-resistant stock, as this method alone assures permanence.

The practical viticultural operations necessarily involved in reconstitution on phylloxera-resistant stock are, apart from the important questions of affinity, selection, adaptation, trenching, and subsoiling, identical with those of ordinary viticulture on European vines and present no difficulty to the average vine-grower. A knowledge, however, of the recent practical advances in reconstructive viticulture is indispensable. To further this object we now offer Australian vine-growers a translation of the sixth French edition of a standard manual on the subject, by Professor Foëx, Inspector-General of Viticulture, France.

Among advanced workers in modern viticulture, Professor Foëx occupies undoubtedly a foremost position. As former Director of the National School of Agriculture, Montpellier, the Professor has carried out, during the last 30 years, numerous epoch-marking studies and investigations on phylloxera-resistant stock and the problems connected with reconstitution. The results of this work are of the utmost importance to all engaged in the world's viticulture, and have already been of inestimable value to French vine-growers.

In his book, *Manual of Modern Viticulture: Reconstitution with American Vines,* Professor Foëx has collected and systematized everything of cultural importance that has stood the test of experience and proved of real utility, and presented the facts to the reader with great clearness.

The translators entertain the hope that this book may prove useful to those engaged in building up the Australian vine-growing industry, and that a spirit of perseverance and energetic enterprise will enable our growers to fully profit from the information it contains, so that they may be better qualified to meet European and American competitors, and gain an ever-increasing share in supplying the demands of Great Britain's wine-market.

RAYMOND DUBOIS.
W. PERCY WILKINSON.

Viticultural Station,
Rutherglen, December, 1902.

AUTHOR'S PREFACE.

Viticulturists are nowadays, so far as choice of remedies against the invasion of phylloxera is concerned, in two distinct situations : some possess vineyards, attacked or not, others do not possess any, as they have been destroyed. The use of insecticides recommends itself to the former, *if, however, the conditions of soil and climate are favorable, and if they are able to provide for the expense of annual treatment.* It is a means of saving considerable capital, and of continuing without interrupting the vintages. This book is not written for those who are fortunate enough to be amongst the former ; they will find in the excellent publications of Marion and Crolas, of the old Viticultural Association of Libourne,* in the more recent works of Crozier† and of Gastine and Couanon,‡ all that they may require with regard to the use of *bisulphide of carbon,* and in those of Mouillefert§ everything concerning the use of *sulfo-carbonate of potassium.* One could only repeat what has been well condensed already in these different books, they have, therefore, been left apart. We intend taking into consideration only those viticulturists who have lost their vineyards, and who cannot hope to succeed with costly insecticides. The replanting of good soils with European vines, with the object of treating them later on with insecticides,

---

* Chemins de fer P. L. M. : *Instructions pour le traitement des vignes par le sulfure de carbone,* année 1878. Paris, imprimerie administrative Paul Dupont, 41 rue J. J. Rousseau. *Instructions relatives a la disposition des trous d'injection,* &c (même edit.).
Crolas et Falières : *Des moyens pratiques et sûrs de combattre le phylloxéra.* Paris, G. Masson, 1878.
† F. P. Crozier : *Phylloxéra et sulfure de carbone.* Paris, 1884.
‡ G. Gastine et Georges Couanon : *Emploi du sulfure de carbone contre le phylloxéra.* Bordeaux, 1884.
§ P. Mouillefert : *Le Phylloxéra ; moyens proposés pour le combattre, &c.* Paris, 1878.

has been advocated; but the irregularity of the results, and, above all, the necessity of reconstituting a vineyard in the state of a patient who has to be doctored all his life, forced the majority of vine-growers to abandon this method, and in districts where practical men have already had a long experience of phylloxera, reconstitution of vineyards on other bases are preferred. These are : *Planting in sand, submersion, and the use of American vines.*

These different methods, the efficacy of which is not contested in regions where they have been experimented with for many years, have entered the period of cultural application. The areas so reconstituted are increasing every year ; we, therefore, deemed it advisable to collect all information resulting from experiments made by viticulturists of the South of France, and also those made at the School of Agriculture of Montpellier. This work, which does not pretend to be complete, was written with the object of preventing vine-growers from groping in the dark as the pioneer experimenters had to do. All facts which seem to be established by practice and justified by theory have been grouped and condensed methodically.

The scheme of this book results from the following considerations :—If one had to classify the different means of reconstituting vineyards, taking only into account the facility of execution, one would naturally place in the first rank planting in sand, which would simply be following the old track ; then would follow submersion, which means yearly cost, special precautions, but which has the advantage of allowing the culture of varieties already known, without being forced to study the question of adaptation and of grafting, and finally, replanting with resistant stock.

Unfortunately, we are not generally able to choose, and circumstances almost always oblige us to adopt a given method. Situations where the two first methods may be applied are very rare, so that the third, which may be applied anywhere, is necessarily the most used, and, therefore, plays the most important part in reconstitution. The American vines will be studied first, at the same time we intend to study the different questions relating to general viticulture, and we will make a rapid survey only of special questions concerning submersion and planting in sand. Such is the idea which originated this work, in which the author has no other object than to facilitate with practical advice the efforts of viticulturists undertaking the great work of reconstituting the vineyards of the South of France. This book is far from being perfect, and would have gained by waiting for longer experience, but it was thought that under actual circumstances it was better to be incomplete than to wait.

G. FOËX.

Colas-Montélimar,
    February, 1899.

MANUAL OF MODERN VITICULTURE AND THE CULTURE OF AMERICAN VINES.

PART I.—AMERICAN VINES.

A.—CHOICE OF CÉPAGES.

CHAPTER I.

DESCRIPTION AND STUDY OF SPECIES AND CÉPAGES.*

The cépages cultivated in America do not descend, as is the case in the old world, from a single type (V. Vinifera). They originate from distinct botanical species, possessing well defined characteristics, and endowing with distinct properties the various cépages springing from them. We do not consider it necessary to give a description of all the forms actually known, as many are of no practical interest. We intend only to study those which gave birth to types presenting some practical value, and to examine the most important forms resulting from them.

1st.—DESCRIPTION OF SPECIES.

The only species which are of value to practical viticulturists, on account of the pure and cross forms to which they gave birth, are the following:—1st, *V. Æstivalis*; 2nd, *V. Riparia*; 3rd, *V. Rupestris*; 4th, *V. Berlandieri*; 5th, *V. Monticola*; 6th, *V. Labrusca*.

(a) **V. Æstivalis.**—The *V. Æstivalis* is generally a vine of medium vigour. Its canes are climbing, large and long,

---

* This word is used as it has no true equivalent in the English language. It is usually translated as *variety*; this, however, does not convey the real meaning, as it may be applied to a species, variety, variation, hybrid, or metis. (Trans.)

and present some analogy to those of *V. Vinifera*. They are deep red when lignified. Upper portion of the growing shoot of a carmine colour; the bursting of the buds and florescence are simultaneous with those of the European vine. Leaves (Fig. 1) generally entire, but often with more

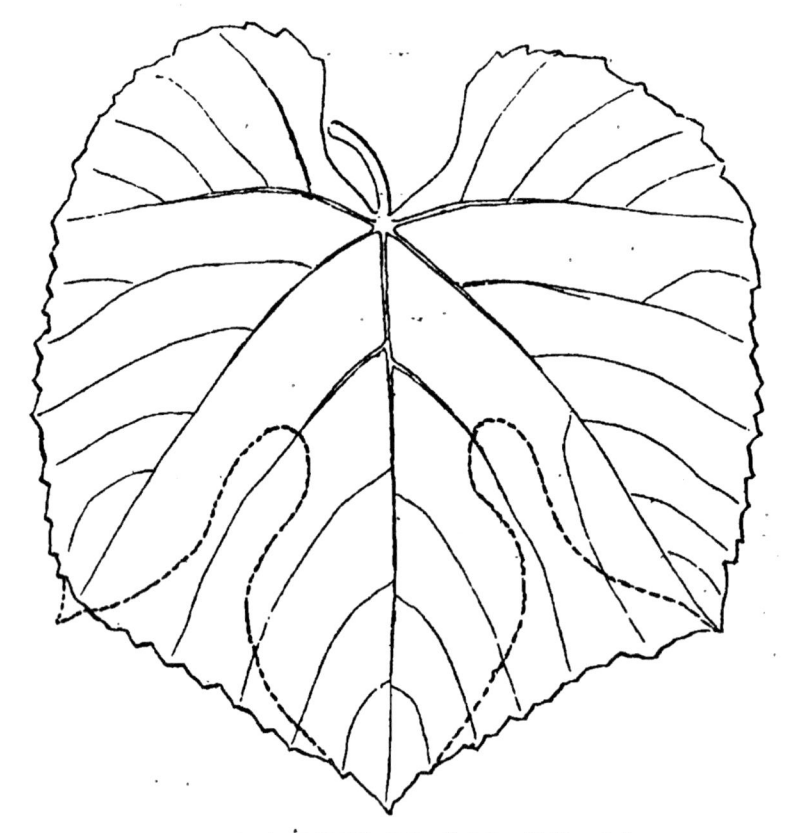

Fig. 1.—Leaf of Wild V. Æstivalis (after M. Mazade.)

or less marked lobes. Teeth blunt, upper-face dull, under-face covered with a white rust-coloured down on the principal and secondary veins. Bunches of very small berries, covered with bloom, of a peculiar taste. Seeds of medium size, from 2 to 3 in number. They are rounded at the top; beak short, blunt; chalaze circular, raphe prominent (Fig. 2).

Fig. 2.—Seed of V. Æstivalis.

This species grows in the central and eastern part of the United States. It was noticed by P. Viala in soils of old formations; it grows in the wild state in pebbly red-coloured soils rich in silica, and is also found occasionally in dry soils formed of calcareous pebbles and rich blue marl.

Fig. 3.—Leaves of Wild Riparia, young and adult (after M. Mazade).

(b) **V. Riparia.**—The *V. Riparia* is generally a slender plant of climbing habit, reaching large dimensions. Its canes are long and slender, with long internodes, cylindrical from one end to the other. The nodes are not protruding, and there are few secondary ramifications. This species is sometimes glabrous, or sometimes slightly tomentose (at the apex at least), varying greatly in colour (white, grey, mahogany colour or purple). The tendrils are discontinuous; the bursting of the buds and florescence takes place early. The young leaves remain a long time folded along the mid-rib, slightly downy on the upper portion of the shoots which curve downwards; adult leaves spread out, cordiform, with rather developed teeth, marking the position of the lobes; teeth sharp, with a few soft hairs over the veins on the under-face (Fig. 3). The bunches generally bear only male flowers, and are therefore sterile. They have the odour of linden. When the flowers are fertile the bunch is small, with small tender pulp berries, possessing a special taste, which is not so accentuated as that of *V. Labrusca*. The chalaze of the seed is not prominent, but long, and confused with the raphe sinking in the median depression (Fig. 4).

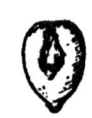

Fig 4.—Seed of Wild Riparia.

The *V. Riparia* spreads over a large geographical area in the continent of North America. It is found 90 miles southeast of Canada, north of Quebec, and in all the United States except Florida, the larger part of Texas, and in almost the whole region west of the Rocky Mountains.

According to P. Viala it grows in alluvial soils formed of rich reddish clay, or in siliceous or clayey-siliceous red soils, pebbly or not, in fertile and fresh sands, in soils formed of hard, calcareous débris, but fresh and rich, and which occupy the largest area in America. In a general way, lime does not suit the *Riparia*, especially if the lime is in a soluble form. It does not grow well in soils which are liable to get very dry in summer.

(c) **V. Rupestris.**—The *V. Rupestris* is a vigorous plant, with a bushy habit resulting from the development of a great number of ramifications. Trunk large and stout. Canes almost erect, with very short and knotted internodes. Tendrils discontinuous. The bud always bursts with young grapes, carmine in colour, emerging from the young leaves, which are shining and transparent. When adult they are small, entire, cordiform or orbiculate, sometimes wider than long, and folded along the mid-rib, parchment-like, very glabrous and very shining on the upper-face (Fig. 5). The

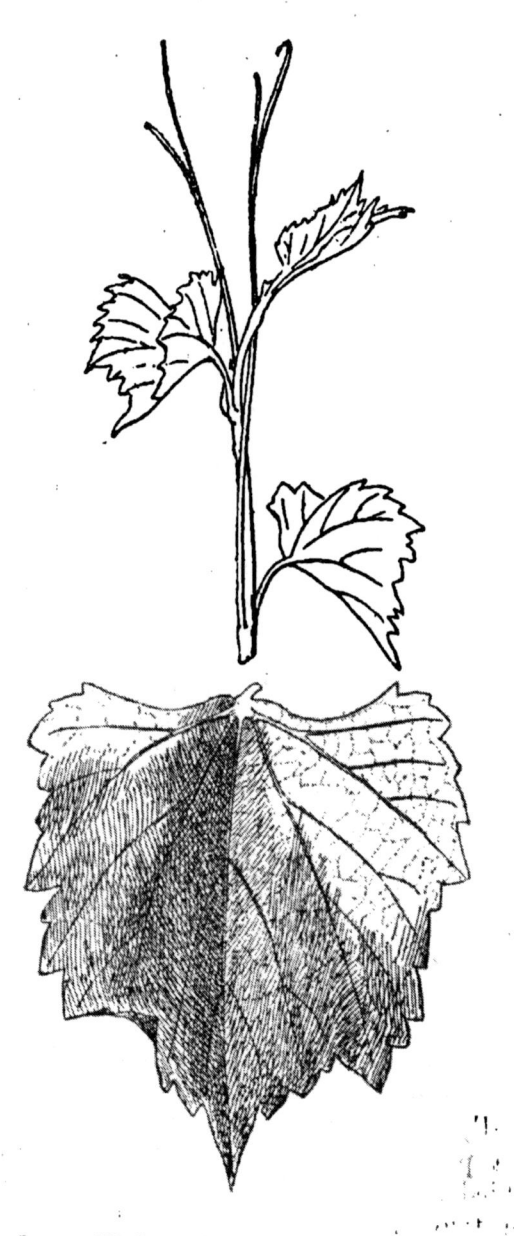

Fig. 5.—Leaves of V. Rupestris, young and adult (after M. Mazade).

bunch generally bears only male flowers, sterile, but sometimes bears small bluish-black berries without any peculiar taste. Seeds small, resembling those of *V. Riparia*, but the chalaze and raphe are less apparent (Fig. 6). Budding and florescence very precocious.

Fig. 6.—Seed of V. Rupestris.

The *V. Rupestris* grows in the southern dry districts of the United States, where it was discovered in more or less clayey soils containing numerous pebbles of silica or hard limestone.*

(*a*) **V. Berlandieri.**—Vigorous climbing habit. Trunk of medium size. Canes with prominent ribs towards their extremity, dull grey, hazel, or reddish, with fluffy hair. Buds ash-grey or slightly violet. Young leaves bronze colour, with brown hairs. Adult leaves of medium size, almost entire, as wide as long, thick, a little parchment-like, dark-green and shining on the upper-face, light-green with stiff hair on the veins and sub-veins of the under-face; margins often curled underneath, teeth blunt and very short (Fig. 8). Bunch medium, compact, elongated. Berries very small, black, with bloom, spherical. Seeds medium, stout, with a short beak, rounded and long, chalaze confused with the raphe, which is not very prominent (Fig. 7).

The *V. Berlandieri* is only found in the south of the United States, where it grows naturally in the hottest and driest soils. It is found in chalky and calcareous soils, where the leaves retain their green colour, as Viala ascertained during the course of his viticultural mission in America in 1887.

Fig. 7 —Seed of V. Berlandieri.

(*e*) **V. Monticola.**—The first forms of this vine imported into France were not very vigorous, but it seems that more vigorous types exist in America. Its habit is semi-erect; canes of medium length, slender, with short or medium internodes of brown mahogany colour, with flat nodes and a few whitish hairs. Numerous secondary ramifications. Leaves small, entire or trilobed, orbicular, or sometimes ended by a point, which gives them a cordiform aspect; slightly folded conically, with very short and blunt teeth, except the two ending the lateral lobes; parenchyma thick, parchment-like, cartilaginous, shining on both faces.

---

* Soils of such description are plentiful in the plains of the North-Eastern districts of Victoria. (Trans.)

glabrous, except at the points of junction of the veins (Fig. 9). Bunch short and conical, with small berries,

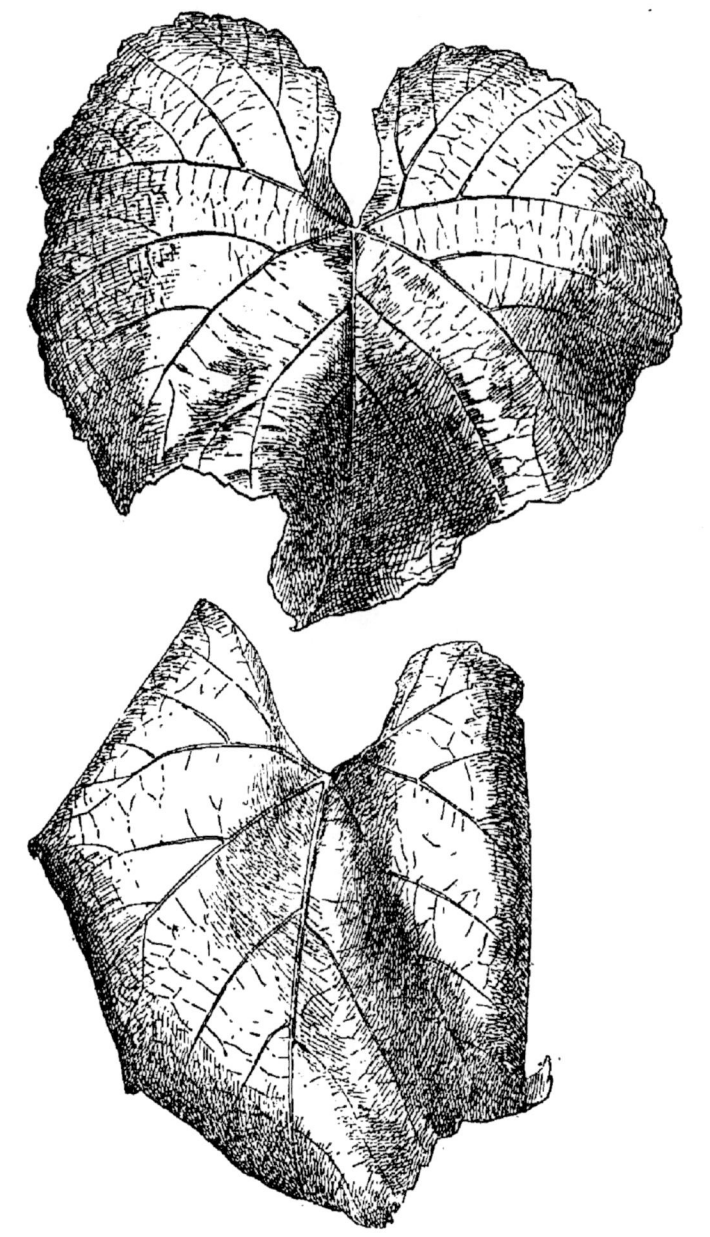

Fig. 8.—Leaves of V. Berlandieri (after M. Mazade).

varying in colour from black to pink-grey, shining, with a fine skin, tender pulp, sweet and without any peculiar taste.

Seeds flat, with very short beak; chalaze circular and protruding; raphe in the shape of a string, rather wide near the chalaze, protruding up to the level of the top depression.

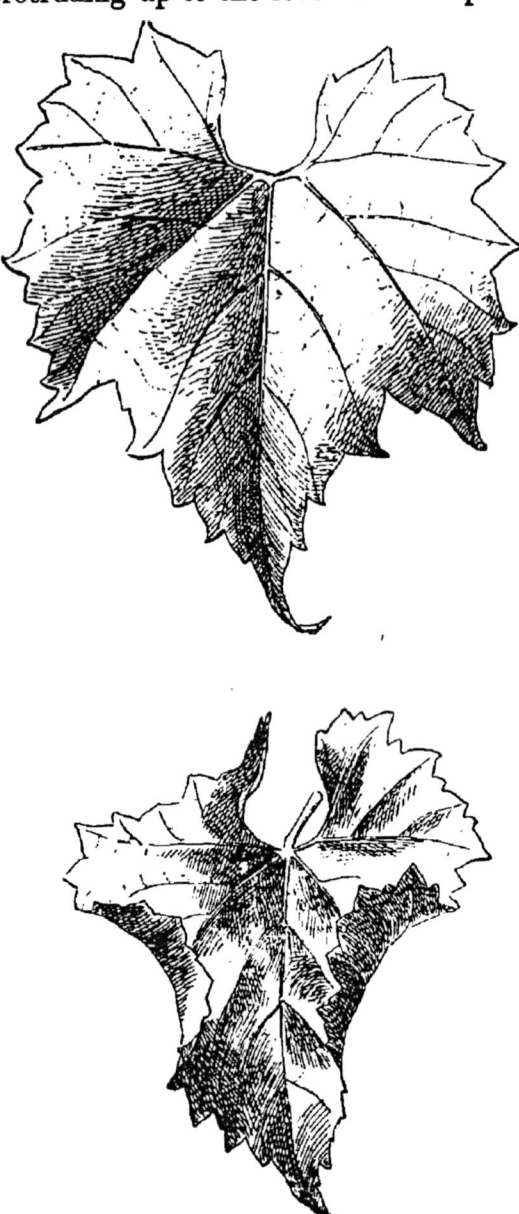

Fig. 9.—Leaves of V. Monticola (after M. Mazade).

According to P. Viala, the *V. Monticola* grows on the dry table-lands of the mountains of Texas. It grows fairly well in calcareous soils without the leaves becoming yellow. However, from this point of view it is not equal to the *V. Berlandieri*.

(*f*) **V. Labrusca.**—Species generally medium in vigour, but climbing sometimes to a great height. Canes stout and long. Sometimes its nodes are covered with glandulous hair, especially in the herbaceous state. Tendrils continuous (this is the only species with continuous tendrils). The buds are pink, and the leaves covered on the upper and under face with dense tomentum, imparting a metallic appearance. The bunches are medium, and generally shouldered with large berries, round or ovate, having a fleshy pulp of very peculiar taste, reminding one of black currants (foxy taste). Skin generally thick, maturation early; seeds large, chalaze and raphe generally slightly or not apparent at all (Fig. 10).

Fig. 10. Seed of V. Labrusca.

The *V. Labrusca* grows in the east of the United States in non-calcareous soils, and more particularly in granitic soils, covered with forests, retaining the moisture in the ground.

2ND.—DESCRIPTION AND APTITUDES OF CÉPAGES.

These different species have furnished graft-bearers either through the selection of certain of their wild forms, or been crossed with European varieties to form hybrids, utilized as direct-producers or graft-bearers. We will now study these different forms and hybrids.

(A).—FORMS DERIVED FROM V. ÆSTIVALIS.

The different forms of *V. Æstivalis* may be regarded as specially fit for direct production. The quality of their fruit, which has no peculiar taste, renders them more suitable than any other for direct-producers. The best known amongst the *V. Æstivalis* hybrids are the *Jacquez, Herbemont, Black-July, Cunningham,* and *Norton's Virginia.*

JACQUEZ.

The Jacquez (Fig. 11), although resisting phylloxera attacks, succumbs and dies if it is not placed under circumstances favorable to its vegetation. For instance, in the department of the Var, where it was cultivated to a large extent, it has generally disappeared in poor and barren regions. On the whole, it gives satisfactory results

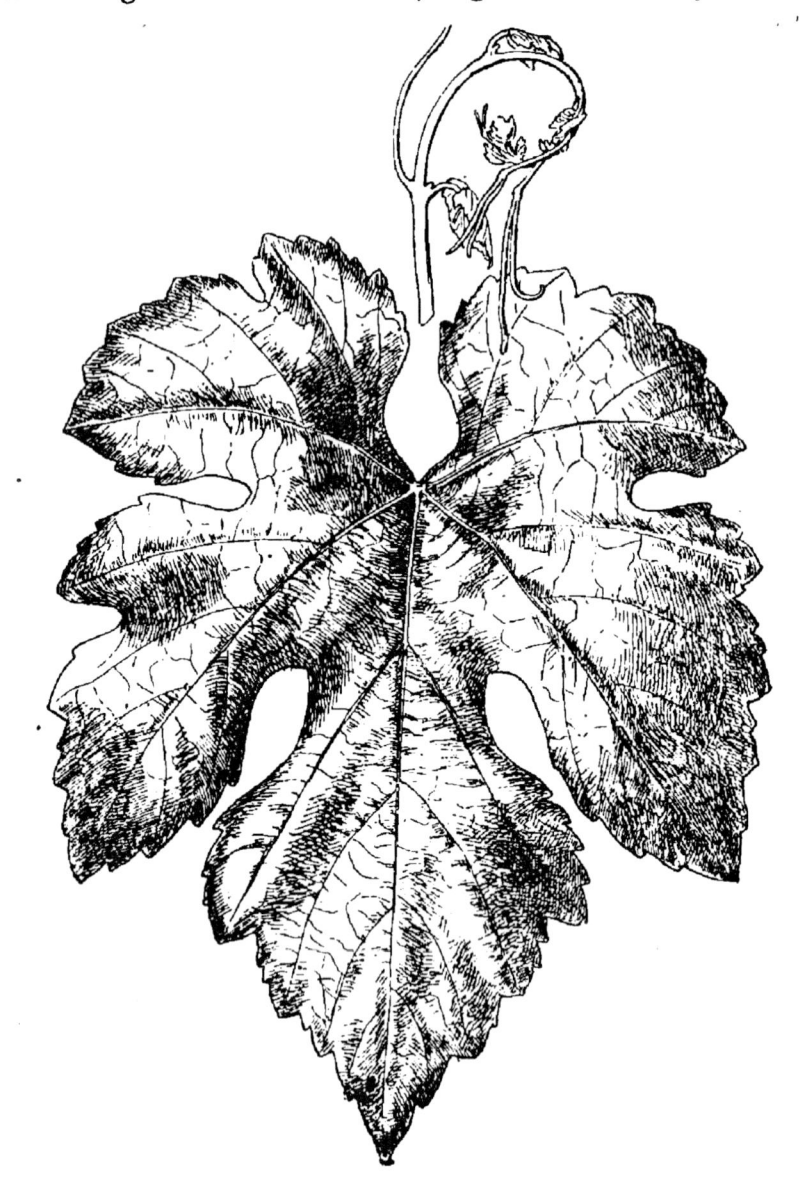

Fig. 11.—Leaf of Jacquez (after M. Mazade).

in fresh and fertile alluvial plains. Viala and Ravaz mark it 12 in the scale of resistance, which is established from 0 to 20 (absolute immunity).

This cépage was, and is even now, used as a direct-producer in some districts of the Var. The wine it yields is rather rough, of a very special taste, which is not agreeable, and is generally flat, but rather strong in alcohol and colour. Its colour, which is rather bluish or violet when the wine is made with very ripe grapes and in contact with the air, becomes of a bright red when it is made with rather early vintage, and when the percentage of acidity is increased by the addition of plaster or tartaric acid to the vat. It would be a very good wine, but is very difficult to make, and its colour is very liable to alter.

The yield of the Jacquez is not, unfortunately, large enough to compensate these disadvantages. Placed under similar conditions, it is inferior to other cépages cultivated in the south of France, such as *Aramon* or *Carignan*. This accounts for it being generally discarded as a direct-producer in countries where the vine is cultivated intensively. It was tried as stock, but its middling resistance to the attacks of phylloxera, which is more apparent after the grafting, do not tend to generalize its use. However, its resistance to lime is greater than that of *Riparia*, and it was not completely discarded until the *Rupestris du Lot* allowed it to be replaced, as this stock is equally adapted to calcareous soils and more resistant to phylloxera.

To sum up, the Jacquez, which had a certain importance at the beginning of the reconstitution of vineyards in the south of France, has been generally abandoned.

Some viticulturists assumed that there were two varieties of Jacquez, one more fructiferous than the other. Nothing up to the present seems to have proved this. We have only seen some vines producing less than others, although they were identical in general characteristics. This can be easily explained by the excessive multiplication to which this cépage was subjected, and which induced the use of cuttings taken trom sterile canes, instead of selecting cuttings only from those which had borne fruit. A sound selection of the cuttings would overcome this defect little by little, and the average yield increased. A Jacquez vine was found at the experimental station of Mas de las Sorres, near Montpellier, with a branch bearing grapes with larger berries than usual. The grafts and the cuttings taken from this branch have given rise to vines preserving this character. Danty multiplied them under the name of *Jacquez with large berries of Las Sorres*.

The Jacquez ripens its fruit at the same time as the Aramon and Carignan. However, as it is advisable to gather the crop before complete maturity, on account of the lack of acidity of its must, it might be cultivated further north and west than the latter if it were not for the attacks of *anthracnosis*, to which it is very liable. In the Gironde it grows well on the high table-lands, but dies, on the contrary, in the plains, succumbing to the attacks of this disease. The same thing applies to the valley of the Rhône and some districts of the Drôme. In the Ohio and Missouri states of the United States it has been discarded for the same reason. It can therefore be considered as a cépage only fit for the south of France, where its limits would be —Nice in the east, Carcassonne in the west, and Montelimar in the north.

The Jacquez is also attacked by *mildew*, especially its grapes, resulting in a heavy loss of crop in seasons favorable to the development of this fungus.

Although the Jacquez does not root as freely as the European varieties and the *V. Riparia*, we may obtain a satisfactory percentage of strikes when lignified cuttings are used, and if proper care is taken when planting, and especially if the cuttings are grafted.

This cépage may be pruned with long rods when cultivated in rich soils. The yield is then greater and its vegetation more vigorous.

HERBEMONT.

Vigorous plant, semi-erect habit, more spreading than Jacquez. Canes long and strong. Leaves with three or five lobes (Fig. 12), deep green, glabrous on the upperface, and light green with hair on the veins of the underface. Bunches large, long, shouldered, compact. Berries small, bluish-black.

The resistance of Herbemont to phylloxera is, like that of Jacquez, rather low (12). Like the latter, it may produce wine; unfortunately its colour is too light, and does not allow it to compete with the wines of the South. The Herbemont fructifies late in the season, and its yield, which is considered large in America—where people are not accustomed to the large production of the cépages of the south of France—is still smaller than that of Jacquez. Finally, this vine does not adapt itself easily to calcareous soils, and is very subject to *chlorosis*.

For these reasons it has been discarded almost everywhere. A few plantations only are to be found in very favorable situations of the department of the Drôme; even there it would be advisable to replace it with grafted stocks.

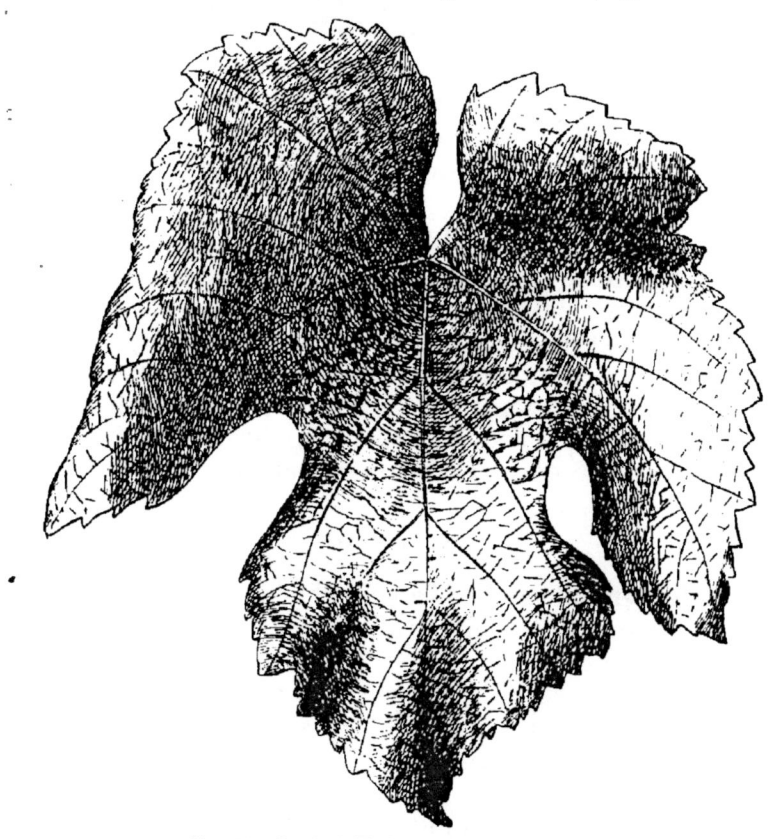

Fig. 12. -Leaf of Herbemont (after M. Mazade).

The Herbemont ripens its fruit at about the same time as the Jacquez, and is not so subject to anthracnosis. It may be cultivated further north and west. Mildew does not affect it.

Herbemont seedlings have given rise to different cépages, known under the name of *Herbemont of Aurelle, No. 1*, and the *Herbemont Touzan;* unfortunately, these variations do not resist phylloxera sufficiently.

BLACK-JULY.

Also known under the names of *Devereux* and *Lenoir* (Bush), was never cultivated to a great extent in France, and is now completely discarded. It is a very vigorous vine of spreading habit, long canes of medium size with numerous ramifications. Adult leaves of medium size, entire or slightly trilobed, deep green and almost glabrous on the upper-face, with very light down on the veins. Lighter green and shorter down forming tufts on the veins of the under-face. Young leaves trilobed, slightly whitish on both faces, with pink margins; bunch small and compact; berries small, deep bluish black.

The resistance of Black-July to phylloxera is 11, according to Viala.

The wine made from the Black-July, although not so rich in colour as that of Jacquez, may be considered as a very good table wine. Unfortunately, the small volume of its bunches and berries does not assure a very large yield. It is less subject to chlorosis than the Herbemont, but more so than Jacquez. It seems to grow in all soils which are not too wet or too cold. It ripens its fruit later than the Herbemont, and roots very well from cuttings.

CUNNINGHAM.

After Herbemont and Jacquez this has been the most widely cultivated of the Æstivalis in the south of France. It has a great analogy to the Black-July, and forms with it a group characterized by their small and compact grapes, and their almost entire leaves (Fig. 13) if compared with the large grapes, and the lobed leaves of Jacquez and Herbemont.

The resistance of Cunningham to phylloxera is 12.

The characteristics of this cépage are a very vigorous stump, a spreading habit, and long ramified canes. The adult leaves are large, entire, or slightly trilobed. The petiolar sinus is generally closed. The teeth are in two series, generally blunt. Leaves slightly goffered between the veins, of a deep green and slightly downy on the upper-face, of a whitish green, and covered with long hair on the under-face. The young leaves are trilobed, downy, and white on both faces. The grapes are very compact, medium in size and shouldered, with small black or slightly grey berries. The wine made from Cunningham, which is rich in alcohol, and possesses certain qualities, is unfortunately deficient in colour, and its grapes can only be used for white wines, which, when well fermented, have a certain value, but the meagre production of this vine does not allow it to be cultivated with advantage.

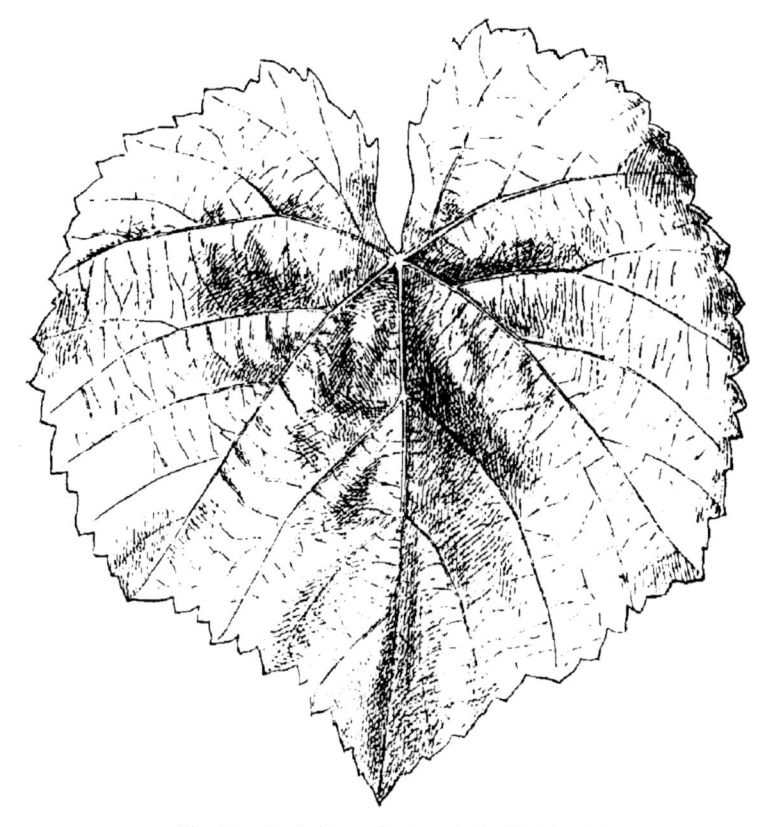

Fig. 13.—Leaf of Cunningham (after M. Mazade).

The Cunningham seems to grow in all soils, provided they are not excessively damp and cold. Among the cépages derived from *V. Æstivalis* it is the most accommodating, from this point of view. It grows better than any other in the soils formed of ferruginous and siliceous pebbles of the *alpine diluvium*. Unfortunately, its maturation is still later than that of the other cépages derived from V. Æstivalis.

Like the Herbemont it does not strike very well from cuttings. All the cépages we have mentioned above, and which had a good reputation at the start of reconstitution as direct producers, are now completely discarded.

(B).—FORMS DERIVED FROM V. RIPARIA.

The forms derived from V. Riparia seem to have been exclusively used as stock, for while the peculiar taste of their grapes and their small fertility, prevent them from being used for the direct production of wine, the facility with which their cuttings root, the small cost of their canes, the rusticity of most of their forms, and, finally, the ease with which they may be grafted with most of the European varieties, give them a prominent rank for that purpose.

Two wild forms of this species occupy an important place in the vineyards recently reconstituted. They are the *Riparia Gloire de Montpellier* and the *R. Grand Glabre*. Different hybrids, resulting from various crossings, more particularly from crossings with V. Labrusca, were used at first by the Americans. Such are *Solonis, Clinton, Taylor, Vialla, Elvira,* and *Noah*. However, they do not occupy a very large area in the new vineyards, but are to be found in certain special situations.

RIPARIA GLOIRE DE MONTPELLIER.

Synonyms: R. Gloire, R. Portalis, R. Michel, R. Saporta, &c.—This Riparia was imported for the first time by L. Vialla, on the property of Portalis belonging to Michel. He drew attention to its vigour, which was far superior to that of other known types. He multiplied it on his property at Saporta. Extended experience has confirmed this opinion, and it is now multiplied almost exclusively among the forms of this species, for the purpose of reconstituting vineyards. Its resistance to phylloxera is 19.

Description.—Very vigorous plant, spreading habit, trunk of medium size (rather large for a wild Riparia), canes long with long internodes, medium in size, flat near the nodes, light hazel colour, with a very thin and very smooth bark, covered with bloom, and with very few secondary ramifications. The young shoots are of a light purple colour. The adult leaves are very large, rounded, dull, with limb regularly goffered between the ribs of the upper-face, and with stiff hair on the veins of the under-face. Petiolar sinus having the shape of a U; sharp teeth; young leaves folded along the mid-rib (Fig. 14); flowers generally male.

Fig. 14.—Leaves of Riparia Gloire, young and adult (after M. Mazade).

RIPARIA GRAND GLABRE.

Synonym: Riparia No. 13 of Meissner's collection.—This form was selected and propagated by Gédéon Arnaud, of Montagnac, who noticed its resistance to chlorosis in the dry and poor whitish soils of that district. It may be considered one of the most robust forms of the species, and one which withstands better than any other a small proportion of limestone. According to Viala, its resistance to phylloxera is 19.

Description.—Vigorous plant, with spreading habit, trunk rather slender, canes long, with long internodes, and numerous secondary ramifications, purple during the herbaceous state, very red when lignified. The leaves are medium or small, long, without being cordiform, the sides being almost parallel. (Fig. 15.)

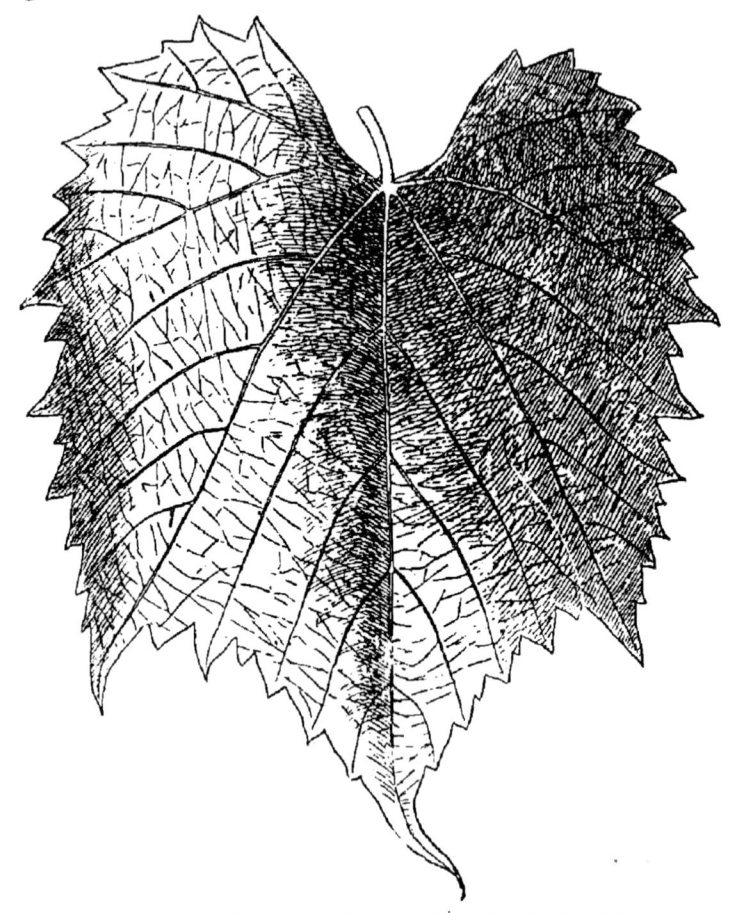

Fig. 15.—Leaf of Riparia Grand Glabre (after M. Mazade).

The *Riparia Grand Glabre* shares many of its qualities with the *Riparia Gloire*. However, it is not so widely cultivated, the latter being often preferred.

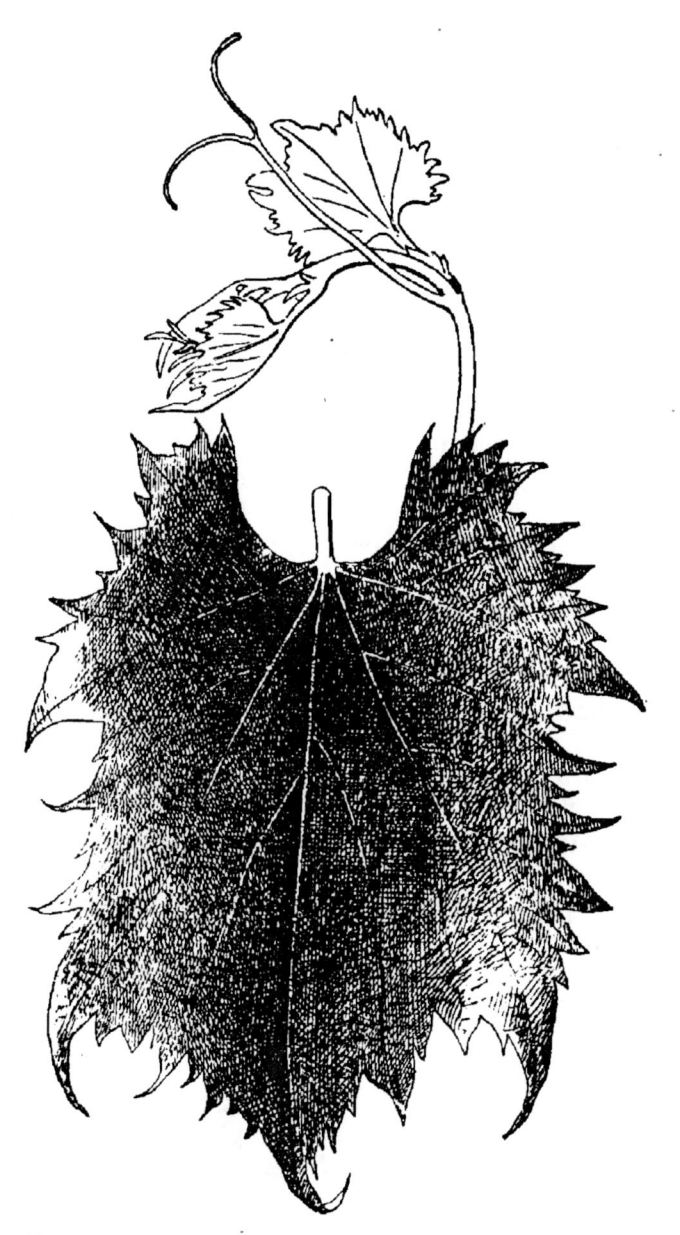

Fig. 16. - Leaves of Solonis, young and adult (after M. Mazade).

SOLONIS.

Synonyms: V. Solonis, Novo Mexicana.—This complex form seems to be the result of crossings between the *V. Riparia*, *V. Rupestris*, and *V. Candicans*. Its inferior resistance to phylloxera seems to be due to the latter. It is only 15, while the *V. Riparia*, and *V. Rupestris* are 19, and the *V. Candicans* 13. The Solonis has been cultivated for a very long time in many botanical gardens in Europe, but the exact date of its importation is not known. Viala found similar forms, or even identical forms in New Mexico. It possesses remarkable properties of resisting limestone, as well as the action of sea salt, and for these reasons it is still used, notwithstanding its inferior resistance to phylloxera.

Its principal characters are: vigorous stump, spreading habit, canes long, with medium internodes, almost cylindrical, slightly sinuous, with long and numerous ramifications, covered with a slight down towards the extremities, and retaining traces of it after lignification. The leaves are medium, entire, with two series of long and sharp teeth, those at the end of the lobes being longer. The three teeth indicating the inferior lobes curl underneath, towards the leaf axis. The leaves are slightly folded along the mid-rib with extremities curled underneath. The young leaves are covered with a whitish down on both faces; when adult they are of a dull green on the upper-face, with straight hair on the under-face, which is slightly lighter (Fig. 16). The bunches of grapes are small and compact, with small black berries.

The Solonis grows in soils containing up to 20 per cent. of lime in its worst form. It grows fairly well in damp and even wet soils. It is only in such soils that it may be regarded as preferable to other stocks, notwithstanding its middling resistance to phylloxera.

In calcareous soils, where it can grow, it should be replaced by the *Rupestris du Lot*, or the *Riparia × Rupestris 3309 or 101-14*, more refractory to the action of phylloxera.

The main defect of the Solonis is in not rooting well from cuttings, especially if these are large. If, however, small cuttings are well preserved and placed under favorable conditions, a strike of 80 to 85 per cent. may be expected.

CLINTON.

Synonym: Plant Pouzin (Ardèche).—The Clinton was one of the first cépages imported to Europe at the beginning of the experiments with American vines. According to the Americans it was considered to be one of the best direct producers, and was cultivated on a large scale as such. Too much was expected from it at first. Vine-growers thought it would make an excellent wine, capable of competing on the French market, that it would be a universal grafting stock, and alone would suffice for all the needs of reconstitution of our vineyards. Unfortunately, although it gives a wine remarkable for its colour and alcoholic strength, it has not been used much as a direct producer, on account of its small yield and its peculiar taste. However, many small growers of the Drôme and Ardèche, plant it on trellises around their houses to make their annual stock of wine for home consumption. Although it roots freely from cuttings, and gives a very good union when grafted, it has been discarded on account of the difficulty of adaptation to soils, and above all on account of its small resistance to phylloxera, which is only 8.

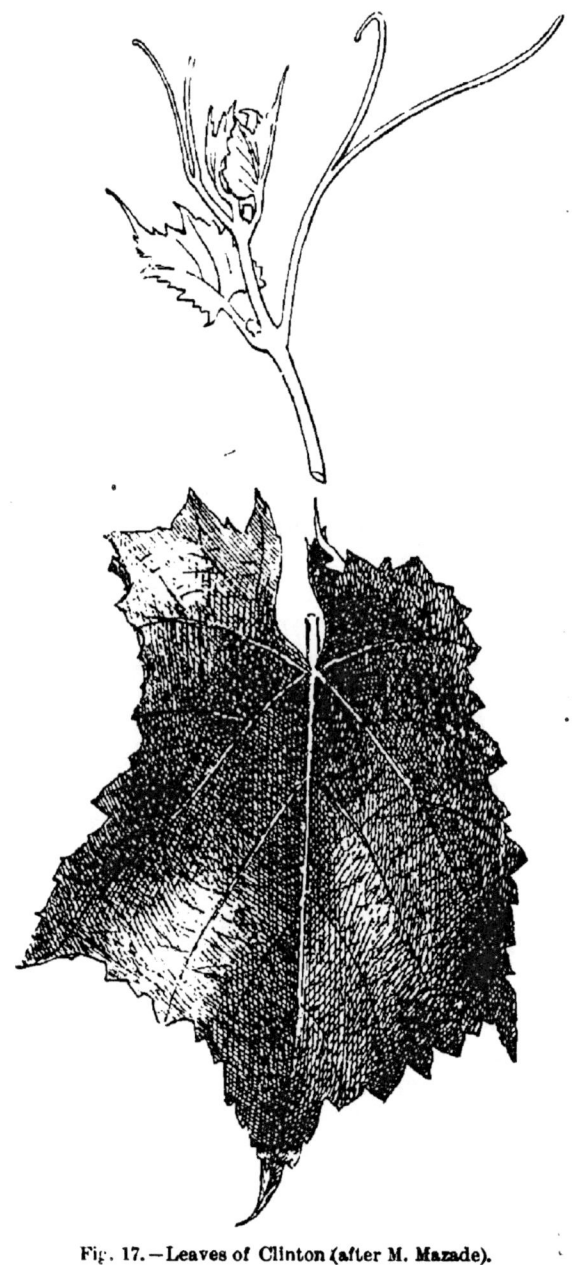

Fig. 17.—Leaves of Clinton (after M. Mazade).

It is a strong and vigorous plant with a spreading and bushy habit. The canes are long and slender with long internodes and numerous secondary ramifications. The leaves are medium, large, or small, generally entire or cordiform, sometimes trilobed, more or less folded along the mid-rib or conical, with undulating margins, deep green and glabrous, the upper-face of a lighter green, with stiff hairs on the veins of the under-face. The young leaves are slightly downy, folded along the mid-rib, but not completely enveloping the apex of the shoot. When the growth is very vigorous, the margins of the very young leaves are pink (Fig. 17). The bunches are medium or small, compact, and not shouldered. The berries are small, black, firm, with a thick skin and a fleshy pulp. The juice is pink, acid, and foxy. This cépage is a good bearer, but it yields a very small quantity of wine on account of the smallness of its berries.

TAYLOR.

This vine, indigenous to America, was the first cultivated there. It was very much extolled by Americans at the beginning of reconstitution of vineyards in France. Its vigour, the large diameter of its trunk, the facility with which it strikes from cuttings, its aptitude to grafting with all European vines, would make it the best graft-bearer if its resistance to phylloxera were higher; it is only 11, and this is probably due to one of its parents, the *V. Labrusca*. However, in certain fertile and fresh sites and not calcareous soils, it has found very favorable conditions of growth, and even now it is to be found in some vineyards bearing fine and very fructiferous grafts.

It resembles the Clinton very closely. However, it is easy to distinguish it by the young leaves of the extremities of the shoots which are always glabrous. The trunk is vigorous and the habit spreading. It is even more robust than the Clinton. The canes are long with medium internodes, of medium diameter and slightly sinuous with numerous and long ramifications. The leaves are fairly large, almost entire or slightly trilobed. The *petiolar sinus* is rather open; teeth sharp, in two series, glabrous on both faces. Bright green on the upper-face, light green on the underface. The point of junction of the veins is generally pink. The leaves are folded along the mid-rib or conically (Fig. 18). The bunches are small and frequently liable to non-setting; the berries are small, amber white.

The fertility of this cépage is small on account of the abortion of most of its flowers.

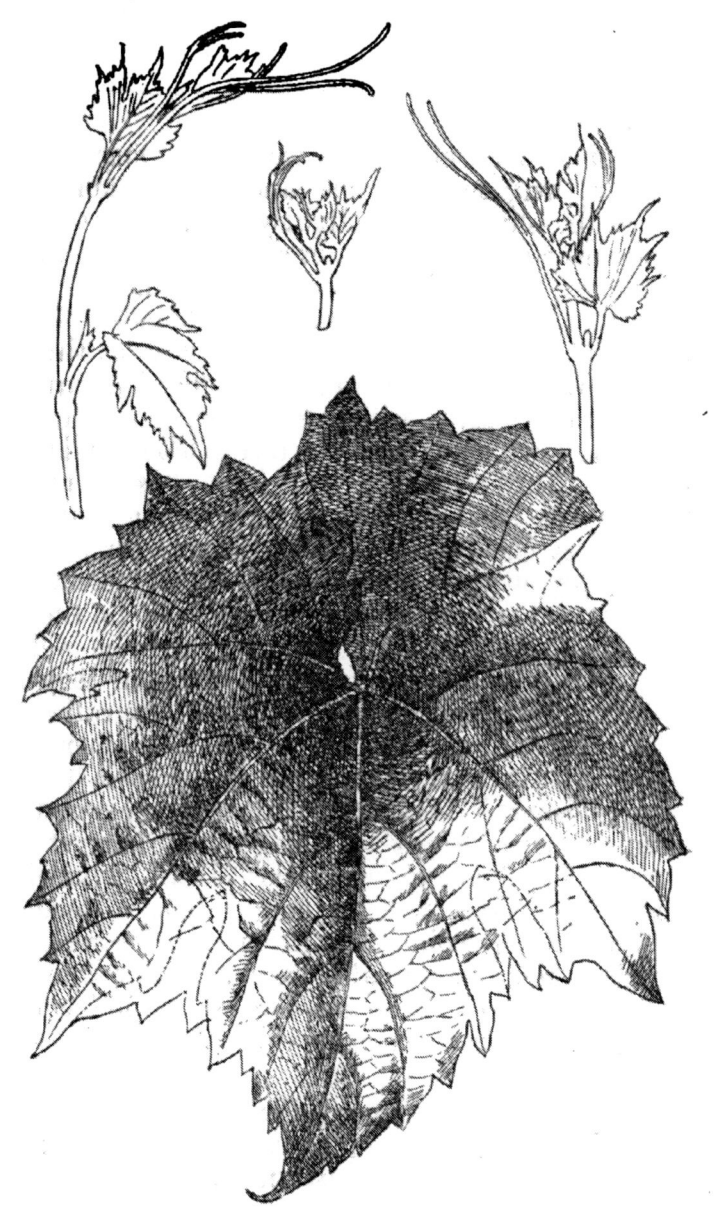

Fig. 18.—Leaves of Taylor (after M. Mazade).

VIALLA.

Synonyms: Clinton, Vialla.—This vine is of no interest as a direct producer on account of the foxy taste of its fruit and of its colour, but it has been used to a certain extent as a graft-bearer in granitic soils, where it roots freely from cuttings and knits well with most European cépages. But its origin (*Riparia* × *Labrusca*) endowed it with a small resistance to phylloxera, 12 only, which prevents its use in dry regions.

Description.—Vigorous plant with spreading habit and robust trunk; long and vigorous canes, of medium diameter, almost straight, shining, and slightly rugose. Green during the herbaceous state and vinous brown when lignified. Internodes medium, finely striated, with large nodes, swollen, covered with a light bloom; continuous tendrils. The buds are brown and become light carmine afterwards, this colour being due to the under-face and the margin of the upper-face of the very young leaves, which are covered on both faces with a dense down, and have the three lobes indicated by longer teeth. They remain a long time closed, enveloping bunches of green flowers, with red tints, which only appear when blooming. The leaves are fairly large, entire, orbicular, of a deep green, almost glabrous on the upper-face, of a lighter green and covered with a whitish down on the under-face. The teeth are blunt and the petiolar sinus well open (Fig. 19). The petiole is strong, medium in length, and covered with tufts of stiff hair. The flowers are rather large, cylindrical with well-marked ribs, green, of a vinous colour on the top, with a nice scent, calyx entire, well developed, remaining adherent a long time, with well separated urceolate discs, yellow or whitish. Ovary with long style and flat stigma. The bunches are rather small, cylindrical, or irregular, always long with a long peduncle, tender and rather swollen at the point of insertion; pedicles rather long, green, with a few disseminated warts. Berries medium or sub-medium, compact, spherical, covered with bloom, of a dark black colour, greenish inside with a few reddish streaks, fleshy pulp.

The use of the Vialla tends to diminish on account of its small resistance to phylloxera, and we do not think it can be recommended in any circumstances.

ELVIRA.

The Elvira is a hybrid of *Riparia* and *Labrusca*, very much extolled by the Americans. Some years ago it had a certain reputation in France, where vine-growers thought it would answer as a direct producer. It is completely discarded now on account of its very small resistance to phylloxera, which is only 8.

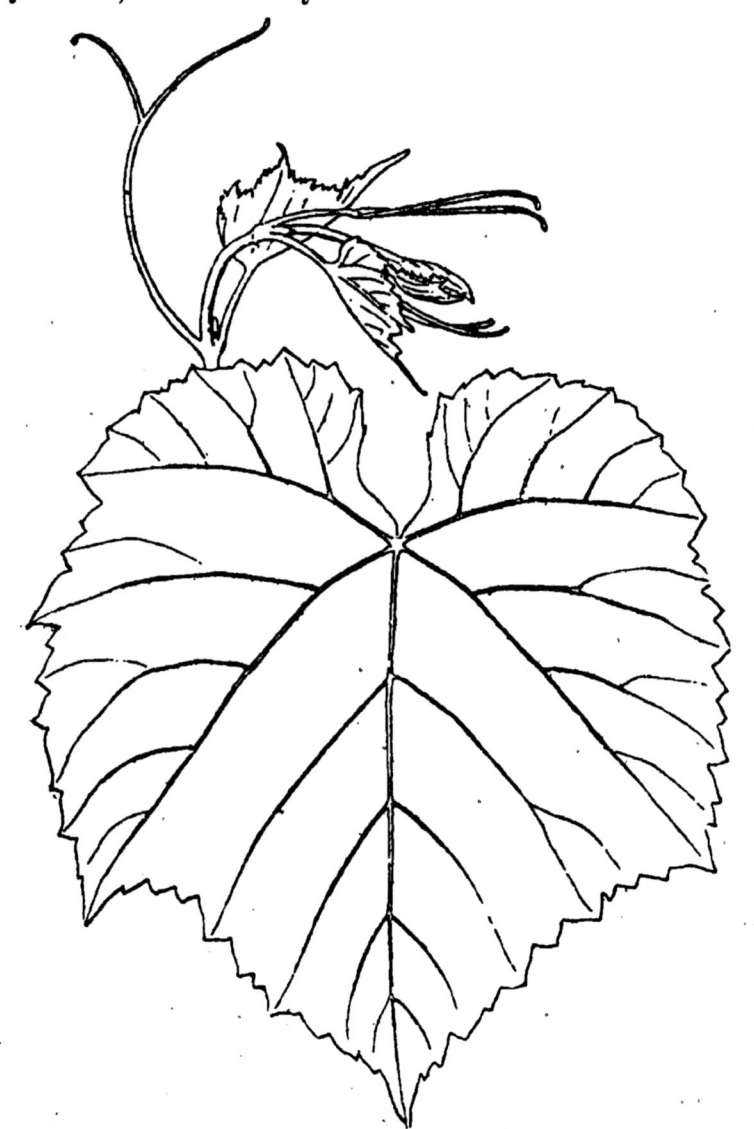

Fig. 19.—Leaves of Vialla (after M. Marade)

Description.—Vigorous plant, with semi-spreading habit, medium trunk, with rough and deciduous bark. The canes are long, large, and slightly sinuous, with a few ramifications, rather brownish during the herbaceous state, with a few short, hard hairs, the extremities covered with a white down, browner around the nodes and at the base of the cane after lignification. The internodes are medium, finely striated lengthwise, with protruding flat nodes, continuous tendrils, long, straight, and trifurcated. Very small buds, often double, deep brown becoming very soon white, with a few pink spots on the outer edge of the leaves, which soon become flat, uncovering bunches of green flowers, with dirty looking brown patches here and there. The young leaves are entire, thick, with whitish tomentum, falling off quickly from the upper-face, remaining adherent longer on the under-face, the veins of which are covered with a slight brownish down. The teeth are provided with green glands, lighter in colour towards the extremity. The adult leaves are large, entire, folded conically, goffered between the veins, deep green, teeth generally blunt in two series, light tufts of hair on the under-face; the veins are wide and straight, covered underneath with stiff hair; petiole strong, covered with numerous stiff hairs, of a light brown hue in places, generally forming an obtuse angle with the plane of the leaf. The flowers are rather small, sub-globular, light yellow, and very odoriferous. Ovaries slightly swollen, surmounted by a long style and a very small stigma. Bunches small, spherical, or cylindrical, rarely shouldered; peduncle strong, of medium length, green, lanigerous; pedicels stout, without warts, berries detaching easily and leaving a light yellow adherent brush. Berries compact, medium, covered with bloom, light pink or light green when they are not exposed to the light, with fleshy pulp and colourless juice, slight foxy taste.

The fertility of this cépage is only middling.

Noah.

The Noah, which was proposed by the Americans as a direct producer, has been brought forward again lately in the south-west, on account of its relative resistance to the attacks of black-rot. But the bad quality of its wine, and its small resistance to phylloxera (13) does not allow it to be used extensively. It is a vigorous plant, with spreading habit, slender trunk, and deciduous bark, falling in irregular lashes. The canes are long and slender, with a few glandulous hairs when herbaceous, reddish brown when lignified; long internodes, finely striated, with slightly flattened nodes and numerous ramifications; continuous tendrils of medium length, bifurcated, becoming purple as they get older. Small pointed buds, covered with rusty down. Young leaves with carmine mid-rib towards the extremity of the under-face, trilobed, covered with a light down on both faces, which quickly disappears; teeth long, undulating. When the leaves become flat, which takes place rather late, bunches of green flowers may be seen wrapped in a white, lanuginous down. Leaves medium or large, entire, rarely trilobed, inferior lobe always marked by a larger tooth, petiolar sinus slightly open, parenchyma thin; deep green, shining and glabrous on the upper-face, under-face covered with a dense white felt, becoming slightly rusty coloured. Straight veins protruding underneath, bright red tint at their point of insertion on the upper face. Teeth generally blunt in two series; petiole straight, covered with stiff hair, and turning purple as it gets older, forming an obtuse angle with the plane of the leaf. Flowers large, cylindrical, elongated, flattened on the top, odoriferous, of a light green, with a finely indented calyx not much developed, stamens with long, slender filaments; nectariferous corona slightly detached, of a yellowish green colour, globular ovary with a slender style, rather long, and surmounted by a large stigma, often bifidate. Large bunches, cylindrical or conical; with large peduncle, ligneous and swollen at the point of insertion, dirty green, rather short and contorted. Small pedicels, short, green, with a few warts, berries detaching easily, and leaving a colourless adherent brush. Berries loose, with thick skin and fleshy pulp; colourless juice, with foxy taste. Cépage of medium fertility.

(C).—FORMS DERIVED FROM V. RUPESTRIS.

The forms generally used for reconstitution are the *R. du Lot, R. Martin, R. Ganzin, R. Mission, R. of Fortworth, R. Metallica, Riparia × Rupestris* 3306, 3309 and 101-14, *Rupestris with Taylor habit.*

RUPESTRIS DU LOT.

Synonyms: *R. Sijas, R. Phénomène, R. Monticola,** *R. Saint-Georges, R. Lacastelle, R. Colineau, &c.*— This form seems to have been imported near Montpellier

---

* The name R. Monticola, given to this form, should be discarded, as it would seem to imply that it is the result of a crossing between V. Rupestris and V. Monticola, which is very improbable.

by Robert Sijas, vine-grower at Montferrier. It proved very hardy and resistant in soils formed from débris of

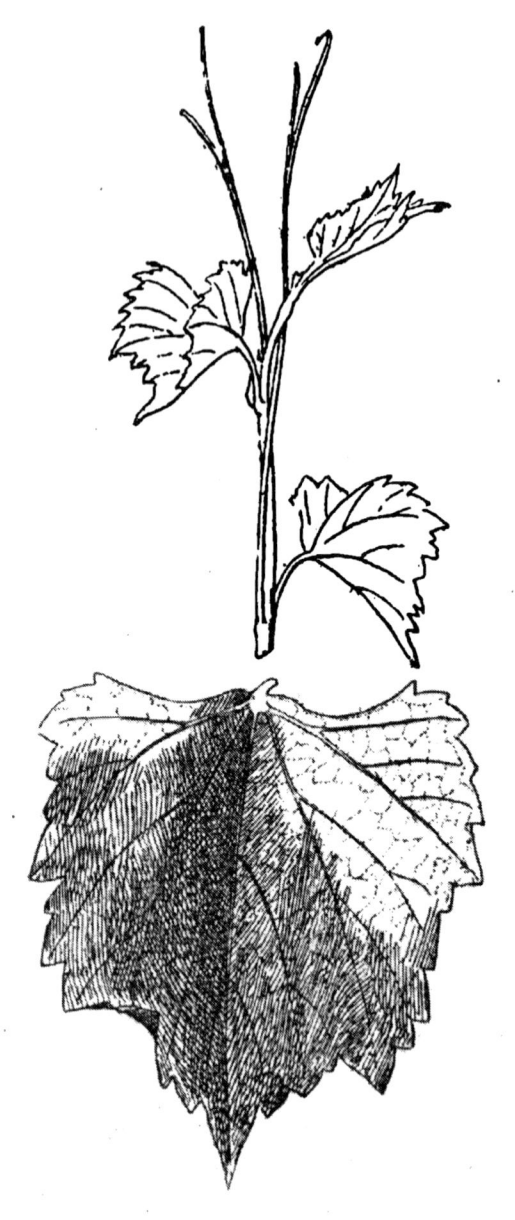

Fig. 20.—Leaves of Rupestris du Lot, young and adult (after M. Mazade).

very calcareous tufa. It seems to withstand lime even better than Jacquez, and has the advantage of being more resistant (19½). It has great vigour, and the way in which it grows in compact, dry, and pebbly soils gives it a great value as a graft-bearer, especially for the eastern districts of France, where it is planted instead of Riparias in many limestone soils too dry and too unfertile for the latter. In damp soils it is much affected by *pourridié*.

Description.—Habit, very erect (the main ramifications alone spreading on the ground); canes knotted, very ramified, with short internodes; leaves very much folded along the mid-rib, with undulating margins, bright, with light metallic sheen, rather thin, petiolar sinus bracket shaped, teeth irregular, rather acute, especially that forming the terminal lobe; leaves of the secondary ramifications sometimes very small, extremities bronze coloured (Fig. 20). If the season is very dry the leaves all fold along the mid-rib and the metallic sheen disappears. Flowers, male; roots rather stouter than those of the other Rupestris.*

RUPESTRIS MARTIN.

The Ruspestris Martin was introduced from Texas in 1874, by Martin, at Montels-Eglise, near Montpellier, and may be regarded as the equivalent of *Rupestris du Lot* for the western regions, where it grows very well in clayey and rather cold soils. It is affected by dry limestone much more than the latter, but it resists phylloxera quite as well (19½), and bears grafts equally well. It is an excellent graft-bearer for non-calcareous or only slightly calcareous soils which do not become dry in summer.

M. Mazade gives the following description of this vine:— Leaves (Fig. 21) cordiform, thick, deep green, wrinkly at the centre, irregularly folded along the mid-rib, margins of the leaf largely undulating and curled up; petiolar sinus V shape; teeth very large and much rounded; wood very sinuous.

RUPESTRIS GANZIN.

According to Millardet, this form was imported from Texas by Charles Martin, in 1874. Dr. Davin and Couderc noticed and propagated it. In 1880 Millardet studied it

---

* Many illustrations and descriptions have been borrowed from M. Mazade's *Guide pour faciliter la reconnaissance de quelques Cépages*, done into English by the present translators, under the title: First Steps in Ampelography. Department of Agriculture, Victoria, 1900.

at Ganzin's vineyard. The *Rupestris Martin* is preferred, as it gives better results in soils where the R. Ganzin also grows.

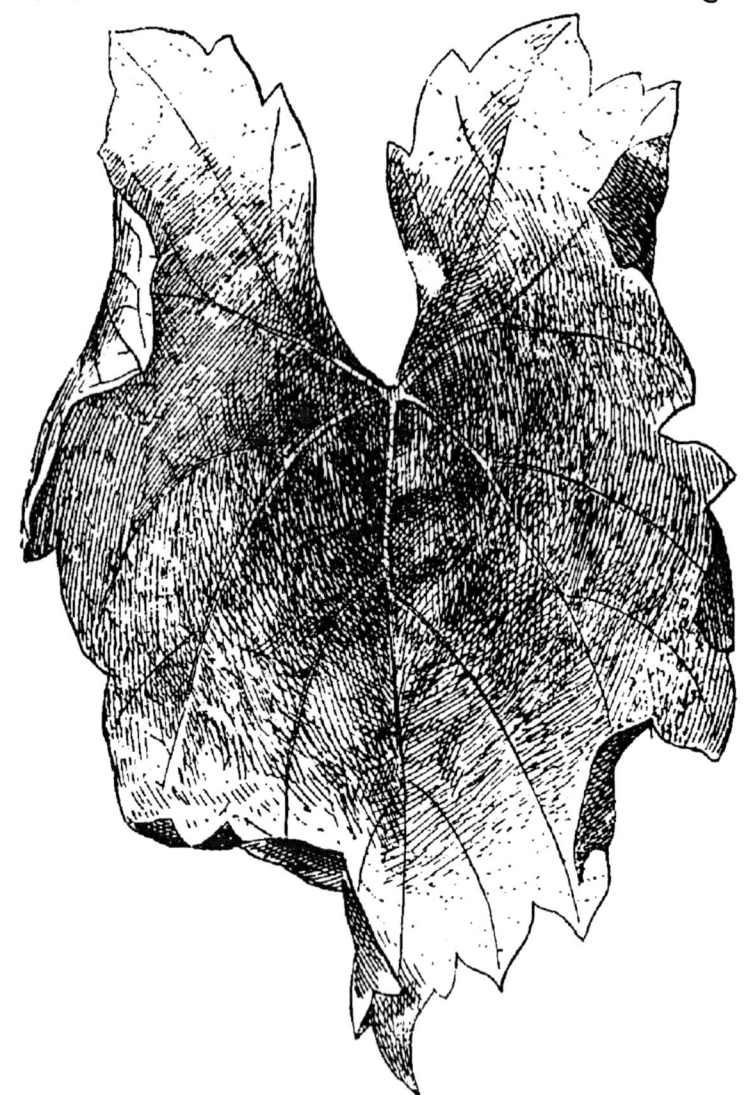

Fig. 21.—Leaf of Rupestris Martin (after M. Mazade).

Description.—Stump, large; habit, bushy; trunk, straight; leaves with undulating margins, regularly folded along the mid-rib; petiolar sinus, very open, varying in shape according to the size of the leaf. Generally yellowish green or orange yellow towards the extremity of the shoots. Numerous male flowers.

Rupestris Mission.

The Rupestris Mission was imported from America in 1887 by Viala. It made a satisfactory growth, and even became vigorous in dry, marly soils with a subsoil composed of calcareous concretions at the School of Agriculture, Montpellier. However, it is inferior to the *Rupestris du Lot* and the *Rupestris Martin* from the point of view of its resistance to limestone, and perhaps even as a graft-bearer.

Description.—Habit, very spreading; canes, large and long; internodes, medium, few secondary ramifications, violet red when herbaceous. The lignified canes are of a light hazel colour. Leaves, small, folded along the mid-rib, margins curled inwards and undulating; petiolar sinus bracket shaped.

Rupestris of Fortworth.

A number of Rupestris sent from Fortworth, in Texas, in 1882, by Jæger, to de Grasset, were grouped under the name of *Rupestris of Fortworth*. They at first attracted attention on account of their vigour. They may be good graft-bearers in *Riparia* soils, but are inferior to the *Rupestris du Lot* in dry and calcareous hilly ground.

Description (according to Viala and Ravaz).—Very vigorous, with strong trunk; canes rather long, light hazel bluish colour, young shoots pink; leaves, very large, thick, light green and shining, goffered along the veins, well folded along the mid-rib, margins slightly curled inwards. Of a yellowish light green and shining on the under-face, veins transparent and yellow, teeth wide and acute in two series; petiolar sinus deep, wide, V shaped, rounded at the base; petiole light pink.

Rupestris Metallica.

This Rupestris appears to be the result of crossing with *Mustang (V. Candicans)*. It seems to resist dry soil, but is inferior to the *Rupestris du Lot*.

Description.—Very vigorous leaves, orbicular, shining, parchment-like, very thick, sombre metallic sheen (hence its name); rather folded along the mid-rib, margins perfectly plane. Teeth regular, petiole forming an acute angle with the limb; petiolar sinus deep, open V shaped, tufts of woolly down disseminated on the canes and petioles; buds whitish.

Riparia × Rupestris 3306 and 3309.

These hybrids, raised by Couderc of Aubenas, have proved very vigorous and resistant to phylloxera. They grow well in calcareous soils, where all Riparias and most of the Rupestris become yellow, and they bear very fructiferous grafts. With regard to resistance to limestone they are equivalent to the *Rupestris du Lot*, and withstand *pourridié* better than the latter. It was noticed in 1897, in the Aude, that *folletage* had generally affected all the vines grafted on *Riparia × Rupestris 101-14*, while those grafted on *3309* were not subject to this accident. Under these circumstances these stocks may be considered as excellent graft bearers capable of giving good results in soils which are too calcareous for *Riparia* and for certain *Rupestris*, and not calcareous enough to necessitate the use of *V. Berlandieri*, and sometimes too wet for the *Rupestris du Lot*.

Riparia × Rupestris 101-14.

This hybrid was obtained by Millardet and de Grasset. It shares the same qualities as the two above described, except that its grafts have a tendency to *folletage*.

Rupestris with Taylor Habit.

This form, selected at Mas de las Sorres, seems to be a hybrid between the *V. Æstivalis* and the *V. Rupestris*. Its resistance to phylloxera is 16. It is a very vigorous plant with strong trunk and spreading habit. Its canes are sinuous, strong, deep hazel colour, with bloom around the nodes. The leaves are large, wide, thin, long, orbicular, thick, fleshy, goffered between the sub-veins, light and dull green on the under-face, with strong veins covered with stiff hair, petiolar sinus deep lyre shaped.

(D).—Forms Derived from V. Berlandieri.

It is only since the viticultural mission of Viala to the United States in 1887, that attention has been directed to the V. Berlandieri, and that a selection to obtain forms more resistant to the action of limestone started. According to Viala the general characters of the forms resisting limestone are: leaves slightly tomentose, of a shining golden yellow. The types most in use are:—*The B. Rességuier No. 1, B. Rességuier No. 2, B. Daignère, B. of Angeac, B. Viala, and B. Ecole.*

BERLANDIERI RESSÉGUIER, No. 1.

This form, selected by E. Rességuier, of Alénya (Pyrénées Orientales), has generally grown well in calcareous soils. The general tint is bright, light-green; wood, hazel colour and shining; leaves, large, elongated, margins often parallel, often regularly folded along the mid-rib, sometimes plain, relatively thin, supple, and smooth; upper portion of growing shoot ashy colour and slightly carmine. Young leaves of a golden yellow passing slowly to the definitive tint; petiolar sinus V shaped; very vigorous form.

BERLANDIERI RESSÉGUIER, No. 2.

Selected by Rességuier like the No. 1. It has been very much propagated, and has given good results as a graft-bearer in soils where vines get chlorosed easily. General tint very deep-green, varnish like, wood hazel colour, strongly striated and excoriated; leaves deep-green, shining as if varnished on the upper face, rounded, thick, margins strongly undulating, often folded conically, teeth very blunt, petiolar sinus U or lyre shaped. Apex of shoot whitish, slightly carmine; young leaves violet bronze, ashy colour, becoming pure bronze, and passing suddenly to the definitive tint.

BERLANDIERI DAIGNÈRE.

Very vigorous and differing very little from the above. Its leaves are more involute. It has generally given good results in calcareous soils.

BERLANDIERI OF ANGEAC.

This form, which resists in the Charentes a high percentage of lime, is very vigorous, and seems to be a good graft-bearer in such soils. Its leaves are rather dull with light-green veins prominent on the limb; teeth well marked, fluffy hair along the veins of the upper-face; buds yellowish-white with a light carmine border more accentuated on the young leaves; wood rather reddish for a Berlandieri.

BERLANDIERI VIALA.

This form, selected and dedicated to Viala by Munson, grows in the most chalky soils of Texas, but its vigour is less than that of those already described, it cannot, therefore, be considered equivalent as a graft-bearer. Its adult leaves are very large, rounded, and thick; petiolar sinus almost closed; young leaves very bronzed and shining.

BERLANDIERI ECOLE.

This form was obtained at the School of Agriculture of Montpellier, from seeds imported from Texas in 1876 by Douysset. It is inferior to the above form, its use is therefore not advisable as a graft-bearer. It is easily recognised by its leaves, which, when adult, are depressed in the centre and very involute.

(E).—VARIOUS HYBRIDS.

Apart from the hybrids previously described, grouping them under the name of the pure form which seems to predominate in their character, there are a great number of other hybrids offered to vine-growers as graft-bearers or direct producers. We only mention those which are of some value and already known:—*Aramon* × *Rupestris Ganzin*, No. 1, and *A. R. G.*, No. 2, *Gamay Couderc* (*Colombeau* × *Rupestris Martin*, No. 3103); *Mourvèdre* × *Rupestris*, No. 1202; *Chasselas* × *Berlandieri*, No. 41, of Millardet and de Grasset; *Tisserand* (*Cabernet* × *Berlandieri*, No. 333); *Alicante-Bouschet* × *Rupestris*, No. 136; *Berlandieri* × *Riparia*, No. 33, and *B.* × *R.*, No. 34; *Petit-Bouschet* × *Riparia*, No. 142, of the School of Agriculture of Montpellier; *Seibel's Hybrids*, No. 1 and No. 2; *Franc's Hybrid, Alicante* × *Rupestris Terras*, No. 20, &c.

ARAMON × RUPESTRIS GANZIN, No. 1.

Obtained by fecundating *Aramon* with *Rupestris Ganzin*.

Description (according to V. Ganzin).—Vigorous plant, strong and stout, with long, spreading canes, buds sombre, carmine, red, bronze, violet; young shoots, carmine, violet, with lighter ribs; leaves medium on the main canes and smaller on the secondary ramifications, almost entire, sometimes trilobed, of a dull green, glabrous; winter wood large and thick, sometimes striated, but rarely ribbed, varying in colour from light brick red to hazel, with a tint of white or yellow dotted with blackish brown spots.

The *Aramon* × *Rupestris*, No. 1, is certainly one of the most resistant Franco-American hybrids. For this reason it has been recommended as a graft-bearer. However, on account of its origin, it offers less guarantee than many other graft-bearers which adapt themselves better to the same conditions. Its resistance to lime is low; it becomes yellow, not only in chalky, but even in the groie soils of the Charentes.

Aramon × Rupestris Ganzin, No. 2.

Resulting from the same seedlings.

Description (according to V. Ganzin).—Vigorous plant, strong and stout, with long, spreading canes; buds, light bronze-green with reddish hue; young shoots similar to No. 1, but with a lighter tint; leaves similar to No. 1; winter wood stout, striated, often ribbed, light hazel colour with a yellowish-white hue, sometimes reddish-brown covered with black spots, and sometimes mottled with yellow, the general colour being lighter than that of No. 1.

This hybrid is affected by limestone more than No. 1.

Gamay Couderc.

Synonym: Colombeau × Rupestris Martin, No. 3103.

Description (according to Couderc).—Very numerous and loose bunches of grapes, 5½in. to 8in. in length, with oval berries (about ½in.), black, very fine, taste resembling European grapes, acid and sweet at the same time, with no after taste, differing only from those of European vines by less freshness. Its wine is good and of a fine colour; the alcoholic strength reaches 11 per cent. (19 per cent. proof spirit); leaves resembling the Rupestris, but trilobed, with characteristic goffered structure towards the centre. Its leaves and semi-erect habit, its large wood with short internodes and large flat nodes, enable it to be easily distinguished, which is of great importance from a commercial and viticultural point of view.

The Gamay Couderc has been recommended as a direct producer and graft-bearer. Unfortunately, its resistance to phylloxera does not seem to be sufficient. It died under the attacks of the parasite at the School of Agriculture of Montpellier, and in other places.

Colombeau × Rupestris, No. 1202.

Description.—Very vigorous plant, with erect habit, trunk large and stout, canes large, straight, or slightly sinuous in places, nodes large, slightly prominent, with short internodes; young shoots slightly violet-purple, with a light fluffy tomentum; tendrils bifurcated, of a vinous red colour when young, becoming bronze-green later on; buds bursting early, young leaves remaining folded along the mid-rib for a very long period; adult leaves orbicular, with deep, acute, and regular teeth, upper face smooth, rather like that of the leaf of V. Monticola; petiolar sinus regular V shape, petiole short, violet colour; flowers generally male; bunches rather small with very small spherical berries, bluish-black, without foxy taste, with a deep colour under the skin, often setting badly.

The 1202 was proposed as a graft-bearer on account of its great vigour and adaptability to limestone soils. Unfortunately, like the Gamay-Couderc, it withered under the action of the phylloxera in the collections of the School of Agriculture of Montpellier.

Chasselas × Berlandieri, No. 41B.

This remarkable hybrid was obtained by Millardet and de Grasset.

Description (according to Millardet).—Very vigorous plant with spreading habit, fertile, resembling at first sight the pure Berlandieri. Wood of the year, large, often bent at the nodes, flattened and often ribbed on one side from one end to the other at the base of the strongest shoots, and rounded towards the extremity. Wood light green or slightly yellow when young, turning to a brown tobacco colour when completely lignified. Internodes long, often irregular (never more than $4\frac{3}{4}$in.). Nodes slightly prominent; buds covered with white down on top, rusty coloured under the scales. Leaves with petiole generally shorter than the limb, of a yellowish-green, often slightly vinous colour in autumn, and slightly downy. Leaves generally larger than long, very flat or only slightly folded, generally pentagonal in shape at the base of the canes and rounded at the extremity, with five lobes at the base, three in the mean part, and entire towards the extremity. Acute lobes on the lowest leaves, often very obtuse on the mean and upper leaves. Lateral sinuses sub-acute or obtuse like the lobes. Petiolar sinus, V or U shaped. Teeth generally in one series, small, obtuse, or rounded, downy on the edge. Limb rather thick, upper-face smooth, shining, almost glabrous, under-face lighter in colour, shining between the veins, which are more or less downy. Hermaphrodite flowers with short stamens.

Notwithstanding its Franco-American origin, the Chasselas × Berlandieri proved resistant to phylloxera, and grew well in limestone soils. It seems, therefore, to be a good graft-bearer for such soils, but unfortunately does not possess very great vigour.

Tisserand.

Synonym: Cabernet × Berlandieri, No. 333.

The *Tisserand* was obtained in 1883, at the School of Agriculture of Montpellier, by fecundating *Cabernet Sauvignon* with *Berlandieri*.

Description.—Plant of medium vigour, trunk of medium size, deciduous bark detaching in fine thongs, long and sinuous canes of medium diameter, nodes slightly protruding, large buds. Wood fairly hard, with very little pith; bark deep red, strongly striated; herbaceous shoots, purple, covered with fluffy hair disseminated towards the extremities, flattened towards the nodes. When bursting, the buds are bright carmine, then become whitish-pink, with large grapes protruding from the centre. Margins of young leaves and petioles pink, with woolly hair, forming a slight down on the upper-face, white hair on the under-face. Adult leaves medium, sometimes orbicular, five lobed, longer than wide, petiolar sinus generally U shaped, the sides of the sinus often overlapping. Inferior lateral sinus fairly deep, teeth in two series, short and blunt, thick and glabrous, of a brilliant green on the top, of a lighter green with stiff hair on the veins of the under-face. Petiole cylindrical, purple, with a few stiff or woolly hairs. Male flowers.

The Tisserand resisted, even when grafted, the action of chalky soils in the environs of Cognac. It bears grafts of a fine green colour, but, unfortunately, its Franco-American origin, and the examination of a few lesions produced on its roots by the phylloxera, do not allow us to recommend it as a graft-bearer.

Alicante-Bouschet × Rupestris, No. 136.

This hybrid was obtained in 1881, at the School of Agriculture of Montpellier, by fecundating *Alicante-Henri-Bouschet* with *Rupestris-Ecole*.

Description.—Very vigorous plant with strong trunk, semi-erect habit, rough bark detaching in irregular thongs of medium length. Long canes, slightly sinuous, rather slender; internodes medium or short, nodes rather flat and rather deeper than the internode in colour; small glabrous buds; tendrils medium, trifurcated, becoming ligneous, light coffee colour, diaphragm thin, flat above, concave underneath. Leaves sub-medium, orbicular or cordiform, or larger than long, like those of the V. Rupestris. Petiolar sinus open, teeth short and blunt, slightly curled. Leaf thick, of a bright green, glabrous and smooth on the upper-face, glabrous and lighter green on the under-face. Petiole rather long, forming a very obtuse angle with the limb. Some of the flowers are male, others are fertile. Bunches, small, long, shouldered, loose, irregular, peduncles and pedicles tender and herbaceous up to the time of maturity. Berries small, spherical, black, with a slight bloom, hard, with fine but strong skin, juice deep red, sweet taste, but slightly acid after taste. Two or three small seeds with short beak, similar to those of V. Rupestris, in each berry.

This cépage is almost sterile.

The *Alicante-Bouschet × Rupestris, No. 136*, has proved very resistant to phylloxera notwithstanding its Franco-American origin, its resistance being 19. It is remarkably vigorous, and is a first-rate graft-bearer, knitting easily. It does not withstand chalky soils, and, when grafted in such soils, becomes yellow in bad seasons. It seems to have the aptitudes of the V. Riparia, but has a larger trunk and greater vigour. However, its superiority is not sufficient to allow it to replace the Riparias.

Petit-Bouschet × Riparia, No. 142—Ecole.

This hybrid, obtained at the School of Agriculture of Montpellier, in 1883, is the result of a crossing between *Petit-Bouschet* and *Riparia*.

Description.—Plant of medium vigour, trunk of medium size, with deciduous bark detaching in long, fine thongs. Canes long, straight, of medium diameter, internodes rather long, nodes small. Tendrils medium, bifurcated, discontinuous, lignifying in autumn. Bark hazel colour, slightly straited; diaphragm thin; leaves medium, thin, five lobed, petiolar sinus U shaped, lateral inferior sinuses fairly deep.

Teeth short and sharp, in two series; lobes slightly revolute, limb very slightly goffered between the veins. Light green and glabrous on the upper-face, lighter green and glabrous with a few disseminated stiff hairs on the veins of the under-face, which are slightly protruding. Petiole of medium size, rather long, slightly purple, forming an obtuse angle with the limb. Grapes small, similar to those of the V. Riparia, loose, with short pedicels; berries small, hard, spherical, with thin skin and umbilic, rather depressed on the side; violet black-colour with bloom, red juice, at first reminding of that of green figs. One to three small seeds, resembling those of wild Riparia.

This cépage is almost sterile.

Although this vine is of Franco-American origin, it has a high resistance like the cépage above described. It grows better in calcareous soils, but the same remarks regarding the opportunities for its utilization also apply.

Berlandieri × Riparia, No. 33—Ecole.

This hybrid and the following were obtained from seeds brought from America by Viala.

Description (according to Viala and Ravaz).—Strong and vigorous plant, habit spreading, shoots straight, cylindrical, large and strong, slightly ramified, internodes rather short, finely ribbed. Lignified canes drab coloured. Young shoots glabrous, yellowish-green and pink in places. Leaves medium, entire, with terminal lobes long and sharp, cordiform, very thick, main veins strong, with a few tufts of hair. Upper-face deep green, shining, goffered between the veins; under-face lighter green, varnish like; petiolar sinus deep V shaped, with a few hairs on the sides. Teeth blunt, in two series, regular; petiole in the same plane as the limb.

The *Riparia × Berlandieri, No. 33*, has very great vigour, resists phylloxera well, and roots freely from cuttings. The first experiments made at Cognac seem to prove that it is well adapted to calcareous soils.

Berlandieri × Riparia, No. 34—Ecole.

Description (according to Viala and Ravaz).—Vigorous plant with stout trunk. Canes cylindrical, largely striated, well-marked ribs on canes of medium size; internodes of medium length; young shoots tomentose, covered all over with numerous short hairs extending to the tendrils and pedicles, of a vinous fawn-brown when lignified; adult leaves large, very thick, sub-orbicular, entire, terminal lobes well-marked, curled underneath, the margin being slightly revolute. Upper-face deep green, varnish like; under-face dull, light green, ribs and sub-ribs covered with short regular brush-like hair. Two series of blunt teeth, petiolar sinus wide, V shaped.

This hybrid seems to have the same qualities as No. 33.

Seibel's Hybrid, No. 1.

This hybrid, like the No. 2, is the result of seedlings of *V. Rupestris* × *V. Linsecomii* (No. 70 of Jæger), most likely fecundated accidentally by a *V. Vinifera*.

Description (according to Rougier).—Medium vigour, trunk strong, habit spreading, bushy. Canes long, slightly sinuous, flattened, medium size, slender; internodes, medium, short, nodes prominent with a protruding pad below the point of insertion of the leaf. Buds small, pointed, chestnut colour, with numerous ramifications like the V. Rupestris. Wood and bark glabrous, shining, hazel colour; buds glabrous, young leaves very shining and glabrous on both faces, of a very light green; leaves shaped like those of V. Rupestris, small, remaining folded along the mid-rib a very short time, entire, with blunt teeth, the lobes being indicated by more developed teeth; petiolar sinus very wide and shallow, U shape; teeth short, wide, and pointed, in two series; upper-face glabrous, light green, varnish like, under-face lighter green, equally glabrous and shining; bunches medium, loose, cylindrical, sometimes shouldered; peduncle long, slender, light red near the point of insertion; berries of medium size ($\frac{6}{10}$in. to $\frac{7}{10}$in. in diameter), rather ovoid, thin skin, persistent umbilic, deep red in color, and becoming rather black at maturity. Abundant bloom, soft pulp, colorless juice.

This hybrid was recommended as a direct producer. It gives a rather fine wine and medium yield. Unfortunately, its resistance to phylloxera is low; it does not even equal that of *Jacquez* (13).

Seibel's Hybrid, No. 2.

Description (according to Rougier).—Very vigorous plant, trunk strong, habit semi-erect. Canes long, straight, stout, almost cylindrical, with deep ribs, internodes medium, nodes stout; buds medium, vinous red, covered with whitish-grey down, few ramifications, tendrils discontinuous, very strong, violet colour when herbaceous; leaves large, orbicular, entire, with more developed teeth indicating the inferior and superior lobes, flat or folded conically; petiolar sinus open, lyre shaped; teeth very irregular, often in several series, wide and blunt; limb thick, tough, upper-face deep green, glabrous, varnish like. In autumn the leaves become red like those of the Tinto's. Veins protruding, strong, covered with a slight, woolly down. Petiole strong, forming an obtuse angle with the limb; bunches large, shouldered, pyramid-shaped, rather compact and regular. Berries medium, spherical, tender when ripe, with thin skins, red, becoming almost black at maturity. Persistent umbilic, juicy, coloured pulp. Very fertile cépage.

Seibel's hybrid, No. 2, was also recommended as a direct producer, but its resistance, which is smaller than No. 1 (about 8), does not allow it to be very extensively used for reconstitution.

Franc's Hybrid.

Obtained by Franc from seeds of Rupestris. In a report to the Minister of Agriculture in 1894, Franc pointed out this hybrid as resisting all cryptogamic diseases and phylloxera.

Description (according to Franc).—Very vigorous plant habit erect, trunk strong, increasing rapidly in dimensions. Shoots strong, with numerous ramifications; buds stout, covered with light red scales; abundant bloom rather late in the season; flowers never affected by non-setting. Leaves deep green, upper-face very shiny, under-face lighter. Luxuriant vegetation. Bunches varying in size; berries black spherical, having a thin skin and a fine bright red juice, sweet, with an agreeable taste.

Franc's hybrid was proposed as a direct producer, but notwithstanding the large number of grapes it bears the yield in juice is small. Its wine is inferior, and the colour, although very bright at first, quickly alters. Its resistance to phylloxera has not yet been ascertained.

Alicante × Rupestris, No. 20, of Terras.

Obtained by Terras, in the Var, by crossing the *Alicante* and *Rupestris*. Very fertile, notwithstanding the bad quality of its wine; this vine has been rather boomed by vine-growers, but its small resistance to phylloxera leads us to think that it will soon be discarded.

CHAPTER II.

CHOICE OF AMERICAN VINES WITH REGARD TO DESTINATION AND SITUATION.

The vine-grower who has decided to reconstitute his vineyard with American vines has to examine different questions before choosing between forms, the resistance of which he is supposed to know. Is he to plant direct producers? Is he to plant graft-bearers? And amongst either of those which are the forms best adapted to his soil and climate? We shall try to solve these different problems in this chapter by grouping under different headings the indications already published on the principal American vines, completing them when necessary.

USE OF DIRECT PRODUCERS OR GRAFT-BEARERS.

Since the resistance of American vines to phylloxera was pointed out, in 1869, at the Congress of Beaune, by Laliman, two solutions to the phylloxera problem were foreseen: First, the substitution of European by American vines; second, the grafting of European vines on American roots, as Gaston Bazille so promptly advocated.

The first solution was naturally preferred, as it seemed to be much easier of execution, and vine-growers were advised to adopt it. Together with the experiments of Laliman and Borty (the two first importers of American vines, with a view to cultivating them for direct production) the Americans, who had since the failures of the *London Company* and of the Swiss colonists of *New Vevey*, only used indigenous vines, assured us that they produced wines equal to those of our best European vineyards. Encouraged by such information, many vine-growers started reconstituting their phylloxera-destroyed vineyards with *Concord, Clinton,* and *Jacquez* (which Douysset had discovered in Texas); *Herbemont, Cunningham,* which were planted extensively; and, later on, with *York Madeira, Norton's Virginia, Vialla, Eumelan, Black Defiance, Autuchon, Cornucopia, Secretary,* and even *Taylor* and *Othello*.

But it was soon recognised that it was impossible to obtain any practical result from such producers. The foxy taste of the wine made from most of them did not suit the French palate, accustomed for a long period of time to the taste of *Vinifera* wines, while those resulting from *V. Æstivalis*, which gave wine of a clean taste, were far from yielding as much as the old European cépages. But the main fact which forced vine-growers to discard them was their insufficient resistance to phylloxera in most soils. These grafted forms resulting from crossings of wild resisting species, such as *V. Riparia* or *V. Æstivalis*, with other species, such as *V. Vinifera* and *V. Labrusca*, which are not resisting, can only thrive well in soils which do not allow the phylloxera to develop freely.

Only a very few of these direct producers are now cultivated, and only a few acres of *Jacquez* are to be found in the most fertile parts of the Var cultivated for wine purposes; all the rest have been either uprooted or grafted. The *Clinton*, which is now called *Pouzin*, only forms a few trellises in front of the houses of small growers of Ardèche and Drôme. A few blocks of *Noah* are yet to be found in the vineyards of the south-west of France. It has been done away with in other parts of France, and grafting is now the general rule, which is not surprising if we think of the immense advantages it affords.

Experience has proved how easy it is to train workmen to perform this operation with success; the use of grafted and knitted cuttings made on the bench and planted in nurseries, enables vignerons to create regular plantations in the first instance by using well-selected stocks; by its use it is easy to produce a wine to which commerce is accustomed, and it endows the grafted vines with a maximum resistance to phylloxera, as it renders possible the use of stocks selected amongst American wild forms, which by the process of natural selection in presence of the insect have become practically immune.

However, the question of direct producers is again brought forward. Those used at first are naturally not mentioned with the exception of the *Noah*, perhaps, but many new hybrids obtained in France, generally from crossings between American and European vines, are offered to viticulturists. Those nurserymen who offer these direct producers to growers do not try to point out the advantage of avoiding the grafting operation, as the argument is played out, but they say that their hybrids resist chlorosis better in limestone soils, and are not affected by black-rot and other cryptogamic diseases.

They have not yet been planted to any extent, but in districts where reconstitution is only starting, and where the work has not yet assumed a decided orientation, small plantations are made with the idea of gradually extending them. If we consider these new trials, we are forced to ask the question—Is it really necessary to modify the basis upon which the reconstitution of vineyards rests, as it is actually done in France? We do not think so; and our opinion on this question rests on the following consideration. As a matter of fact, it would only be necessary if:—

- 1st. The direct producers had an equal or superior value from the point of view of quality and quantity of their produce to our grafted cépages, and if they offered the same guarantees as the latter with regard to their resistance to phylloxera.
- 2nd. If the graft-bearers were not sufficiently resistant to phylloxera, and if they could not adapt themselves to certain soils for which direct producers would be better adapted.
- 3rd. Finally, if no remedy be known against black-rot, a given direct producer had better qualities of resisting this disease than any other European vine of equal value.

We think that, so far, neither of these hypotheses have been realized; and we may say that up to the present no American producer has given wines equal in quality to those of the fine European cépages, neither do they produce it in an equal quantity. No direct producer would bear comparison with *Burgundy*, *Cabernet*, or *Shiraz* with regard to quality, or with *Aramon*, *Terret-Bourret*, and *Carignan* with regard to quantity. We must not forget that their resistance to phylloxera is generally low on account of the strain of *V. Labrusca* and *V. Vinifera* which they contain, and that the higher the quality of their wine and their fructivity the lower the resistance.

On the contrary, the graft-bearers now in use answer all the requirements of viticulture so far as phylloxera is concerned. The tendency to discard types of low resistance, such as Taylor, Vialla, Solonis, Jacquez, &c., has increased every year; and only a few wild forms have been retained after long and careful selection. These are *Riparia Grand Glabre, R. Gloire de Montpellier, Rupestris du Lot, R. Martin, Berlandieri* (for calcareous soils), or spontaneous or artificial crossings between these species (*Riparia × Rupestris, Riparia × Berlandieri, Rupestris × Berlandieri.*

The problem of adaptation to calcareous soils has been solved by the use of well-selected *Berlandieris*, or hybrids *Americo × Berlandieri*, which, if necessary, are treated by the Rassiguier process. It has at least given results equal to those obtained with certain direct producers, which never possess a resistance to phylloxera equal to that of Berlandieris; and we must never forget that *maximum resistance* to phylloxera should always be the first item considered in planting American vines. As a matter of fact, if under certain exceptional conditions, and for reasons it is not always easy to ascertain, a small resistance to phylloxera is sufficient; in the majority of cases the use of vines of low resistance has always resulted in failure, and compelled resorting to new and expensive planting. To quote an instance already mentioned: If in certain parts of the Var, fine Jacquez, producing abundantly, are to be found in fresh and fertile soils, it does not follow that in other parts where the soils are dry and poor the *Jacquez* (which does not resist phylloxera well) will succeed, and those viticulturists who planted it under such conditions regret now that they were unacquainted with the *Rupestris du Lot*, a graft-bearer growing in most soils, which would have prevented very many failures.

Finally, with regard to resistance to *black-rot*, there is no reason to think that our cépages of good quality will be replaced by direct producers resisting this disease better, as these would always yield an inferior crop. We know the results obtained by treatments with copper salts, and we think it will be possible to obtain still better results in future, and to save expenses by following the prescription published by the Commission appointed to study the black-rot disease. It is only in cases where all means of combating the disease must be abandoned, which would be absurd, that the use of *Noah*, for instance, should be advocated, as was done in the south-west of France.

We see from this that none of the direct producers actually known can be recommended, and it is towards European vines grafted on American stocks, strongly resistant to phylloxera, and well adapted to given soils, that vine-growers must exclusively turn their efforts, if they desire to make a success of reconstitution of phylloxerated vineyards. We will, therefore, only study the selection of graft-bearers fulfilling the conditions indicated:—

1st.—RESISTANCE TO PHYLLOXERA.

So far as resistance to phylloxera is concerned, the graft-bearers actually in use may be classified as follows, the scale of resistance ranging from 0 to 20, 20 being absolute resistance:—

	Resistance.
Alicante-Bouschet × Rupestris No. 136	17 ?
Aramon × Rupestris Ganzin No. 1	16 ?
Aramon × Rupestris Ganzin No. 2	16 ?
Berlandieri (selected forms)	17
Chasselas × Berlandieri No. 41	17 ?
Jacquez	12
Petit-Bouschet × Riparia	17
Riparia × Berlandieri No. 33	17
Riparia × Berlandieri No. 34	17
Riparia Gloire de Montpellier, or R. Portalis	18
Riparia Grand Glabre	18
Riparia × Rupestris 101-14	18
Riparia × Rupestris 3306	18
Riparia × Rupestris 3309	18
Rupestris du Lot, or R. Phénomène	18
Rupestris Martin	18
Rupestris Metallica	18
Rupestris Mission	18
Solonis	14
Taylor	13
Taylor-Narbonne	17
Tisserand (Cabernet × Berlandieri No. 333)	16 ?
Vialla	14

The natural tendency of vine-growers to use only those vines offering high resistance has caused a great many graft-bearers used at first to be eliminated. These graft-bearers have in some special cases succeeded, but in the majority of cases succumbed. They are given in the above list with marks below 14. Such are *Jacquez, Taylor, Vialla,* and *Solonis*, except in soils where they could not be replaced by any other, as we will see later on. It is not advisable to use Franco-American hybrids, for even if their resistance to phylloxera seems satisfactory their European strain is not in their favour, and they may sometimes result in grave failures. It is only in cases where vines of pure American origin cannot adapt themselves to the soil that the above hybrids may be used, but these circumstances seem to be very exceptional, and, in a general way, we may say that we possess pure American graft-bearers for all varieties of soils where the vine is generally cultivated, as we will show in the study of adaptation to soil.

2nd.—Adaptation to Soil.

With a few exceptions, the species of American vines growing in the United States do not thrive in limestone soils, especially if the limestone is in an easily assimilable form. They become more or less yellow when there is a small proportion of this substance, and die if there is a large percentage of it. Sometimes chlorosis brings about complete discoloration, and even the destruction of the *parenchyma* of the leaf, prevents the cane from lignifying, the vine becoming stunted and dying if the evil lasts several consecutive years. The reconstitution of vineyards on limestone soils has been one of the greatest difficulties vine-growers had to contend with; therefore an exact knowledge of the quantity of limestone different American graft-bearers can stand is of very great importance with regard to the study of adaptation to soil.

At the beginning of this question the percentage of carbonate of lime contained in soils where American vines grew well or became chlorosed was simply measured, and after the mission of P. Viala, in America, in 1887, B. Chauzit gave, in 1889, the following table, showing from personal analysis, the percentage of lime which different American vines could stand:—*

Percentage of Carbonate of Lime in Soil.	American Vines Growing Well.
Less than 10 per cent.	Most American Vines.
From 10 to 20 per cent.	Riparia, Taylor, Vialla.
From 20 to 30 per cent.	Jacquez, Rupestris, Solonis.
From 30 to 40 per cent.	Champin, Othello.
From 40 to 50 per cent.	V. Monticola.
Over 60 per cent.	V. Berlandieri.

* B. Chauzit: *Étude sur l'adaptation au sol des vignes Américaines*, in *Une Mission en Amérique*, by Pierre Viala. Montpellier, 1889.

These indications are now considered as insufficient. In the first place, they do not give any indication with regard to new graft-bearers studied since, and which have real value; further, they do not give any information with regard to the nature of the lime contained in the soils analyzed. We know now that the peculiar state of limestones of different physical nature affects American vines differently, assuming the percentage of carbonate of lime to be equal. They are more affected by soft and friable limestone, such as chalky, pebbly, or pulverized marl, and can, on the contrary, grow without becoming yellow in soils containing a high percentage of lime if this lime is in a crystalline or saccharoidal state, forming a sandy débris, and not paste or mud in the presence of water.

It would seem that in this latter form limestone is generally more soluble. Montdésir and Bernard have shown that it is possible to gauge the assimilability of limestone by the rate of disengagement of carbonic acid gas resulting from the action of acids on it. Houdaille and Semichon have continued this study, and made much progress. Bernard invented a *calcimeter* (Fig. 22), with which it is possible to rapidly ascertain the limestone contained in the soil, and to judge approximately from the rate of disengagement of carbonic acid gas, the more or less facility with which the limestone is decomposed.

This apparatus, which is easy to manipulate and costs very little, should be in the hands of all viticulturists who wish to study their soils themselves with the object of ascertaining which graft-bearer will give the best results. Houdaille's *calcimeter* is more complicated and provided with a self-registering curve-marking device, with the aid of which it is easy to ascertain the rate of disengagement of carbonic acid, and, therefore, the rate of decomposition of the carbonate of lime, but it is rather a laboratory instrument giving very complete indications.

The rate of decomposition, however, is not always sufficient to explain certain facts, such as the presence in soils of humus furnishing carbonic acid, decomposing limestone, and water which dissolves it. Most of the soils of the Charentes, in which vines become chlorosed, contained a high percentage of humus, which, according to the analysis of Chauzit, varies between 0·412 and 0·803 per cent.

Many other soils in which vines become chlorosed do not contain a very high percentage of lime, but they always contain a very high percentage of humus. Finally, the presence of clay closely united to lime seems to be a cause of diminution in the dangerous action of carbonate of lime upon American vines.

Certain soils, such as the blue marls, near Montpellier, grow (owing to the large proportion of clay which they contain) Riparias, which do not become yellow even grafted. When the sub-soil is at a depth of less than 20 inches, it has an action of the same order upon vines.

The good growth of many Franco-American hybrids in calcareous soils and their ready adaptation to grafting with American vines, which was pointed out by Viala and Ravaz, induced many

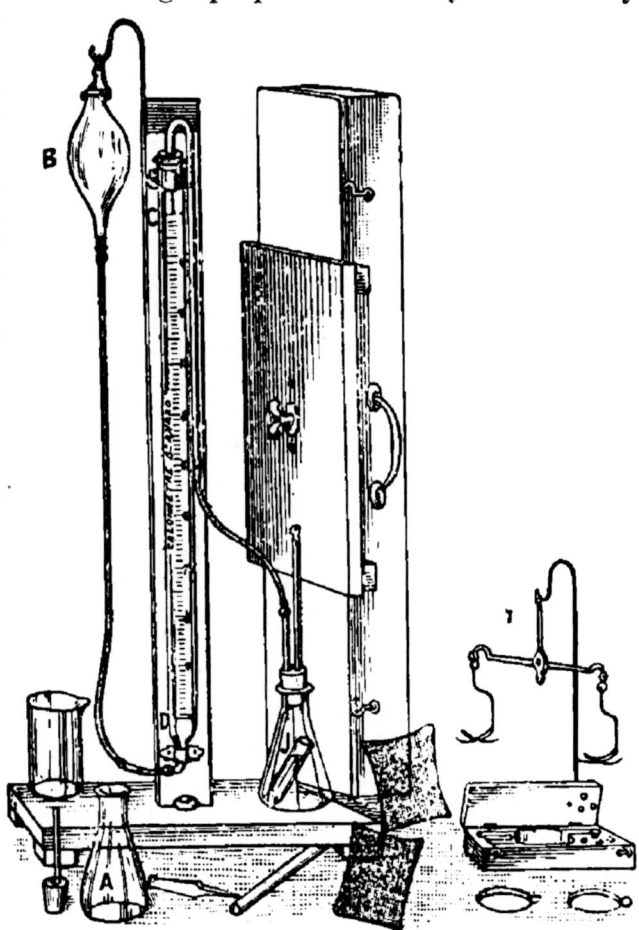

Fig. 22. Bernard's Calcimeter.

to work in that direction. Millardet, de Grasset, Couderc, Castel, Terras, Malègue and ourselves at the School of Agriculture of Montpellier, with many others, have made experiments in that direction. We tried by fecundating V. Vinifera with American species, such as the V. Berlandieri and V. Monticola, having already the power of resisting limestone, to obtain graft-bearers adapting themselves easily to such soils. Unfortunately, although in many instances we were successful in obtaining plants resisting chlorosis, we always failed to obtain vines having sufficient resistance to the action of phylloxera in soils in which it multiplies easily; and this is not surprising, as the strain of *Vinifera* has always a chance *à priori* of diminishing the resistance of the American parent. But now the time has come when we cannot sacrifice the resistance to phylloxera in favour of resistance to lime, and this is the reason which induced us to abandon the *Tisserand (Cabernet × Berlandieri No. 333)* of the School of Agriculture of Montpellier, which always bears in every soil perfectly green grafts, and seems more resistant than *Jacquez* to phylloxera, that is to say, sufficient in many cases, but not always. We cannot state that the Franco-American hybrids already created will not realize the desired conditions, but we feel convinced that the solution to the problem must be looked for in another direction.

American hybrids have been created without any strain of *Vinifera* whatever. Some of these resist limestone to a high degree, but those so far created do not resist it as well as the Franco-American (Franco × Berlandieri) hybrids, one of the parents only being resistant.

However, we can quote amongst these, remarkable types which may render real services in soils in which vines only get slight chlorosis, such as the Groies of the Charentes (*Riparia × Rupestris No.* 101-14, of Millardet, and de Grasset; *Riparia × Rupestris* 3306 *and* 3309, of Courderc; *Belton* or *Candicans × Monticola*). Further, certain types, such as the *Riparia × Berlandieri*, created by Millardet, de Grasset, Courderc, Malègue, &c.; the *Berlandieri × Riparia Nos. 33 and 34*, of the School of Agriculture of Montpellier, and a few others, will, perhaps, possess both qualities of resistance to lime and phylloxera, but they require further experimentation. It is self-evident, however, that it is amongst wild species living naturally in chalky soils in the United States that we have the best chance of finding types resisting chlorosis, and from this point of view the only two deserving to be studied are the *V. Monticola* and *V. Berlandieri*.

They both grow in Texas, and seem to be endowed with great power of resistance to phylloxera, drought, and chlorosis. The *Monticola* resists a little better, but, unfortunately, it does not root freely from cuttings, and the forms imported have not up to the present proved very vigorous.

Many forms of *Berlandieri* are vigorous, and furnish large and fructiferous graft-bearers. Unfortunately, they do not root freely when the usual method of planting is followed. However, some nurserymen, such as Euryale Rességuier, of Alénya, have succeeded in obtaining 50 per cent. of strikes. Viala and Mazade have proved, by experiments conducted at the School of Agriculture of Montpellier, that the grafting of *Berlandieri* cuttings increases the strike in a large proportion.

Although we may hope that certain Franco-American and Americo-American hybrids will enable vine-growers to obtain satisfactory results in calcareous soils, it is better to use *Berlandieri*, which has already proved its good quality.

We may, therefore, in the actual state of our knowledge, consider this vine as giving the best solution to the question of reconstitution of vineyards in limestone soils. The practical difficulties which are met with reside principally in the choice of types. We must, according to Viala, look for the following characters:—Vigorous vegetation, very thick leaves shining on both faces, with extremities of shoots only slightly tomentose, and young leaves golden brown.

These characteristics are to be found in the forms already selected, which we have previously described:—*B. Rességuier Nos. 1 and 2, B. Daignère, B. of Angeac, B. de Lafont No. 9, B. Mazade.*

We have no doubt that if the selection is continued new types of equal, if not superior, value will be found.

Unfortunately, good Berlandieri forms are expensive, and this prevents their general use, for growers will not risk money if they are not certain of the resistance of the stock offered to them, especially when they know that a less resistant graft-bearer may do.

No doubt, the grafting of buds on old stumps is a rapid means of propagating cuttings. However, as cuttings of other species are placed on the market at a small cost growers generally prefer buying them if they are adaptable to their soil. For this reason we will study the value of the different stocks most generally used, showing the quantities of limestone they can stand. These indications have only an approximate value, as the nature of the lime and the numerous conditions already explained (depth of soil, presence of humus, presence of free carbonic acid, clay, humidity, &c.) may greatly vary the effects of this substance. Humidity seems to have a greater influence than any, and the limits of limestone given hereafter, which were established from experiments made in the dry parts of the Mediterranean region, must be reduced in damper countries.

V. Riparia.—Two wild forms have been retained, the *Riparia Gloire de Montpellier* and *R. Grand Glabre*, which may be regarded as equivalent. Like all Riparias they have the inconvenience of forming a trunk of smaller diameter than that of the scion (Fig. 23), but they certainly constitute the best graft-bearers in the majority of soils on account of the abundance of their production. Therefore, whenever the drought and the percentage of limestone is not too great, they should be preferred. They may be used with almost every chance of success in soils containing up to 20 per cent. of carbonate of lime. In the Mediterranean region we may even use them in soils containing 25 per cent., under the condition that the subsoil is at a depth of at least 20 inches, and that the soil is fertile.

Fig. 23.—V. Vinifera grafted on V. Riparia, showing almost normal difference between size of stock and scion

V. Rupestris.—Again two forms have been selected as superior: the *R. Martin* and *R. du Lot*. The former is very resistant to phylloxera, and succeeds under conditions similar to those suiting Riparias. In calcareous soils they bear less fructiferous grafts, but as they can grow in poorer and more pebbly soils, they are preferred under certain circumstances. It grows better than the latter in rainy and damp climates, such as the centre and west of France.

The *Rupestris du Lot* is remarkable for its resistance to limestone; it withstands 40 per cent. in the Mediterranean region, and sometimes 50 per cent. when the soil is deep and the limestone not too soluble; therefore, it would be advisable to use it in the damper climates of the south-west in soils containing more than 25 per cent. It bears grafts of great vigour, but which (probably on account of the excess of vegetation) are sometimes little fructiferous. It is, therefore, in poor, pebbly soils that is should be planted; in such soils it presents advantages, and is equal, if not superior, to Riparia so far as the fructification of its grafts is concerned. Heavy clayey soils do not affect it provided, however, that they are not too damp, for it is easily attacked by *pourridié* (*Dematophora necatrix*). It has sometimes been stated that its resistance to phylloxera is not perfect; but, although we have seen a few tuberosities on its roots, they were never numerous or sufficiently developed to become dangerous.

The *Riparia × Rupestris* 101-14, of Millardet and de Grasset, and the 3306 and 3309 of Courderc, are less known as graft-bearers, but, however, have certain real qualities. They seem to be endowed with great resistance to phylloxera, and, with regard to limestone, may be regarded as equivalent to the Rupestris du Lot. They can even withstand a high percentage of limestone, and bear very fine European grafts. They should be used instead of the Rupestris du Lot in damp soils, where the latter might be attacked by *pourridié*, or in soils so rich that they cause a powerful vegetation resulting in diminished fructification of grafts.

V. Berlandieri.—The well-selected forms of this species resisting limestone well are also remarkable for their great resistance to phylloxera, the facility with which they knit with Vinifera grafts, their abundant fructification, and great resistance to drought. They may be used in soils containing more than 25 per cent. of limestone in the west, and more than 40 per cent. in the south of France, or in all soils where limestone is in the dangerous form, or where local conditions increase its action.

Salt is also an objectionable substance in soils, and, if the proportion of it is large enough, may render soils unfit for vegetation.

The graft-bearer withstanding the greatest percentage of this substance is the Solonis, and it is alone used for reconstitution in the saline soils of the Aude and the Pyrénées-Orientales. As it is impossible to use any other stock, one does not take into account its resistance to phylloxera, which, however, is not of such great importance in this case, salt soils being unfavorable to the development of the insect.

To sum up, the following is a list of the soils in which certain American vines may succeed :—

- 1st. Fresh, fertile, deep soils, containing less than 25 per cent. of limestone: *Riparia Gloire de Montpellier*, and *R. Grand Glabre*.
- 2nd. Fresh soils but slightly fertile, and of little depth, clayey, containing less than 25 per cent. of limestone: *Rupestris Martin*.
- 3rd. Clayey soils, not too damp or not too pebbly, poor, containing up to 40 per cent. of limestone in the south and 25 per cent. in the west of France, or up to 80 per cent. in certain well-drained tufas: *Rupestris du Lot*.
- 4th. Clayey soils more or less damp, containing up to 40 per cent. of limestone: *Riparia × Rupestris, No. 101-14, 3306, 3309*.
- 5th. Calcareous soils of a chalky nature, pulverized white marl, &c : *Berlandieris*.
- 6th. Salt soils, or *pourridié* soils : *Solonis*.

B.—METHODS OF MULTIPLICATION.

CHAPTER III.

METHODS OF PROPAGATION APPLICABLE TO VINES.—PROPAGATION BY SEEDS.

The vine, like most plants of the upper scale of the vegetable kingdom, may be multiplied by *seeds* or by different methods of segmentation, *cuttings*, *layers*, and *grafts*. All these methods are of different value in different cases, and it is by a sound choice between these that the success of the plantation often depends. We will shortly study them, examining their various applications, and the special care they require.

Propagation by seeds.—We may sow vine seeds with the object of obtaining: first, new cépages; second, resistant graft-bearers.

The creation of new cépages is very tedious work, which cannot be performed by most viticulturists, who generally desire to obtain as quickly as possible a vine with known qualities. However, it possesses a certain interest, and the Americans have by this means obtained, in a relatively short time, many meritorious cépages from their wild types. We think it advisable to describe it for those who would feel disposed to enrich viticulture with new forms perhaps better adapted to special conditions.

While the different methods of multiplication and segmentation simply consist in placing a portion of the plant under conditions allowing it to continue the life begun in common with the mother plant, without modifying it, those of multiplication by seed give rise to a new vine, differing in certain measures from those which produce it, although resembling them in its general characters; for instance, many are unfertile or inferior to their parents, preventing this mode of reproduction being used with direct producers. But this variation, which is a great obstacle when we desire to preserve a good type, becomes a condition of success when new types are to be created. Viticulturists select amongst the new types produced in this way those which seem best adapted to given soils and conditions, and multiply them afterwards by the ordinary process of segmentation.

If the variations are too frequent and too considerable in seedlings to allow this method to be used for the production of fruit, we may, however, by observing certain precautions, avoid modifications of the root system special to each vine, and upon which their resistance depends. We can therefore utilize it to create graft-bearers for our European vines, especially in districts not yet infected, where the introduction of rootlings would be inadvisable.

(A.) *Choice of Cépages.*—With the object of obtaining new types of direct producers, it is advisable to use cultivated varieties having already some of the required characters, but which do not possess such fixed characters as wild types, and which consequently are able to furnish offspring preserving the good qualities of their parents, and at the same time able to acquire additional qualities. Unfortunately, the varieties thus attained do not generally resist phylloxera well, as was proved in the case of *Saint-Sauveur*, obtained from *Jacquez* seedlings by Gaston Bazille, and the *Herbemont of Aurelle* resulting from *Herbemont Touzan seedlings*. We may, by crossing varieties offering qualities which we would like to see united in a single individual, try to obtain an intermediate variety, possessing them all. Crossings between V. Vinifera and certain American species were tried, with the object of obtaining direct producers, endowed with an abundant production of grapes of good quality and sufficient resistance to phylloxera. The *V. Vinifera* and the *V. Berlandieri* were also crossed, with the idea of obtaining graft-bearers, thriving well in limestone soil. A great number of hybrids obtained in this way will certainly resemble either one or other of the parents, and lack in some qualities, but it is not impossible (although very improbable) to obtain an individual possessing all the good qualities of both parents. However, it was noticed that the prevailing characters were always those of the male parent; therefore in a crossing between Vinifera and American vines the latter must always be used as male, so as to diminish as little as possible the

PROPAGATION BY SEEDS.

qualities of resistance to phylloxera. We have in a previous chapter, when describing direct producers and graft-bearers, explained the value of the association of different species.

Hybridization.—The operation is carried out in the following manner :—The flower of the vine presents a peculiar disposition ; its petals, instead of opening at the top, become separated from the calyx at their base, and remain united at the top, forming a kind of hood maintaining the anthers in contact with the pistil (Figs. 24, 25, and 26). The hood of

Fig. 24.   Fig. 25.   Fig. 26.
Different stages in the opening of a normal Vine Flower.

each flower must therefore be removed before the petals become detached. When this is done we must ascertain that no pollen has fallen off from the anthers ; the stamens are then removed with special scissors and forceps (Fig. 27)

Fig. 27.
Scissors and Forceps used for the removal of corolla and stamens.

Fig. 28.
Gauze Bag used for protecting flowers from contamination.

Fig. 29.
Gauze Bag kept open with a spiral wire.

to prevent accidental fecundation. The flowers of the variety which is to play the part of male are then rubbed or shaken above the former so as to cover them with pollen. The fecundated flowers are then covered with a gauze bag (Fig. 28) so as to protect them from contact with any foreign pollen. When the periods of florescence do not correspond, we may forward that of late varieties by growing them under glass, or retard that of early varieties by planting them in the shade and sheltering the bunches of flowers in paper bags.

After the fecundation has been performed, it is advisable to take some precautions to avoid non-setting, which may result from the washing away of pollen by rain or from a sudden fall in the temperature. To remove the first cause of this accident we must keep the bags open by placing a spiral piece of wire inside (Fig. 29), or sheltering them with little hoods made of paper dipped in linseed oil. The second cause may be removed by repeated sulphuring or by annular incision.

Sometimes one may be induced to use, not only seeds resulting from direct hybridization, but also those variations produced by hybridized varieties; unfortunately, such offspring always resemble one or other of the parents and are therefore of no interest.

When seedlings are used with the object of creating graft-bearers, we should, on the contrary, avoid as far as possible these variations, so as not to lose the quality of resistance to phylloxera, which is after all, the only reason for their existence. We must therefore use wild types, the main characters of which have been fixed by long natural selection, and among these we should choose those of very early florescence, rendering spontaneous fecundation with less resisting species impossible. Wild *V. Riparia*, *V. Rupestris*, and *V. Berlandieri* seem to fulfil these conditions, and experience has proved the wonderful permanence of these general forms in their offspring. Therefore we think it advisable to use these only when we have not an opportunity of studying the resistance of others by growing them in soils infested with phylloxera.

(B.) *Selection of seeds.*—The seeds used for propagation must be gathered the same year, from berries which have reached complete maturity. Experience has proved that those fermented with the must germinate in the same proportion as those removed from the berries.

(C.) *Preparation of seeds.*—Seeds planted without any special preparation generally germinate irregularly and successively. With the object of avoiding this we must stratify them in winter in sand kept damp during March.[*]

---

[*] Corresponding to September in Victoria.

If this is not possible on account of the seeds having been received too late, they should be soaked in water for two or three days; however, stratification is preferable.

(D.) *Sowing.*—The sowing is done in April* so that the young plants will not suffer from spring frosts.

The seeds are buried about $\frac{1}{10}$ inch deep in well-mellowed and manured soil, or covered with from $\frac{1}{10}$ to ½ inch of loose soil or sand if the soil is compact. They are planted in lines 1 to 2 feet apart, and every 6 inches on the lines. Experience has proved that the development during the first year is proportionate to the distance between the plants. Finally, it is advisable to cover the bed with a light mulching.

(E.) *Care.*—Watering every two or three days with a very fine rose, and careful hoeing are necessary. The germination generally takes place a month after the sowing; the young plants are often very sensitive to the action of the sun; they must not be watered in the day time, and it is even advisable to shelter them with canvas during the hot hours of the day.

(F.) *Lifting.*—The seedlings of *V. Riparia* frequently reach 4 to 5 feet in length the first year; those of *V. Æstivalis* rarely exceed 18 inches to 2 feet. However, it is necessary in both cases to lift them at the end of the winter and plant them out, as they suffer if left longer in the seed bed.

(G.) *Study and Utilization of Seedlings.*—When the object of hybridization is to obtain new direct producers, the florescence of the young seedlings should be forwarded as much as possible so as to assist the study of their fertility and the quality of their fruit. The time necessary for the young seedlings to fructify has been greatly exaggerated. Some *Clinton* seedlings produced fruit the third year at the School of Agriculture, Montpellier, and most other seedlings fructify at the fourth or fifth year. Further, there are different means of forwarding fructification: layering, inarching, annular incision, or ligature of a long rod preserved for the following year, or still better, grafting a bud of a young seedling on an old stump. Generally the fruit

---

* Corresponding to October in Victoria.

does not acquire at first the size and abundance it would reach in years to come; we must assist the development of these qualities by the selection of cuttings, repeatedly grafting and layering, rather short pruning, and cultivation in first-class soil.

When the object is to obtain graft-bearers, the young plants may be utilized in two ways, as it is possible either to use the young plant itself or cuttings from it.

Seedlings of forms growing rapidly, such as wild *Riparias, Solonis,* &c., can often be grafted with the cleft method the first year, but the vigour and the aptitude of each plant not being equal the resulting plantation would be irregular. It is preferable to use cuttings only, these cuttings being selected amongst the strongest and those having the greatest vegetation.

However, before using seedlings we must ascertain their degree of resistance to phylloxera. The use of a rapid and sure method is necessary, for the fact of a vine dying in phylloxerated ground does not mean that phylloxera is the cause of its death; it might be a defect in the adaptation, or any other cause. Further, the action of phylloxera is very slight, and sometimes *nil* in certain soils, so that if trials are made in such soils we may conclude that the resistance is sufficient when, in fact, this is not the case. The study of the lesions produced by phylloxera on the roots is the only means of ascertaining quickly and surely the degree of resistance of each type. When the roots of a vine recently attacked by the insect are examined a great number of swollen radicles are to be seen, distorted and forming *nodosities;* the larger roots bear protuberances, which have been termed *tuberosities.* These different swellings alter with time, and penetrate more or less deeply into the tissue of the root, resulting in the death of the root when they develop in great numbers and acquire considerable size. The degree of probable resistance to phylloxera can, therefore, be ascertained by studying the number and the size of these tuberosities. Vines not bearing any trace of the action of phylloxera, although growing in phylloxerated land, may be regarded as indemnified. (*V. Rotundifolia* alone fulfils this condition.) The others may be classified according to the *scale of resistance* which we have mentioned already. The indemnified vines come first, then those bearing more or less numerous nodosities on the rootlets without *tuberosities* (these give practically the highest degree of resistance); finally, those bearing numerous *tuberosities*. The larger and the more penetrating these lesions are, the lower the variety must be placed in the scale of resistance.

A longer study made in different soils and climates eventually enables the nurseryman to gather more exact and complete data, but although it may result in his discarding a few types which, for various reasons, do not show at first very important lesions, it never results in his taking back types eliminated after examination of the lesions of their roots.

To sum up, seedlings may be used to produce resistant graft-bearers in countries not yet infested with phylloxera; their other applications are rather within the domain of nurserymen or amateurs than in that of vine-growers.

CHAPTER IV.

PROPAGATION BY CUTTINGS.

Propagation by cuttings is the oldest and most generally used method of multiplication. It is considered by the majority of viticulturists as superior to any other in practice, and certain types of vines are rejected simply because they do not root freely from cuttings. As a matter of fact, it is very easy of execution and has the property, like any other method of propagation by segmentation, of preserving the characters of the type from which the cutting has been taken, and even sometimes the characters of one single branch which differs from other branches on the same plant. The only differences which may arise between the mother plant and the plant resulting from its cuttings are produced by differences in soils and climates, and are generally shown only by modifications in the development and vigour, not altering the fundamental properties of the original type, such as resistance to phylloxera, taste of fruit, &c.

The facility with which all the *V. Vinifera* varieties grow from cuttings contributed to the generalization of this method in Europe. Since it has been applied to American vines, certain forms have been found to strike with difficulty, but vine-growers, far from discarding this method of multiplication when using American vines, have, on the contrary, made a more complete study of the means of insuring its success.

The art of the viticulturist consists in promoting the growth of roots on the fragments of cane used as cuttings (after selecting the best cuttings capable of producing plants of good quality) by placing these under special conditions. We will study the following items with regard to this method of multiplication:—1st, Choice of canes, care to be taken for their preservation in transit; 2nd, best type of cuttings; 3rd, means of promoting root growth; 4th, time of planting; 5th, choice of soil (planting out or nurseries).

1st.—Choice of Cuttings; Care to be taken in Preservation and Transit.

(A.) *Selection of Cuttings.*—The canes should only be cut when they are well lignified. This precaution should be more specially observed when we have to deal with vines lignifying late in winter. We should also discard all cuttings from plants attacked by any of the different cryptogamic diseases, such as *anthracnosis, mildew*, &c. They are generally not well developed and are liable to carry disease into a new vineyard.

Experience has proved that the mean part of canes of medium development with rather close nodes offers the best chances of strike, and produces the most fructiferous plants, becoming rapidly fertile. The large canes do not root as freely, and grow wood rather than fruit, while those too slender are liable to dry before even throwing roots. They often do not lignify sufficiently, and generally give weak plants.

When we propagate direct producers we should always choose canes which have borne flowers, which are not subject to non-setting, and which have given abundant and fine fruit.*

These characters, peculiar to each cane, get well fixed by selection of this kind, and a considerable increase in the production is thus obtained. On the contrary, when we propagate graft-bearers our only object should be to obtain vigorous plants, and we need not take into consideration the above indications.

(B.) *Preservation of Cuttings.*—The canes cut just before planting offer the greatest chances of success. It is well known that cuttings which have travelled a long distance, such as those sent from America, are under very unfavorable conditions when compared with those gathered in the vineyard where they are to be planted.

Packing.—However, as it is often necessary to send cuttings abroad or to use cuttings which have travelled, we think it useful to give a few indications with regard to packing, and the care to be given to them when they arrive.

---

* These indications must be more particularly followed when multiplying *Jacquez*, as the variations of this cépage, which are not very fertile, actually tend to predominate on account of the indiscriminate use of its cuttings.

To obtain perfect preservation of cuttings they should be placed under such conditions that they neither dry nor absorb more water than they naturally contain. Desiccation kills the cuttings by removing their water of vegetation. An excess of water induces the development of bacteria and moulds which may injure the cuttings. Sometimes, if this does not take place the tissues of the wood, gorged with water, dry away very quickly when exposed to the air.

Packing in fresh, light, almost dry soils realizes the best conditions. Unfortunately, the weight of such packages renders them impracticable. When the cuttings have not to travel very far the best way is to surround the bundles with straw, after wrapping the base in slightly damp moss. For longer voyages the bundles may be completely surrounded with moss or saw-dust, mixed with powdered charcoal, the cases being lined with oil paper.

Care to be given on arrival.—On arrival the cuttings should be unpacked and dipped into water for one or two days, or better, stratified in slightly damp soil. The cuttings sent from America are often packed in damp *sphagnum;* this, however, has the defect of being too wet. If the cuttings packed in this way have not suffered during the voyage they should be stratified in almost dry sand and removed in small lots prior to planting out. It is also advisable to keep them in a bucket with water at the bottom until the moment of planting. When these cuttings have to be kept a certain time before planting the best means of preserving their vitality is to stratify them in sand in the cellar or in a shed.

2ND.—BEST TYPES OF CUTTINGS.

(A.) *Different Systems.*—The types of cuttings most generally used are those known as *Crossettes* (mallet-cuttings),[*] that is to say, those having a small piece of wood attached obliquely at their base (Figs. 30 and 31), and those which consist of any part of the cane (Fig. 33). In Crossette cuttings the lower end of the cane is very favorable to the growth of well-placed roots. They have been used for a long time almost exclusively on account of this, but, however, have the defect of not being easily planted with a dibble on account of the slanting disposition of the two-year-old wood;

---

[*] Columella (2 B.C.–65 A.D.) mentions this type of cutting as *malleolus*. Publii Virgilii Maronis Georgicorum, Libri quatuor. Trans. by John Martin, London, 1755. (Transls.)

PROPAGATION BY CUTTINGS.

and, further, the latter is too old to root well, and often rots, injuring the whole plant. To prevent this accident the piece of two-year-old wood is removed, preserving only the swelling formed by the ring of latent buds (Fig. 32).

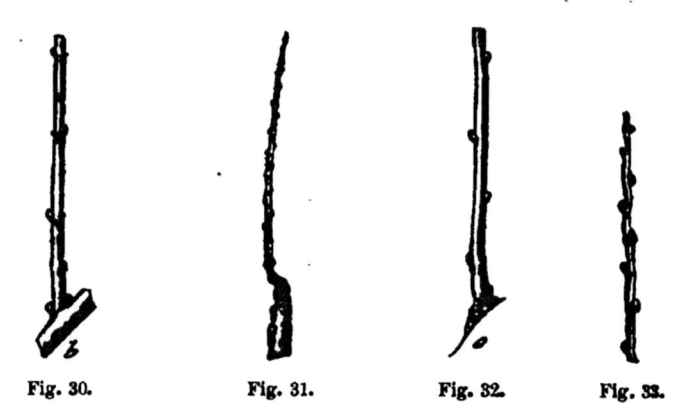

Fig. 30.   Fig. 31.   Fig. 32.   Fig. 33.

Figs. 30 and 31.—Mallet Cuttings. Fig. 32.—Cutting with two years old wood removed. Fig. 33.—Ordinary Cutting.

Unfortunately, the scarcity of certain American varieties and the necessity of utilizing all the wood from the base to the extremity does not allow the use of this method, and generally we have to be content with cuttings taken from any part of the shoot. The latter, which are easy to procure, give satisfactory results in most cases.

(B.) *Length of Cuttings.*—As a principle, when the future development and good constitution of the plant alone are taken into consideration, the shortest cuttings are best. Cuttings with a single bud, for instance (Fig. 34), give a bundle of very powerful roots in the prolongation of the stem, and produce plants of remarkable vigour (Fig. 35). Very long cuttings, on the contrary (Fig. 36B), grow a large number of tufts of roots at each node. They do not make very large individual development, and, as shown in the figure, diminish in length towards the base, which is incapable of growing roots with any vitality, and often rots and dies away. But the question is not

Fig. 34.
One-eye Cutting.

as simple as it appears at first. The necessity of placing the cutting in a sufficiently damp surrounding to insure its strike is a complication; in most cases the required moisture is only found at a certain depth in the soil, and therefore we must make the cutting a greater length than seems preferable at first.

The drier the soil the longer the cutting should be.* Their length generally varies between 10 and 14 inches. One or two buds only are left above the surface of the ground.

The use of single-eye cuttings, or herbaceous cuttings, has also been recommended, the former being sown with drills and covered with an inch or so of soil. This method is also used to strike rare varieties under glass; but, unfortunately, the cépages, which, on account of their great value only, allow the expense of glass frames, do not, even with this method, give a satisfactory percentage of strikes. As for herbaceous cuttings, it can only be practically done with suckers taken off the grafts, planted in light soil, watered, and shaded. They strike easily, but never give such strong plants, and their wood is never well lignified.†

Fig. 35.
Young plant of average vigour obtained from a one-eye cutting of V. Vinifera.

Therefore, in many cases we are forced to use any part of a shoot (Fig. 37). We will now study the means of promoting their root-growth.

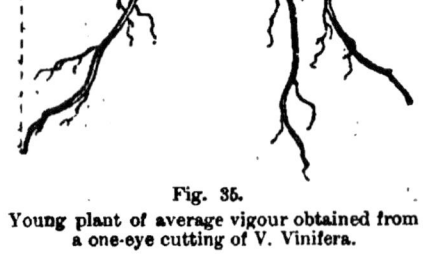

---

* If the soil is very dry, it is better to root the cuttings in the nursery the year before, and plant them out as rootlings. The inconvenience resulting from the use of long cuttings is thus avoided.

† The Duchess of Fitz-James obtained excellent results with this method, using hothouses established for the purpose.

3rd.—Means of Promoting the Root-Growth on Cuttings.

The evolution of roots can only take place in sufficiently warm and moist surroundings, without, however, being excessively so. In practice, the greatest difficulty met with, is

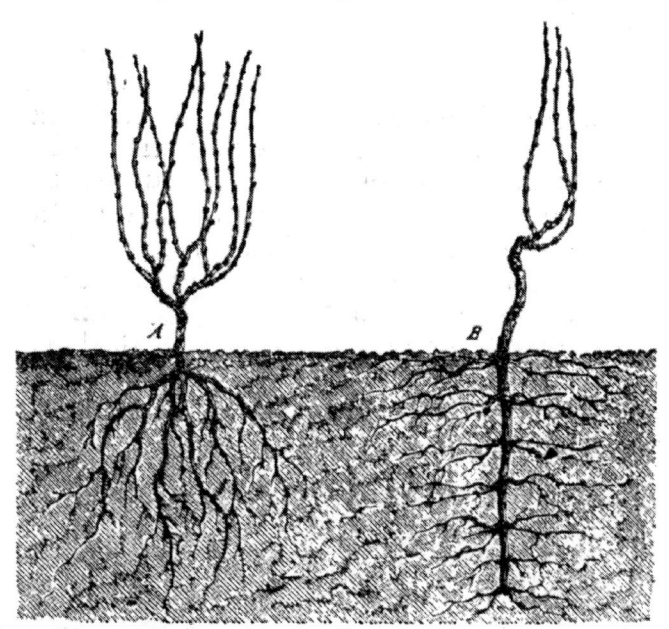

Fig. 36.—A. Vine resulting from a short cutting. B. Vine resulting from a long cutting.

to prevent the cutting from drying before it is able to provide for the water it evaporates. Certain American species are very refractory on account of the time elapsing between the bursting of the buds and the development of the roots; this forces the plant to evaporate largely before it is able to draw the necessary water from the soil. For instance, while the *V. Riparia*, *V. Labrusca*, and *V. Rupestris* strike easily from cuttings, *V. Æstivalis*, and more especially

Fig. 37.—Ordinary bent cutting.

V. Berlandieri, strike with difficulty; while *V. Candicans* and *V. Rotundifolia* are almost impossible to multiply from cuttings.

The means of remedying this difficulty have been studied with great care, especially with regard to the *V. Berlandieri*, which contains, as we have seen, most valuable forms for calcareous soils. These means may be grouped in two classes—1st. Those which hasten the development of the roots ; 2nd. Those which prevent desiccation till the roots start to grow.

The first means can be arrived at by stratification, soaking, barking, torsion or bruising.

(A.) *Stratification.*—This consists in burying the cuttings during winter in very light soil or slightly moist sand, so as to determine the formation of *callus.* It has been recommended to strike the cuttings vertically and upside down, as it was thought that it would cause the sap to run towards the upper bud, which, when planted, would be the lower bud, and furnish the roots with abundant food. The experiments carried out at the School of Agriculture of Montpellier with this object did not show any difference between this method and the ordinary horizontal method of stratification. When the cuttings are taken out of the heaps of sand, they should be dipped in water to prevent them from drying before planting.

(B.) *Soaking.*—The soaking of cuttings in water produces effects similar to those of stratification, but, if prolonged, may cause disadvantages which never happen with the latter process. The wood is liable to lose, through maceration, a part of the soluble matters it contains, or to rot ; therefore, it must only be used when stratification is impossible, and should not last more than five or six days.

(C.) *Barking.*—This is done with the object of inducing the formation of *callus*, which seems to play the part of roots for a time, and to lay bare the layer of cells from which the roots are thrown. It is done by removing two thongs of bark on the part which is to be buried ; a small tool, made by Leydier and Lencieux, enables this operation to be performed rapidly. We may arrive at the same result by torsion or bruising, but the water always penetrates through the splits, reaching the pith and causing it to decay, so that by the use of the latter method we rarely obtain healthy plants. To sum up, barking, which has been used for a very long time in the South of France, is preferable, and can be applied together with stratification.

(D.) *Watering, &c.*—Watering and mulching fix in the soil the water necessary to the growth of the cutting, but can only be used practically in nurseries. It greatly increases the percentage of strikes. The water should be allowed to percolate through the soil. If the soil is very compact and if the quantity of water used is considerable the cuttings will rot.

Complete covering with sand checks the growth of the buds and consequently the formation of leaves, which are the principal organs of evaporation, but does not prevent the formation of roots. It also acts as a kind of mulching, preventing the desiccation of the soil. If the cuttings are at a certain distance apart a small mound of sand is formed round each of them, and if they are planted close together in lines, continuous ridges are formed in that direction.

Shade greatly diminishes evaporation through the leaves; it may be obtained by canvassing or by placing the nursery under trees with light foliage; the green rays of light which alone pass through the leaves are not conducive to evaporation.

We should not forget, however, that although shade helps the strike greatly, it ultimately prevents the development of young plants, which must transpire abundantly to obtain food and rapidly increase in size; therefore it should only be used as a temporary means.

4TH.—MOST FAVORABLE TIME FOR PLANTING CUTTINGS.

It was formerly thought, in the South of France, that the earlier the cuttings were put into the ground the larger the percentage of strikes, except in very damp soils, and, as a matter of fact, early planting gave the result vine-growers now obtain by stratification, *i.e.*, *callusing*. But, when cuttings are planted out early, they are liable to suffer from the excess of humidity during winter, and from the action of frosts. It is evidently preferable to stratify the cuttings in sand and to plant them out rather late, when the temperature is high enough to induce prompt vegetation.

It is towards the end of March and the beginning of April[*] in the Mediterranean regions that these conditions seem to be realized. However, the time for planting depends also on the nature of the soil; light, warm, well-exposed soils should always be planted earlier than cold and damp soils.

---

[*] September and October in Victoria.

Finally, Viala and Mazade have shown that with *Berlandieris*, which are naturally very difficult to strike from cuttings, a large proportion (40 per cent., instead of 6 to 8 per cent.) is obtained if the canes are only pruned when they have herbaceous shoots 3 to 4 inches in length, these being cut away before planting.

This method, unfortunately, rapidly exhausts the mother plants.

5TH.—SELECTION OF SOILS FOR CUTTINGS.

Cuttings may be planted out direct, or in nurseries, where they will root, and then be planted out the following year as rootlings.

(A.) *Planting out.*—The direct planting out of cuttings offers the following advantages:—It saves the expense of transplanting and the check in the development of the plant which results from this operation, but it generally has the disadvantage of placing the cutting in unfavorable conditions for rooting. It should only be adopted in light, fresh, and fertile soils with varieties striking easily.

(B.) *Planting in nurseries.*—Planting in nurseries enables vine-growers to place their cuttings in more favorable conditions for development, by selecting the soil and giving special care to the nurseries. Further, it diminishes the cost during the first year, for the plantation being more compact, the cultural operations are conducted on a much smaller area. It should always be used when a vineyard is to be established in clayey soils, or in dry, pebbly, shallow soils, or when rare varieties are to be propagated. Nurseries should always be established for the purpose of replacing "misses" in a young vineyard. We will see how this is done when studying the establishment of the vineyard.

(C.) *Establishment of a nursery and care to be given to it.*—A nursery should be established as far as possible in light, warm, well-drained soil with means of irrigation. The soil should be perfectly cleaned and disturbed to a depth of from 1 to 2 feet; manured with easily assimilable fertilizers, such as decomposed stable manure, old fowl-yard manure, guano, or chemical fertilizers. The planting is done in the following manner:—The cuttings are placed upright in small trenches with vertical sides (Figs. 38, 39,

PROPAGATION BY CUTTINGS.

and 40); a part of the mellowed soil is pressed on the base of the cutting with the foot, and the trench completely filled with the rest of the soil (Figs. 41, 42, 43). The distance generally left between the cuttings is not sufficient to allow the plant to reach complete development during the first year. The most favorable distance would be 20 inches between the lines, and 6 to 8 inches in the lines.

Fig. 38.
Open trench for the plantation of cuttings.

Fig. 39.
Sand placed at the bottom to promote root growth.

Fig. 40.
Cuttings placed along the side of the trench.

When there is no means of irrigation, and when the soil is not naturally moist, it is advisable to cover the whole surface with a mulching. The care to be given to these cuttings simply consists in hoeing to destroy weeds, without, however, removing the mulching during the whole of the summer. When, on the contrary, it is possible to irrigate, the plants are slightly earthed up, so as to leave little drains between the rows in which the water may flow, percolate through the soil, and reach the roots. Frequent hoeing should take place after each watering so as to keep the whole surface loose.

Fig. 41.
Soil (T) rammed above the sand.

Fig. 42.
Mellowed soil (U) placed above the rammed soil.

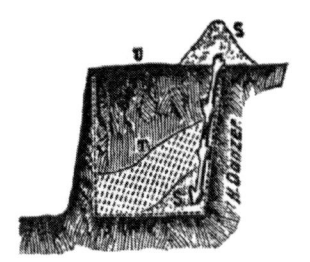

Fig. 43.
Ridge of sand (S) covering the tops of the cuttings.

The cuttings may be left one or two years in the nursery. Those left two years are naturally stronger, but they do not acquire all the development they would if planted out, on account of the small space available. Further, the size and the length of their roots renders transplanting rather difficult; they have to be cut or broken, and, finally, when planted out, their growth is checked to such an extent that no advantage is derived from it. Therefore it is preferable in most cases not to leave the cuttings over a year in the nursery.

Such are the main results of experience with regard to the propagation of American vines by cuttings. Although this method may be considered as the most important, and is the most used, American vines may be propagated by layering.

CHAPTER V.

PROPAGATION BY LAYERS.

Layering consists in inducing the growth of roots on a cane before it is separated from the mother plant. This method, which, like propagation by cuttings, preserves all the characters of the mother plant and even those of the cane, offers the advantage of better insuring the strike of the young plant, as it is only separated from the mother stock when it is provided with all organs necessary to its existence. Therefore it should be preferred, although rather complicated, for species not rooting freely, such as *V. Candicans* and *V. Berlandieri*, or for rare and expensive cépages. We will study successively the following items:—1st. Types of layers. 2nd. Means of promoting their root growth. 3rd. Best time for layering.

1st.—Principal Types of Layers.

These are:—A. *Ordinary layering;* B. *Complete burying of the mother plant;* C. *Multiple layering;* D. *Reversed layering.*

(A.) *Ordinary layering.*—This may be used for the production of rootlings, filling up a vacant space in a vineyard, liberating an American variety grafted on a European vine, or for rooted nodes used as stock for bench grafting. When rootlings alone are required a portion of the cane is buried underground as close as possible to the mother plant, leaving two eyes projecting from the soil at a certain distance from it. All the intermediate buds between the mother plant and the point where the cane enters the soil are removed, to prevent the development of shoots at the expense of the layer. The part in the ground must be as short as possible so as to save wood and use the extremity as a cutting, and also to avoid the formation of a great number of tufts of roots, with small individual development.

This layering may be done with lignified or herbaceous shoots. In the latter case we gain time as we obtain rootlings the same year; when such rootlings are to be transplanted, it is necessary to prune them before planting out, so as to leave only two tufts of well-constituted roots. These acquire much larger size than if they had all been allowed to remain on the rootling.

Ordinary layering can also be adopted for filling up vacant places in an old vineyard, or for liberating American canes grafted on European vines. In both these cases the layer has to remain in the place where it is performed. Its execution is shown in Fig. 44; after having dug out the dead

Fig. 44.—Ordinary layering.

stump and carefully removed all the roots, a trench is opened between the mother plant and the place where the dead vine was growing; this trench is deep enough to allow the ploughing to be performed in the vineyard without touching the cane (about a foot). A cane sufficiently long is selected in such a position as not to alter the shape of the mother plant after it is cut away. It enters the soil as close as possible to the mother plant, is buried at the bottom of the trench, the extremity turned up vertically and tied to a stake, leaving two buds free above the ground. The trench is filled with mellowed soil well rammed against the cane.

Manure is often put into the trench so as to promote the development of roots. However, it seems preferable to manure only the mother plant the first year, and to manure the layer after it has been separated from the mother plant. One avoids in this way a growth of roots from the mother plant towards the trench, which would withdraw assimilable matters before the layer had time to produce roots large enough to allow it to compete.

When the cane is not long enough to reach the place where the young plant is to be established, successive layers may be resorted to, or the grafting of another cane by the whip-tongue system, the layering being performed in the usual way.* Further, it is possible, with the layering method, to change the nature of the vine by grafting a cane from another cépage.

The ordinary layers made in the vineyard are generally separated from the mother plant when two years old. If this operation is done earlier it produces a check in the growth, diminishing the fructification. In certain parts of the valley of the Rhône this method is used to replace a " miss " by a cane of European vine grafted on an American plant. If the graft is well knitted, and if the roots are carefully removed during the two first years, those growing on the European cane are quickly destroyed by phylloxera, and the new plant lives at the expense of the American graft bearer. It goes without saying that in this case the layer must not be separated from the mother plant. This method also enables nurserymen to obtain a great number of rooted eyes by lifting canes buried during the spring. These rooted fragments or rooted nodes may be grafted with every chance of success. (Champin method.)

(B.) *Complete burying of the mother plant.*—This method may be used to replace " misses " in a vineyard, or to liberate American vines grafted on European stumps. It is generally considered as inferior to all others ; it yields plants of little vigour and very short life. This is the result of the bad distribution of the root system, partly grown on the old wood, and spread over too great a length of cane. Further, it is more expensive than the above. It should only be used when we wish to obtain several plants from a single mother plant, in which case it is better than any other.

These layers are made in the following manner (Fig. 45) :—A deep trench is formed reaching from the mother plant to the spot where the new plant is to grow ; the main roots of the stump are cut away to allow it to bend down without breaking ; two canes selected for the purpose are brought down and buried at the bottom of the trench, allowing the two extremities to project out of the ground, one

---

* We may also mention Hardy's system of training the layering shoots along a stake for two or three years, as described in *The Australian Garden and Field*, 1901. (Transls.)

in the place where the new plant is to grow and the other in the place where the mother plant was; manure is then added, and the trench filled with mellowed soil. By making

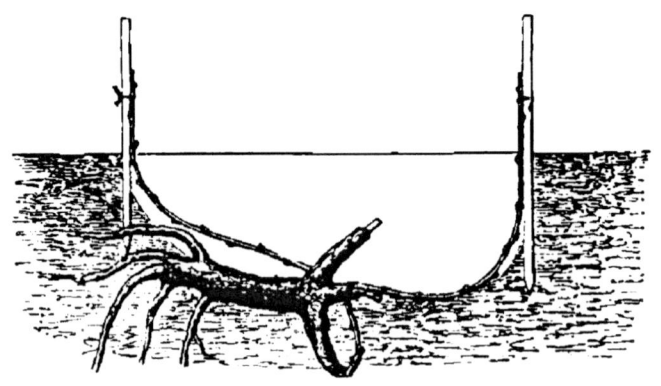

Fig. 45.—Complete burying of the mother plant.

trenches radiating from the old stock it is possible to establish many new plants by the layering several shoots from a single stock.

(C.) *Multiple layering.*—The multiple, or *Chinese* layering, is used to obtain rootlings, and offers the advantage of allowing these to be raised in one season, that is to say, in the time usually necessary to obtain one cutting, and this without wasting any wood.

The operation is conducted in the following manner (Fig. 46):—A trench, 10 inches deep, is formed, starting from the mother plant; a cane, selected for the purpose, is stretched at the bottom of this trench, and kept in position with little pegs at a depth of $2\frac{1}{2}$ to 3 inches. All the buds between the old stock and the place where the cane enters the ground are removed; when vegetation starts each bud develops, and as soon as they reach 6 to 8 inches the trench is carefully filled with soil mixed with manure and sand if the soil is naturally stiff. When it is not naturally moist the surface should be covered with mulching. Numerous roots develop on the cane at the base of each shoot during summer, and when the time for planting out has arrived the cane is unearthed and divided between each node, forming so many healthy rootlings.

This practice may be considered as the most practical and the most economical for multiplication of species rooting with difficulty, such as *V. Candicans* and *V. Berlandieri*.

(D.) *Reversed layering.*—Reversed layering may be used for replacing "misses," or for establishing an American

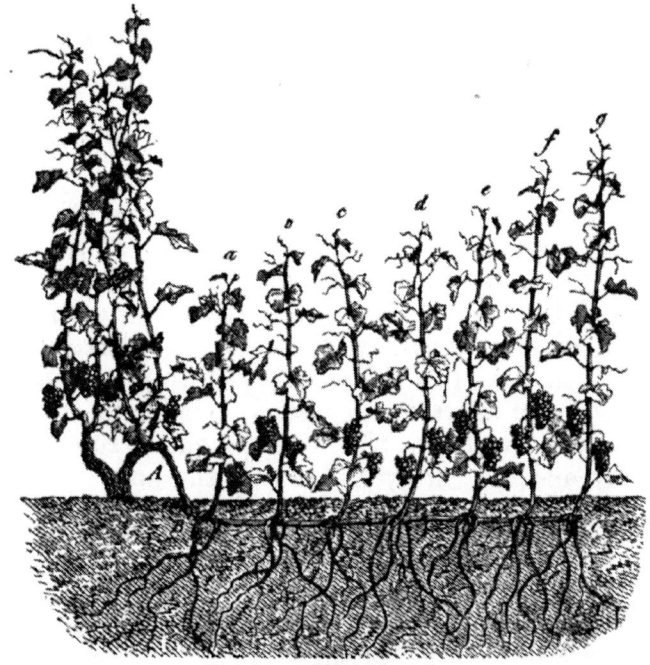

Fig. 46.—Multiple Layering.

rootling by means of an American scion grafted on a European stock. A cane (Fig. 47) is selected on the mother plant, its extremity bent and driven down in the ground to a depth of 8 to 10 inches, the soil having been dug up and manured. All the buds between the mother plant and the soil, except those two nearer the soil, are removed. Rooting takes place within a year, and it

Fig. 47.—Reversed Layering.

is cut from the mother the following year. Strange as it may seem, no ill effects result from the turning up-side-down of the stem of the young vine which this process entails, the young vine is well constituted, and even bears fruit the very year the operation is performed. To sum up, this method may be considered as superior to any other, its only faults being that it prevents cross ploughing, and requires a great length of wood.

2ND.—MEANS OF PROMOTING ROOTING OF LAYERS.

Although layers generally root freely when planted in mellowed, moist soil, some means of promoting the growth and development of their root system can be recommended—such are: 1st. A ligature made with a piece of wire towards the middle of the underground part of the layer; 2nd. A split kept open with a small wooden wedge; 3rd. A tongue separated with a part of the wood, or simply barking. The principle of these operations consists in inducing the formation of *callus* favorable to the development of roots.

Watering and mulching to prevent the soil from drying also greatly helps the development of young plants.

3RD.—BEST TIME FOR LAYERING.

The most favorable time for layering lignified canes is immediately after the fall of the leaves. The cane buried at that time is submitted to a kind of stratification, and throws roots quickly and freely when the vegetation starts again. However, an exception must be made in the case of soils remaining too damp in winter, in which the buds may rot.

When herbaceous shoots are used they should be buried as soon as they are not too brittle, and can be bent without breaking. The more tender and greener a shoot is the more easily it throws roots.

To sum up, from the above descriptions we see that layering is generally a more complicated and more expensive method than propagation by cuttings, and this accounts for it not being generally used. However, it can render real services, as it insures a strike of every bud, even with varieties which do not root at all from cuttings.

CHAPTER VI.

GRAFTING.

The object of grafting is the propagation of a plant by fixing it on another plant called a graft bearer, which furnishes it, by means of its roots, with the nourishment necessary to its life. The graft-bearer is termed *stock*, and the fragment to be propagated is called the *scion*.

Grafting, like other methods of multiplication by segmentation, insures the preservation of all the qualities belonging to the scion; the stock can only influence the scion in-so-far as vigour and development are concerned, but special properties, such as the constitution of the flowers, colour, shape, and taste of fruit for instance, cannot be modified. Sometimes the size and the saccharine strength of the grape are increased; this happens even if a variety is grafted on its own roots. All that has been alleged with regard to the sterility of scions grafted on unfertile stocks, the alteration in the taste of fruit of European varieties grafted on American species having *foxy* grapes, or of the non-affinity between stocks with white fruit and scions with black grapes is *quite erroneous*, and must be regarded as *simply dictated by ignorance*. The same thing applies to the stock which, when grafted with another variety, never modifies the nature of its roots or stem tissues.

Grafting can only take place between plants belonging to closely related botanical families; with regard to vines, the limit of affinity seems to remain within the genus. Inter-grafting of the different species of the genus *Ampelopsis*, as also of the genus *Cissus* and *Ampelocissus*, has always failed, and *a fortiori* also when the grafting of vines on plants belonging to other families (*mulberry, whortleberry, blackberry, clematis*) was tried. Even the *V. rotundifolia*, with its peculiar characteristics, does not knit with other species of the same genus.

The knitting which unites stock and scion is effected by the contact of the *generative layers*, the tissues of which unite and become modified for that purpose. The surrounding conditions necessary for the performance of this phenomenon are first, sufficient moisture to prevent the desiccation of the tissues of the graft; second, sufficient temperature to promote the rapid formation of new cells within the generative layers.

The first condition is so very important with vines that the graft can only be performed with success underground, the surrounding soil preserving the necessary amount of moisture which cannot exist in the surrounding air.

The Romans grafted vines, and this operation was formerly exclusively used in the South of France. It is possible with this method of propagation to change the nature of a vineyard without wasting any time, and it was used in the Hérault to replace old cépages by *Aramon*, or cépages sensitive to *mildew (Carignan, Grenache)* by others resisting this disease better. Grafting also hastens the fructification of varieties naturally ripening their fruit late in the season. Cazalis-Allut recommended it for *Muscat of Frontignan*, which only gives a complete crop the fifteenth year.* It rapidly recuperates the production of vines weakened by age, and is, as we have already seen, the best method of hastening the florescence of young seedlings. It may be used for the rapid multiplication of rare and expensive vines. Finally, by grafting European varieties on American resistant stocks, it prevents the extermination of the former by *phylloxera*, and preserves their undoubted superiority. The reconstitution of vineyards by this means gives to this operation greater importance than ever.

(A.) *Grafting operation.*—We will study the following items :—

    1. Age at which the stock can bear the graft.
    2. Selection of scions.
    3. Best time for grafting.
    4. Different methods used.
    5. Grafting machines and implements.
    6. Ligatures and waxing.
    7. Care to be given to grafts.
    8. Conditions of application of grafting.
    9. Value of different stocks with regard to their knitting power.

---

* *Memoires sur l'Agriculture, la Viticulture et l'Œnologie*, by Cazalis-Allut; Montpellier, 1848, p. 73.

1st.—Age at which Stock can bear Grafts.

It is possible to graft a vine at any age, from the time when it is a simple cutting till it is exhausted by many years pruning and production; in the latter case it imparts new youth and new fertility by replacing old foundation wood with healthy young wood. But during this long period all ages are not equally favorable to the success of the operation; the grafting of cuttings, for instance, gives a lower percentage of strikes than the grafting of rooted vines, which is easily explained when we remember that a cutting has not only to knit with the scion, but also to root. Notwithstanding this, the grafting of cuttings tends to be generalized, as it enables growers to obtain results quickly, and gives a sufficient strike in certain climates if proper care be taken.

As far as rootlings are concerned, it may be stated that the younger the plant the greater the proportion of knittings. This is explained by the freshness of the tissues in contact, which is favorable to the prompt formation of abundant cells necessary for the knitting to take place, and probably also by the system of grafting used in these cases, cleft graft or whip tongue graft, it may be considered as the best. The importance of grafting young stocks is more apparent with graft-bearers belonging to certain species, such as wild *Riparias*, with which the percentage of knittings diminishes as the plant grows older. However, the herbaceous grafts, which theoretically realize the best conditions, have the disadvantage of being more difficult to perform, but of giving rise to more vigorous vines. As, therefore, they have been so far very little used in France we will study more especially the grafting of lignified canes.

2nd.—Selection of Scions.

(a) *Selection of Canes.*—As grafting preserves the characteristics of the mother plant, and in a certain measure those of the cane itself, it is important to select canes amongst the most fertile and healthier shoots, showing well defined characteristics of the variety to be propagated. Those having borne non-setting flowers and badly-coloured grapes should be discarded. Further, they should be well lignified, bearing all their buds, of medium development, and containing as little pith as possible. These latter conditions, which are met with on the canes of old stumps, are important, in so far as their wood is not liable to dry before knitting takes place, or to split when the cleft is made ; the strength of the joint, and, therefore, the knitting, are assured. The canes of young plants are softer, dry easier, and offer less chance of success.

(b) *Best Time to Gather Canes.*—Experience has proved that to insure the success of this operation the vegetation of the scion must take place later than that of the stock. Knitting can then take place before the leaves have developed sufficiently to evaporate water, and, consequently, desiccate the scion. It is therefore important to gather the canes before the sap has started rising, and to preserve them until the moment of grafting.

(c) *Preservation of Scions.*—The conditions for good preservation of scions are similar to those indicated for cuttings ; they should be prevented from growing to avoid the above-mentioned dangers. To realize these conditions we may, as is done in the South of France, place them in bundles of 50 in cellars where the temperature remains low, and cover them with almost dry sand (10 per cent. of water only), or again, place them vertically in trenches 3 to 4 feet in depth, sunk in a shed or exposed to the south near a wall, the cuttings being covered with sand first and earth on the top. We must take the same care as with cuttings when removing them from the stratifying beds.

(d) *Means of Ascertaining the Vitality of Scions.*—Accidents may happen which prevent the perfect preservation of canes. It is therefore important to be able to ascertain before the grafting operation if such canes are capable of knitting. The following processes may be used with this object :—A section is made through a cane, and if the green layer placed under the bark has become dry and black we may be sure that it has lost all its vitality. But this does not mean that the canes which have remained green are capable of knitting. Under these circumstances, the best means of ascertaining their quality consists (as recommended by Louis Vialla) in placing a few canes taken here and there from the bundle in a bucket of water kept slightly warm for a few days, by exposure to the sun or placing over a range in the kitchen. If the buds swell and open, and if drops of water are seen on the top section of the canes, we may be certain that the wood is in good condition.

GRAFTING.

3RD.—BEST TIME FOR GRAFTING.

After the graft is made it must knit as quickly as possible, therefore it should always be performed during the period of vegetation, that is to say, in spring. However, autumn grafts have often been recommended; these give more time to perform the operation, and enable vine-growers to employ fewer operators. These grafts give excellent results in certain years when growth lasts long enough to allow the knitting to take place before winter. They have also resulted in dismal failures in years of early frosts or abundant rains. We must not forget that grafts remaining a long time before knitting are exposed to various dangers. The tissues left bare dry away, and other deterioration capable of preventing the knitting takes place. Further, spring frosts may destroy the young buds or suddenly arrest the growth, causing grafts to die. It is therefore in spring, from the middle of March to the end of May (about September to November in Victoria) that circumstances are most favorable.

Dull weather with slight showers preventing the desiccation of the scion, but not checking its evolution through excessive humidity, should be preferred, when possible. Dry north winds or abundant and continuous rains are, on the contrary, unfavorable conditions.

4TH.—DIFFERENT METHODS USED.

Vines may be grafted by all systems used for other woody plants, but a few only give practical results. We shall rapidly survey the different methods recommended, only describing in detail those which have proved successful and are generally adopted.

In France grafts made on lignified wood are practically alone used; experience has proved that if they are made above ground they do not succeed on account of the rapid desiccation of the sections exposed to the air. Underground grafts have therefore been almost exclusively adopted.

It has also been proved that grafts by approach generally give more vigorous plants and more perfect knitting. We will therefore study the different methods of cleft grafting, the most used being: (*a*) *Ordinary cleft graft;* (*b*) *English cleft graft;* (*c*) *Whip-tongue graft;* (*d*) *Side cleft graft;* (*e*) *Cutting graft*. However, as *budding* and *herbaceous grafts* have attracted attention lately, we will say a few words about them also.

(*a*) *Ordinary Cleft Graft.*—This is the oldest graft used, and has for a very long time been the only one. The soil is dug away from the stump down to the level of the first large roots; the trunk is cut 1 or 1¼ inches above the surface of the soil (Fig. 48) so as to avoid as much as possible the liberation of the *V. vinifera* scion when grafted on American stocks. The section is cleaned and smoothed with the grafting knife. It is then split along its diameter with a special chisel, or knife, if the trunk is not too large. In the first case the chisel is placed a little sideways (Fig. 48*a*), and when the cleft is made

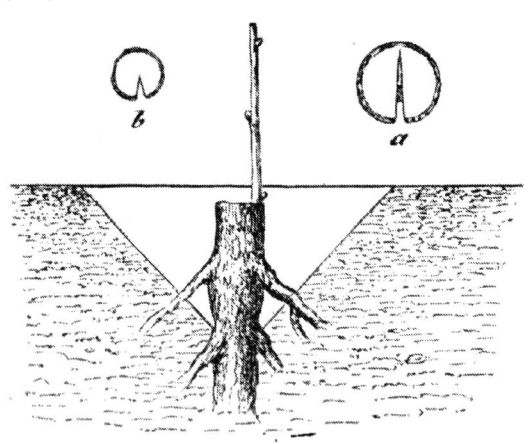

Fig. 48.—Ordinary cleft graft. (*a*) Section of large stump cut with a chisel. (*b*) Section of a small stump cut with a pruning bill.

the upper part is slightly widened by cutting away two tongues of wood on each side, the thickness of which depends on the size of the scion. A more regular and neater section is thus obtained, and the crushing resulting from the pressure of the sides of the cleft is thus avoided.

Fig. 49.—Scion used for ordinary cleft grafting.

The scion usually carries three buds and an internode below the inferior bud. This internode is cut wedge-shaped, the two bevels of the wedge being closer together on the side opposite the eye. One of the bevels must be more slanting than the other, so as to avoid cutting into the pith on both sides (Fig. 49); by doing so a continuous piece of wood is left strengthening the wedge. This scion is inserted into the cleft, forcing the under-bark to correspond everywhere. This is the main condition of success. Many operators are contented to make the bark correspond outside, but as the bark of old stock is thicker than that of the young canes, it may happen that the generative layers be parallel without coinciding. To avoid this difficulty the scion should be placed slightly oblique, so as to allow the inner bark to correspond in one point at least. When the scion is in its proper position the chisel is taken out of the cleft. When the stock is very large it is better to insert two scions to sustain proportion between the aerial growth and that of the stock (Fig. 50). The chance of success is thus doubled, and if both scions knit the weaker is removed the following winter.

Fig. 50.—Cleft graft with two scions.

Fig. 51.—English cleft graft.

This method of grafting is generally used for old stock. For young vines of smaller diameter we may ligature so as to obtain sufficient pressure, or only make a cleft on one side with the grafting knife (Fig. 48 b).

(b) *English Cleft Graft.*—This method (Fig. 51) is very extensively applied for young rootlings, on account of its easy execution and the double chance of success it offers if properly performed.

The soil is removed from the young rootling as in the previous case; it is cut level or slightly above the surface, but low enough to allow the soil to be mounded round the joint, and is split with a chisel or knife. The scion is selected of an equal diameter, so as to obtain knitting on both sides. It is cut wedge shape, the two bevels being equal and inserted in the cleft, being careful to allow both sides to coincide outside, as in this case the bark of both stock and scion is practically of the same thickness. The results obtained with this method are satisfactory, and it is quite equal to the whip-tongue graft. However, the joint is not as strong the two first years, and it produces large pads of knitting tissue.

(*c*) *Whip-tongue Graft.*—It is only since the grafting of European vines on American species was started that the whip-tongue graft was invented. It may be considered as giving the best results when well performed, and when the stocks are young enough to allow the grafting of scions of an equal diameter.

The soil is removed as in the previous case, and the stock cut at a bevel, level with the soil (this is done with a special knife), and a vertical cleft made towards the centre of the section. Formerly this bevel was made very long (Fig. 52) so as to increase the surfaces of contact as much as possible, and obtain good knitting and a small pad, but experience has proved that long bevels form long tongues, which dry very easily, and therefore cannot knit. Further, the bevels are not rigid enough, and the joint is weaker. Pulliat* advocates a bevel of 28 to 32 per cent., which corresponds to an angle of 16° to 19°, and a tongue about a quarter of an inch in length

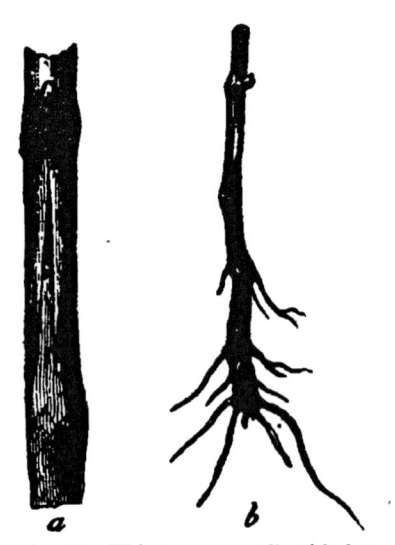

Fig. 52.—Whip-tongue graft with long bevels:—(*a*) on cutting; (*b*) on rootling.

(Fig. 53). The scion is prepared in exactly the same way, being careful to make the section as close as possible to the bud; it is assembled with the stock, so that each tongue is inserted in each cleft. If the graft is properly performed all

---

* V. Pulliat, *Manuel du greffeur de vignes.* Bibliothèque du *Progrès Agricole*, rue d'Albisson, 1, Montpellier, 1885, pages 19 and 20.

the sections should coincide, not leaving any part exposed to the air. It should be assembled in such a way as to keep quite rigid without the aid of a ligature. Whip-tongue grafts, which can only be made to coincide with the aid of a ligature, rarely give good knittings; in this case the ligature simply serves to prevent the displacement of the joint in case of knocks.

About one-fifth of an inch is the minimum diameter for a stock to be grafted, the operation being rendered too difficult if it is smaller. The maximum diameter is limited by that of the scion. However, it is possible to graft with this method a stock larger than the scion, but the beneficial effect of the double knitting is then lost; two to three eyes are left on the scion; this depends on the length of the internodes. However, in the case of grafted cuttings, one bud only is left, so as to keep a certain proportion between the outside growth and the development of the roots at the start, and avoid the desiccation which would result from the evaporation caused by too large a number of leaves.

Fig. 53. — Whip-tongue graft with short bevels.

The whip-tongue graft, which generally enables growers to replace European vineyards by American vines within a year, gives the best results with regard to the proportion of knittings and the constitution of the plants. This seems to be due to the large area of the surfaces of contact, which allows better knitting, facilitates the exchange of food material between stock and scion, and forms a long and flat cicatrice, which does not injure the ultimate development of the plant. The whip-tongue graft, on account of these advantages, will always be the most used in reconstitution of vineyards, as soon as the number of operators capable of performing it increases.

The *Champin Graft* (Fig. 54) is only a modification of the whip-tongue; it is more difficult to perform; it gives less satisfactory knittings, for a part of the section is exposed to the air; and, moreover, it facilitates the growth of roots on the scion.

The *Saddle and Camuset* grafts (Fig. 55) are the reverse of the cleft graft. These grafts are difficult of execution, and do not form such good unions as the cleft graft.

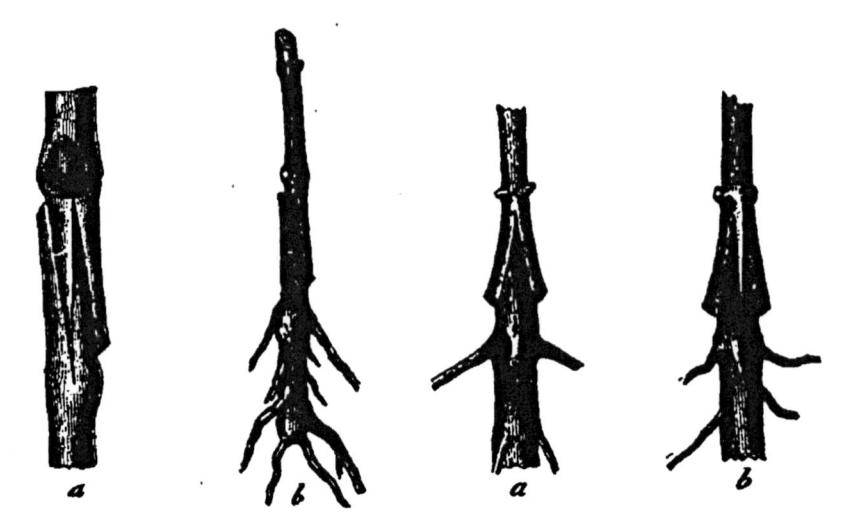

Fig. 54.—Champin graft:—(a) on cutting (b) on rootling.

Fig. 55.—(a) Saddle graft; (b) Camuset graft.

(d) *Side Cleft Graft.*— Several methods of side clefts have been recommended; they do not differ much from one another. The most used are those due to Gaillard, Brignais, Dauty, of Montpellier, and Constant Ballan, of Omey, also known under the name of Cadillac graft.

These methods consist in placing the scion in a cleft made on the side of the trunk, the head of the stump being retained. According to their promoters, they possess the following advantages:— By preserving the head of the stock a better vegetation is secured while the knitting takes place; in case a graft misses it renders further grafting possible, this being impossible with beheaded stocks, and it preserves the crop of the stock until the scion is capable of yielding fruit.

Gaillard's graft is performed in the following manner:— Level or slightly above the soil a horizontal and shallow cut is made with a saw (Fig. 56 *B*), a chip of wood is detached from the top by means of a chisel held slantingly. On the horizontal section thus exposed a cleft is made parallel to the axis of the trunk, in which two scions are inserted (Fig. 56 *e*, *f*). The joint is then strongly bound.

GRAFTING. 97

Dauty's graft is similar, but in this case the graft is made with a bent secateur S (Fig. 57), which makes a kind of notch, and the cleft at the same time.

Cadillac's graft only differs from the two above-mentioned in its cleft, which is made slanting instead of vertical, without previously making a notch. The stock *c* (Fig. 58) is cut on the side at *b* about an inch above the level of the soil; the scion *a*, cut wedge shape, is inserted in this cleft with the usual precautions; the joint is bound with raffia so as to prevent the scion from being displaced. One bud only is left on the scion so as to prevent the joint from splitting under the weight of long shoots. Finally, the soil is mounded round the joint to prevent it from drying.

Grafting tools have been invented to render this operation easier. The first is a kind of forceps with flat jaws (Fig. 59). A long opening, *d e*, is made in one of the jaws, to allow the passage of a triangular blade of a special knife (Fig. 60). The cane *b c* is kept in position by the pressure of the jaws and two small pins, *d* and *e*; the cleft is made very neatly by sliding the blade of the knife into the opening. Other methods of grafting or budding, such as the graft by approach, the end to end graft, have been recommended, but very soon discarded on account of the small percentage of strikes.*

Fig. 56.—Gaillard graft.

(*e*) *Cutting Graft.*—This system is only used in very special cases when the graft has to be liberated after the knitting. The stump in this case is only used to temporarily feed the scion which grows independently when it has thrown

---

* A. Champin: *Traité théorique et pratique du greffage.*

its own roots. It is sometimes useful for the propagation of American vines. However, to obtain good results this

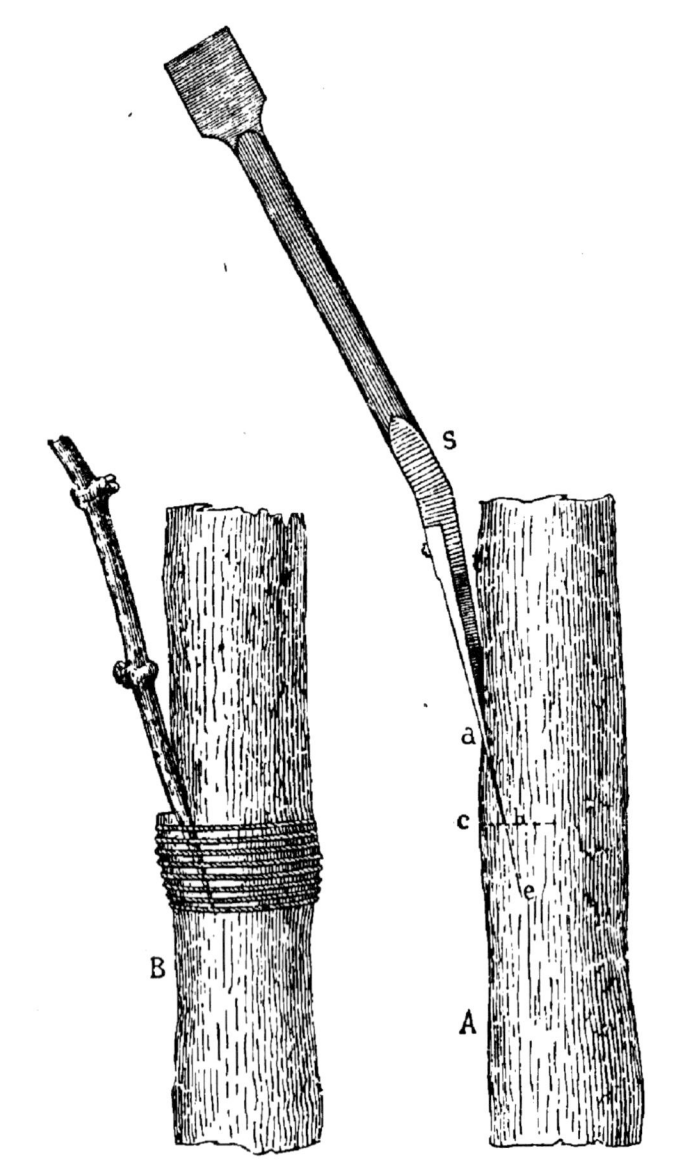

Fig. 57.—Dauty graft.

graft should be performed in very mellow, rich soil, capable of feeding the new plant in the place where the old stump grew previously.

GRAFTING. 99

The soil is removed, and the stock cut, as in the case of an ordinary cleft graft; a slightly bent cutting, with a piece of

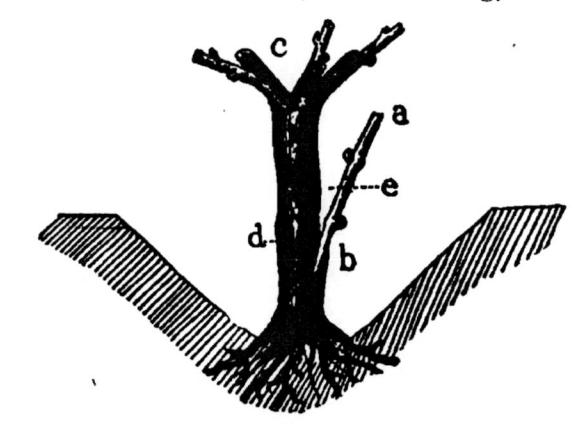

Fig. 58.—Cadillac side-cleft graft.

two-year-old wood at its base, is selected; two slices of bark are taken away on each side, forming like the blade of a knife (Fig. 61). This blade is inserted into the cleft, the inner bark corresponding on as great a length as possible, and the joint bound if the pressure of the sides of the cleft is not sufficient.

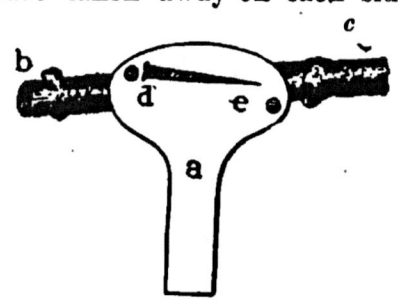

Fig. 59.—Forceps used for side-cleft grafting.

(*f*) *Budding.*—The advantages derived from budding, in the case of many plants, induced viticulturists to apply this method to vine stocks or cuttings. The first trials were not very encouraging, the proportion of strikes being very low.

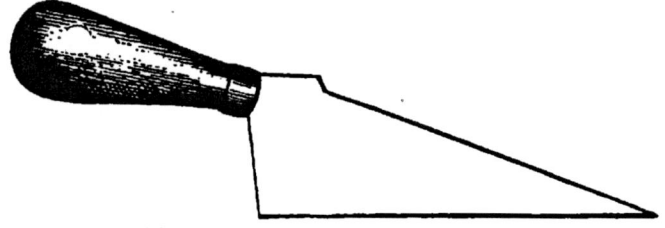

Fig. 60.—Knife used for side-cleft grafting.

However, better results are obtained now, especially in Hungary, where this method of grafting has been advocated by

G 2

Professor Horváth. In France it is used under the name of Salgues graft (Figs. 62 and 63). Lapparent, Inspector-General of Agriculture, and E. Marre, who experimented with it in the Lot, obtained good results.

Budding of the vine may be done with either growing or dormant eyes. The latter mode seems preferred in Hungary, as it gives stronger and better constituted plants. The budding is done in the following manner :—
The bud or eye used as scion is taken from the mean part of a shoot which has reached complete development. Alazard,

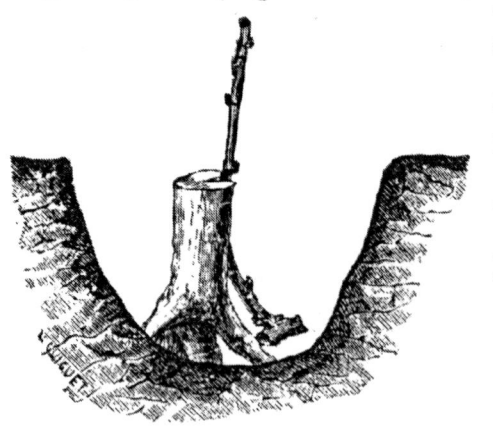

Fig. 61.—Cutting graft.

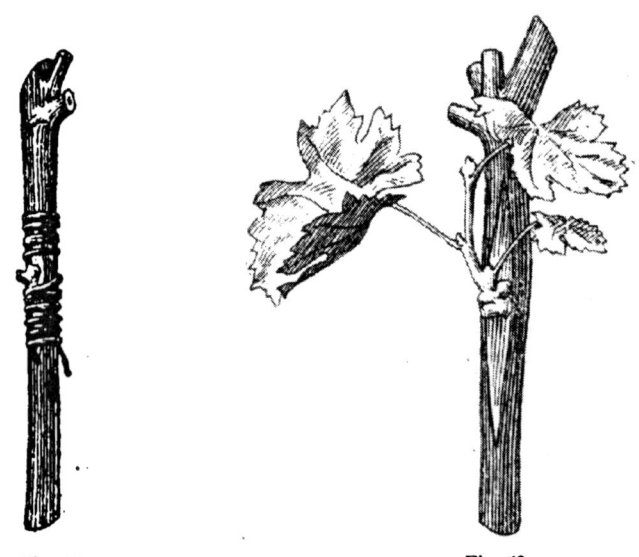

Fig. 62. Salgues Graft.

Fig. 63. Salgues Graft knitted.

who has had great experience in budding vines, recommends "*to take the buds from nodes in which the wood and the diaphragm are only slightly apparent, and the pith completely green and swollen with water.*" The scion-bud is ¾ to 1¼

GRAFTING. 101

inches in length, and ·04 to ·08 inch of cellular tissue is preserved under the bark. This is to avoid the desiccation of the bark. Half or a third of the petiole is preserved.

The stock may be a shoot of the year well developed and well constituted, a lignified cane, an ordinary cutting, or the shoot of a young rootling; the only condition required is that the bark separates easily.

On the selected spot, which in herbaceous shoots must be below the last bud, a longitudinal slit 1 to 1½ inches in length is made, the sides being lifted with the grafting knife.

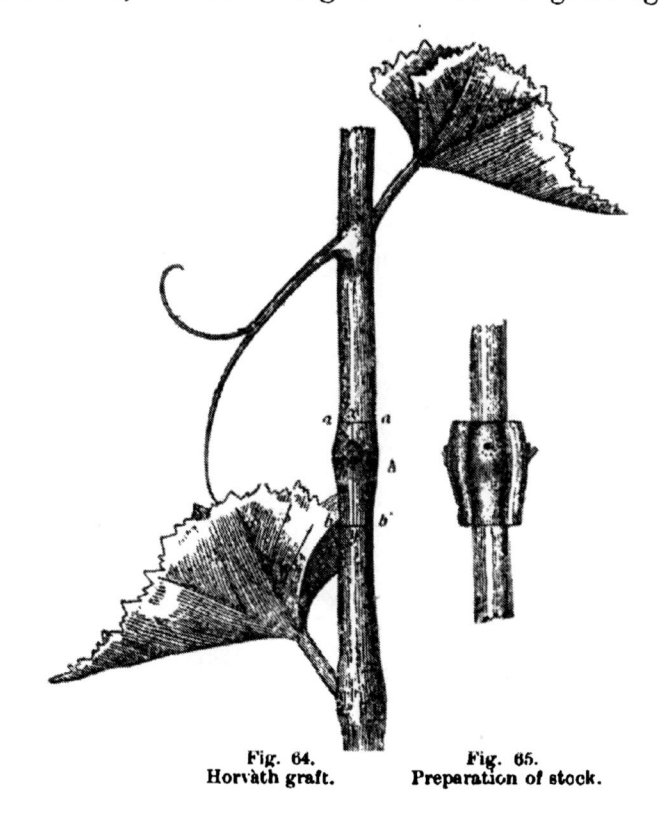

Fig. 64.
Horváth graft.

Fig. 65.
Preparation of stock.

The bud is inserted under the bark, which is raised by bending the shoot inwards. The joint is bound with wool or cotton (Fig. 62).

Horváth[*] recommends, as very important, the grafting of the bud on the place ordinarily occupied by an eye. He operates in the following way: A leaf is removed from the

---
[*] Professor at the School of Viticulture, at Tarczal, Hungary.

shoot used as stock, and an annular incision cutting into the bark only is made above and below a node (Fig. 64 *aa' bb'*). A third vertical incision passing through the centre of the eye is made joining the two annular incisions *x y;* the two flaps of bark are lifted (Fig. 65), the bud (Fig. 66) fitted underneath, and the joint bound (Fig. 67).

Although the budding of vines is performed with success with these new methods, it unfortunately seems to give plants of short life, and always inferior to those obtained with the cleft methods.*

(*g*) *Herbaceous Grafts.*—Herbaceous grafts have not generally succeeded in France, while, on the contrary, they

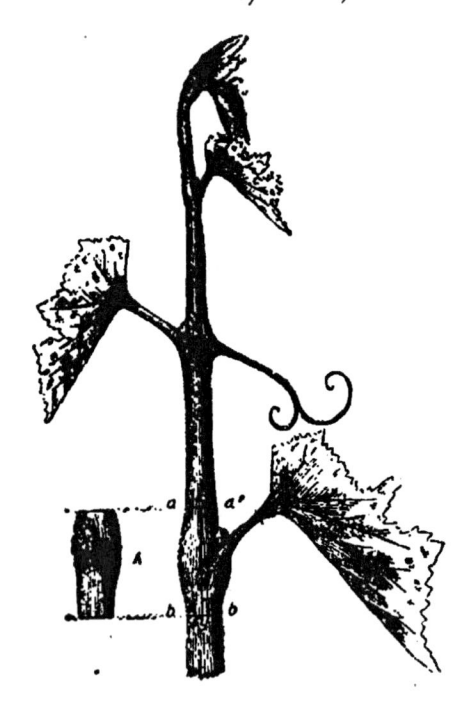

Fig. 66.—Horváth method. Preparation of scion

have generally been applied successfully in Hungary, where this method of grafting was used very long ago for fruit trees.

Herbaceous grafting may be done—1st, with a simple cleft ; 2nd, with a whip tongue ; 3rd, with an English cleft ; 4th, with a side cleft.

---

* For further information see *New Methods of Grafting and Budding as applied to Reconstitution with American Vines*, by the present translators, Department of Agriculture, Melbourne, 1901.

GRAFTING. 103

E. Jouzier,* who was appointed to study and report on the viticultural methods of Hungary, describes the herbaceous cleft graft as follows:—

"This graft is made on very young shoots. It may be performed when the extremity of the young shoot between the second and third leaf, counting from the top, is still soft,

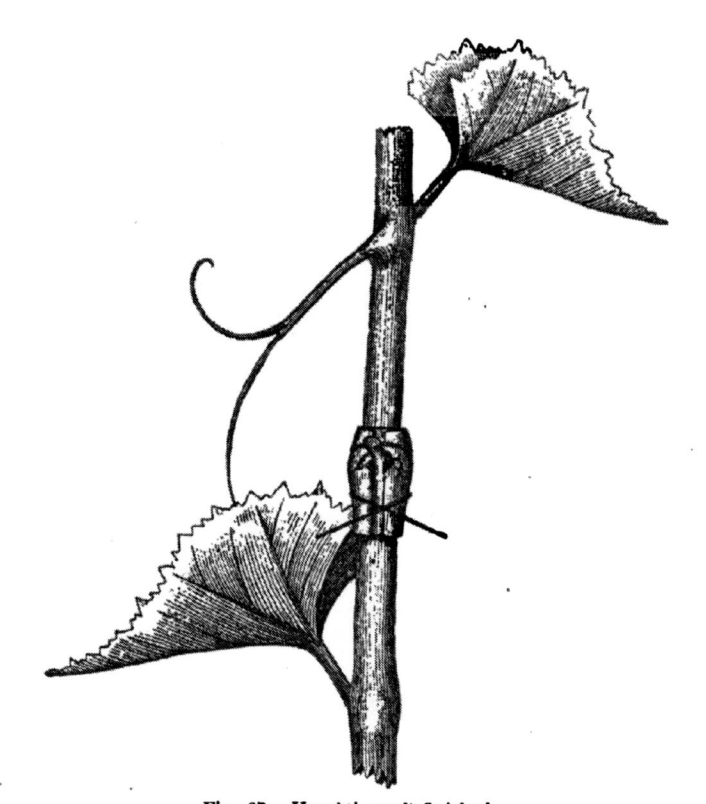

Fig. 67.—Horváth graft finished.

but already flexible (Fig. 69 *a* and *b*). This does not happen before the beginning of June, when the shoots are 16 to 24 inches in length. Until then the extremity is very soft and too brittle.

"When the young shoot is fit to be grafted, the apex between the second and third leaf is cut away (Fig. 69 *a a'*) leaving about 1½ to 2 inches above the last leaf (Fig. 69 *x y*), which is cut away, leaving a small part of the petiole (*b b'*).

---

* Late Professor at the School of Viticulture, Ondes; now Professor at the School of Grand-Jouan.

A cleft is then made, splitting the shoot down to the first retained node; the cleft must cut into that node, but not overreach it (Fig. 68 *m n*)."

"The scion is selected amongst similar shoots of the variety to be propagated (Fig 72). The extremity is cut in such a way as to preserve the top bud and two open leaves (*x y*).

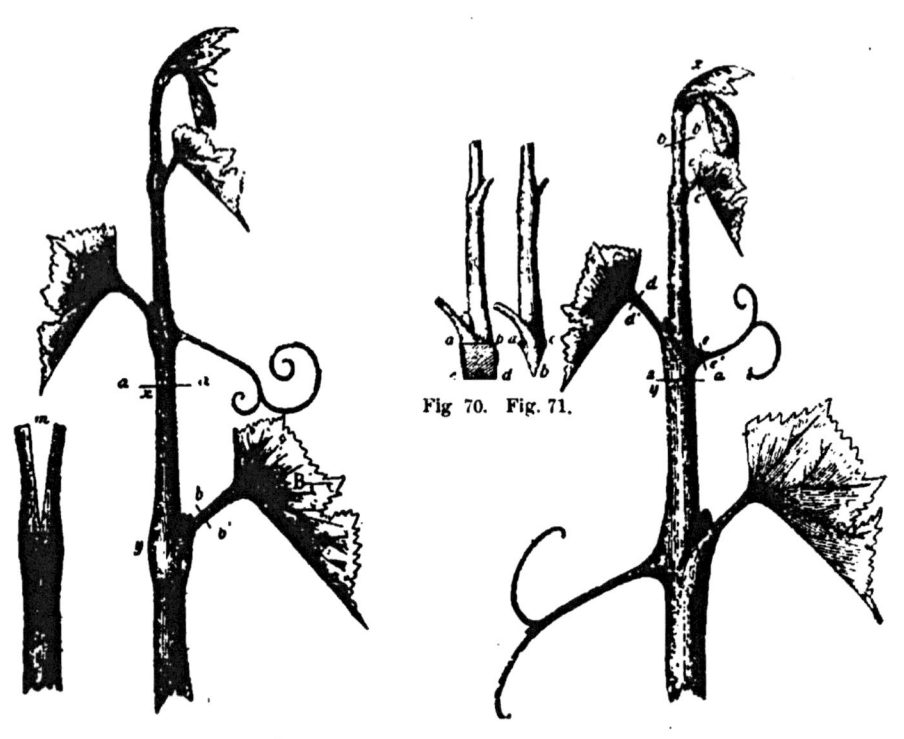

Fig. 68.　Fig. 69.
Herbaceous Graft.—Preparation of stock.

Fig 70.　Fig. 71.

Fig. 72.
Herbaceous Graft.—Preparation of scion.

These two leaves are cut away, leaving a small part of the petiole (*c c'* and *d d'*), the tendrils *e e'* are also cut away with the terminal bud (*b b'*), and the bottom of the scion is cut wedge shape (Figs. 70 and 71). The angle of the wedge (*a b c*) should not be too acute—that is to say, that the sides (*a b c d*) should be rather short; the wedge should be cut in the node itself, being careful not to touch the eye and the petiole.

"The scion thus prepared is fitted into the cleft so as to replace the eye of the stock by that of the scion (Fig. 73), and the joint is bound with wool or raffia.

GRAFTING.

"The most practical way of binding consists in making two or three turns round the top of the cleft (Fig. 74A) without tightening it, then, keeping the ligature lightly between the fingers, the scion is adjusted so as to allow its bark to coincide with that of the stock; the tie is then tightened, and continued downwards so as to completely

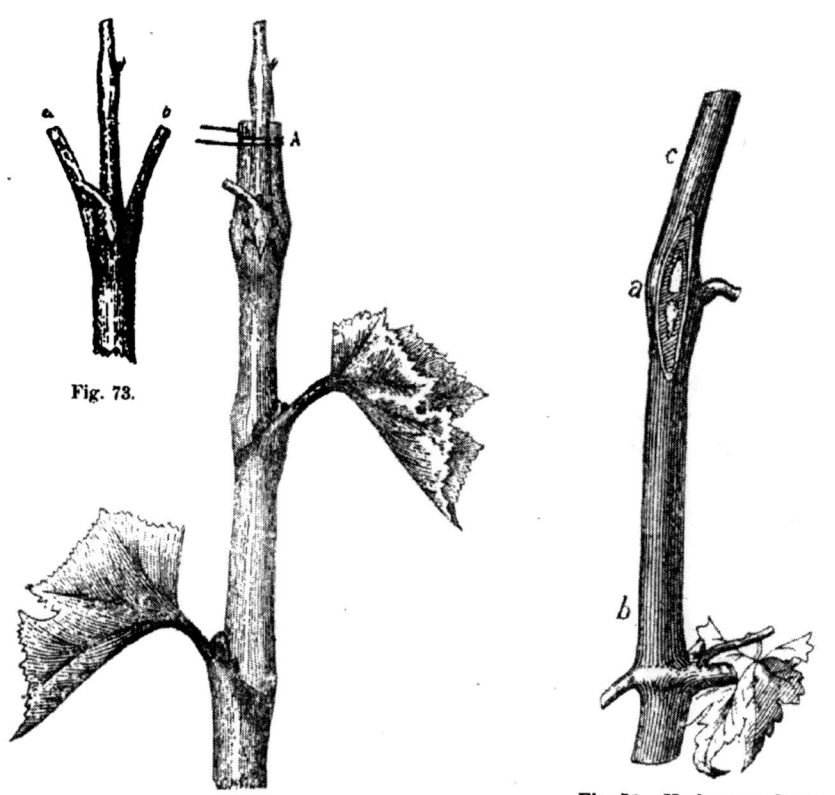

Fig. 73.

Fig. 74.—Herbaceous Cleft Graft completed.

Fig. 75.—Herbaceous Graft (after H. Goethe).

cover the joint, leaving the eye out. If wool is used, the most practical way of fastening the ligature consists in simply twisting both ends together. It goes without saying that a very sharp grafting knife with a very thin blade should be used."*

The ordinary herbaceous cleft graft, or the English herbaceous cleft graft (without tongue), are performed in the same way as with lignified wood. The side cleft graft is made

---

* E. Jouzier, *Greffage de la vigne en écusson et en fente herbacée;* in *Annales de l'Institut Agronomique*, vol. xii., 1887, page 152.

as shown in Figs. 75 to 78. The sections on the stock and scion are made upon the node, thus greatly increasing the strike.

Herbaceous grafts should be made in June.* With the side cleft graft, the extremity of the shoot of the stock is pinched. The buds of the scion develop two or three weeks after the operation, and its shoots lignify well.

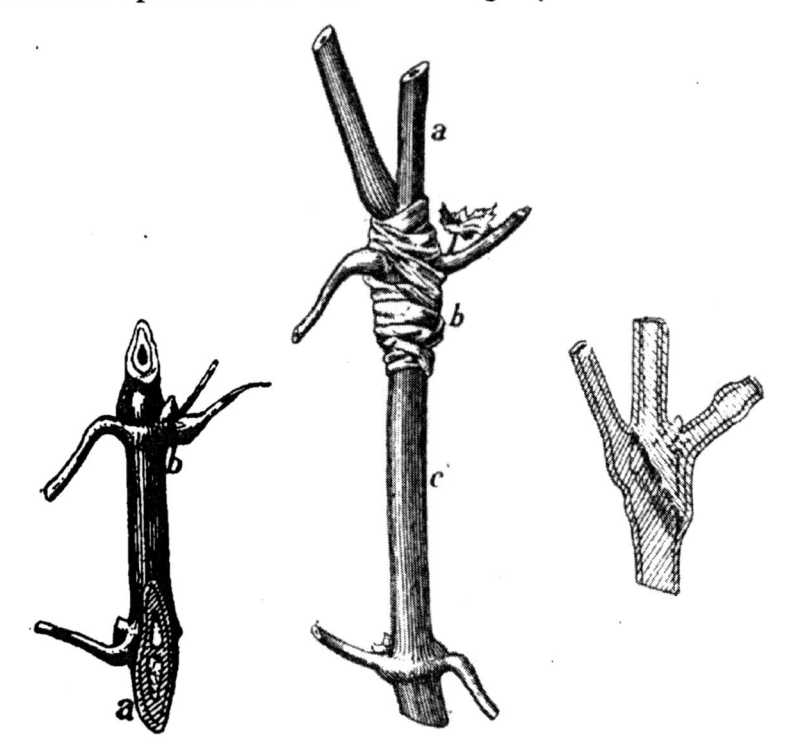

Fig. 76.
Herbaceous Graft a, b, Scion (after H. Goethe).

Fig. 77.
Same after tying.
a, scion; b, ligature;
c, stock (after H. Goethe).

Fig. 78.
Section of union (after H. Goethe).

Herbaceous grafting, notwithstanding the success obtained in Hungary, is a delicate operation, and belongs rather to the domain of horticulture. It certainly cannot be used in extensive viticulture, as proved by experience in the South of France.

5TH.—GRAFTING MACHINES AND IMPLEMENTS.

(a) *Tools used for Cleft Grafting.*—1st, an iron saw (Fig. 79), used for cutting large stumps; 2nd, a secateur,

---
* November or December in Victoria.

GRAFTING.

used for young plants; 3rd, an iron chisel, described hereafter; 4th, a hammer, or rather a small mattock, which is used for driving the chisel and to clear the soil away from the plant (Fig. 80); 5th, a strong grafting knife, used for smoothing the sections and to prepare the scions.

All these tools are known, and the illustrations are sufficient to give an idea of them; however, attention is drawn to the grafting chisel, which must be made so as to perform several operations. As a matter of fact, the grafting chisel may be simply considered as a wedge used to split a piece of wood, and if necessary the ordinary cold chisel could be used. But, as we have already seen, in the case of a single

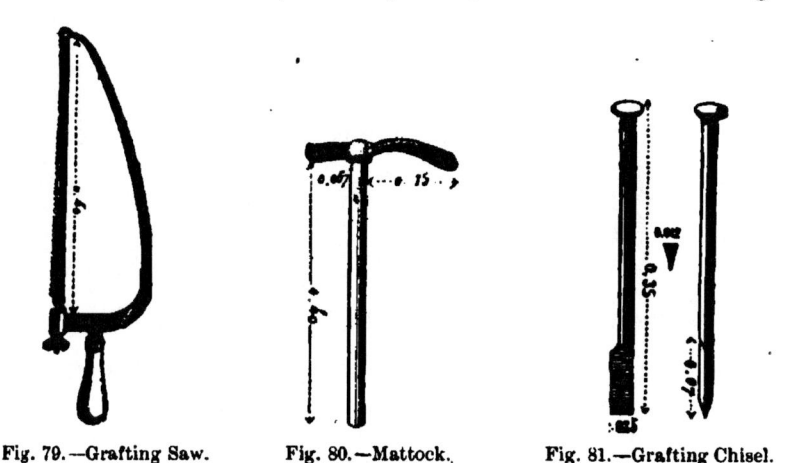

Fig. 79.—Grafting Saw.   Fig. 80.—Mattock.   Fig. 81.—Grafting Chisel.

scion being grafted on a stump, the cleft is only made on one side, so as to preserve the stock and allow the side of the cleft to press against the scion. For this purpose the blade of the chisel should not be of the same thickness on both sides; sometimes it is the shape of a knife having one side sharpened to allow of a cleft being made on the young stumps (Fig. 81).

(*b*) *Tools used for Cleft-grafting Young Plants.*—In this case a cleft is made with a strong grafting knife. However, Comy, of Garons, has invented an arrangement greatly facilitating the execution of this operation, and allowing it to be made with great perfection. Comy's arrangement comprises:—1st, A gauge; 2nd, a scion box; 3rd, a grafting knife for the scions; 4th, a stronger grafting knife for the stocks.

The gauge is made of a brass plate, on the side of which eight notches are cut varying from ⅓ to 1⅓ inches in width, for measuring the diameter of the scions (Figs. 82 and 83 *j*). Each notch bears a number corresponding to the numbers on each compartment of the scion box.

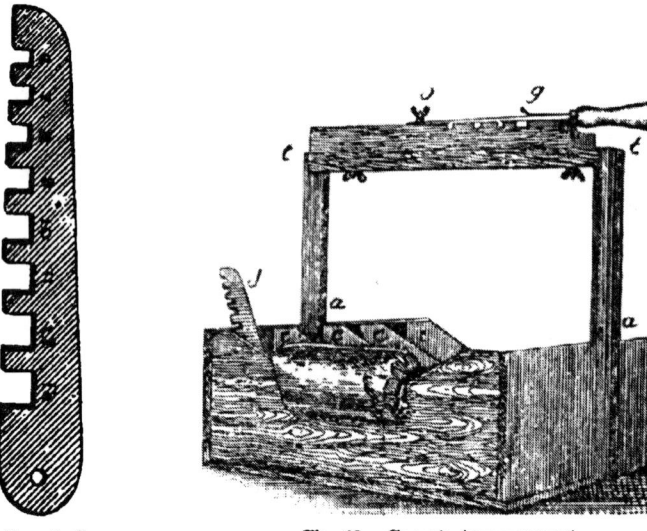

Fig 82.—Comy's Gauge.   Fig. 83.—Comy's Arrangement.

This box is divided into eight equal compartments, into which the scions are placed after being gauged; the larger compartment is used to carry the tools and accessories. On the top of the wooden handle (Fig. 83 *t t*) a wooden block is fixed, and a blade *o b*, having one extremity fixed on a pivot *o*, round which it revolves, the other extremity is provided with a handle *b*. A horizontal brass guide keeps the blade flat on the wooden block, which is made of oak, on the side of which are 16 inclined grooves, allowing the making of both sides of the wedge for cutting scions of different diameters. The numbers on each pair of notches correspond to the numbers on the gauge.

The grafting knife (Fig. 84) is of special construction. On the blade is a small brass knob *a*, and a brass slide *b*, which can be easily moved with the thumb; a graduation corresponding to that of the gauge enables the operator to measure the distance between the knob and the slide.

Comy's arrangement is used in the following way:—The scions are first sorted with the gauge and placed in each corresponding compartment in the box, which is taken on

GRAFTING. 109

the ground where the young plants are decapitated and the cleft made with the grafting knife. One must be careful while making the cleft to measure the diameter of the stock with the slide. A scion of equal diameter is taken out of

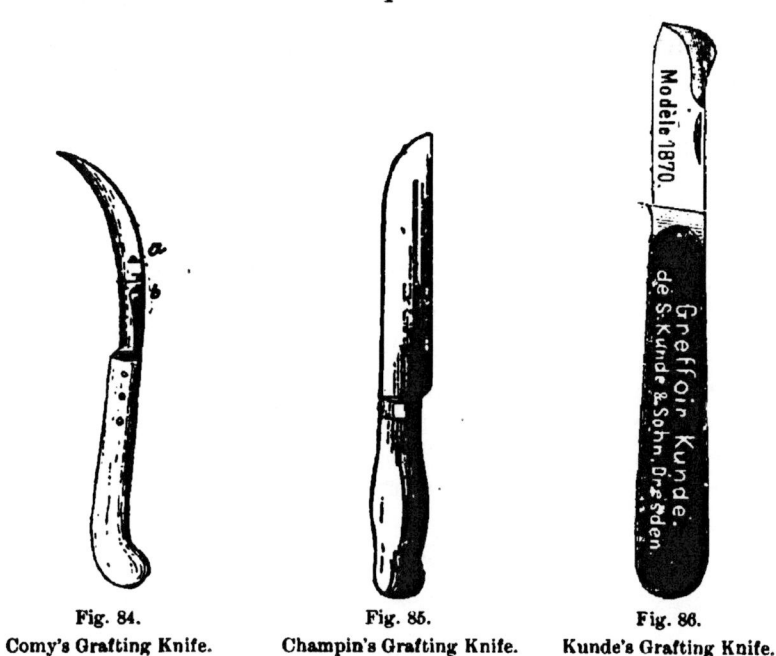

Fig. 84.
Comy's Grafting Knife.

Fig. 85.
Champin's Grafting Knife.

Fig. 86.
Kunde's Grafting Knife.

the compartment corresponding to the measurement read on the blade of the knife. This scion is placed in each of the two grooves on the handle corresponding to the number of the compartment, and the two bevels are made with the sliding knife. The scion thus prepared is inserted in the cleft and bound in the usual way.

The use of this arrangement presents the following advantages:—1st, it allows one to rapidly find scions of diameter exactly equal to that of the stock; 2nd, to make perfectly plane and exactly symmetrical sections.

(c) *Tools used for Whip-tongue Grafting.*—This graft is easily made with an ordinary grafting knife. The only special feature of this knife is that the blade is flat on one side (Fig. 88) so as to allow the making of a perfectly plane section. This can only be insured by sharpening the knife on one side only, for the sharpening of the blade always causes it to become convex near the edge (Fig. 87), inducing the knife to oscillate and making uneven sections. This is avoided if the flat side of the blade alone is used (Fig. 88).

The grafting knives most used are those of Champin (Fig. 85) or Kunde (of Dresden) (Fig. 86). The grafting knife of Rolli, Lausanne (Switzerland), is equal in strength and has the advantage of being cheaper.

Guides may be used to enable the operator to make very regular plane sections and always obtain the same bevel. Castelbou's guide (Fig. 89) is in the shape of a pentagonal

Fig. 87.—Section of a blade sharpened on both sides.

Fig. 88.—Section of a blade sharpened on one side only.

frustrum, on the face of which holes are bored reaching the base. These cylindrical holes vary in diameter and are made parallel to the axis of the frustrum, so that their section is oblique on the face. Steel springs fixed at the bottom of

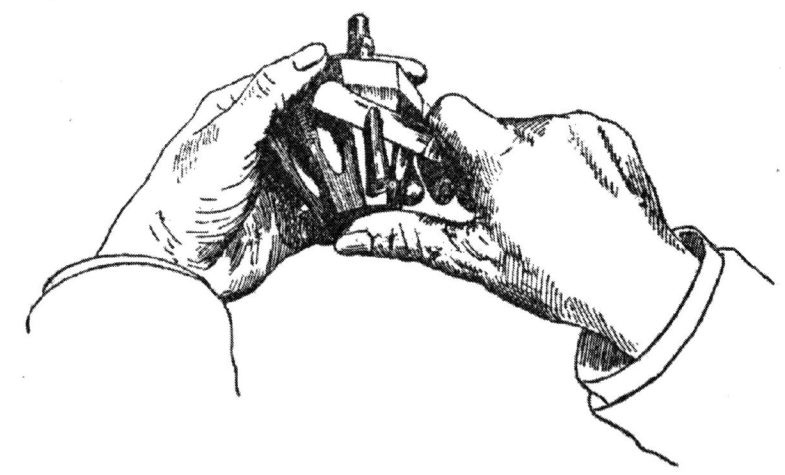

Fig. 89.—Castelbou's Guide.

each face form two kinds of guards, which press against it when submitted to a slight pressure, but remain slightly away from it when in a normal state.

This guide may be used for out-door grafting or bench grafting. In the latter case it is fixed on a kind of stand, and is used in the following manner :—The stock or scion is placed in one of the holes corresponding to its diameter,

GRAFTING. 111

the blade of the grafting knife is slided against the face and above the springs of the frustrum, making an oblique and plane section; the knife is then turned over and placed between the face and the spring, making the cleft in the right position.

F. Richter makes thousands of whip-tongue grafts every year, and uses a still simpler guide. Each operator has before him three brass tubes, varying in diameter, with one end cut bevel shape at the required angle and fixed on a stand bolted on the table (Fig. 90). The canes are passed through one of the tubes corresponding to its diameter, and the bevel made by sliding a Kunde knife over the side of the tube. A woman makes the tongues by hand with a small knife.

Fig. 90.—Richter's Grafting Knife.

Finally, a great number of machines have been invented to help the making of the whip tongue graft. The only one generally used now is that devised by Petit, civil engineer at Langon (Gironde).

This machine (Fig. 91) consists essentially of two blades, one G, used to make the bevel, the other F, used to make

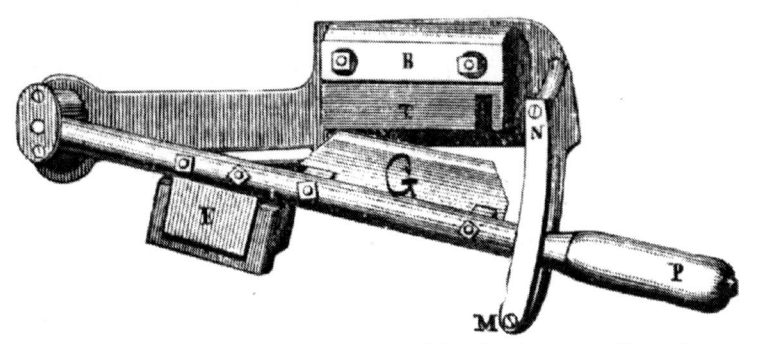

Fig. 91.—Petit's Grafting Machine, used for whip-tongue grafting.

the tongue. They are both fixed on a lever provided with a handle P, at one of its extremities, revolving round a pivot at the other extremity. This lever works between the two parallel guides M N, keeping it in a horizontal position and limiting its movement sideways. The blade used for the bevels is fixed on the front; the blade F, used for the tongues, is smaller and placed at the rear.

Under the blade G is a brass socket T (Fig. 91), and (*a b c d* Fig. 92), forming an inclined winding plane. On the top of the socket is a horizonal stop B, limiting the movement of the blade in front. This arrangement of the socket allows the same length of bevel to be obtained with cuttings varying in diameter by placing them in different points on the socket.

Fig. 92. - Inclined Socket of Petit's Machine.

Under the blade F is a second wooden socket similar to the former. These different tools are bolted on a cast-iron frame fixed on the side of the bench by a strong vice.

The machine is used in the following way :—1st, a cane is placed on the socket T in a suitable position, the extremity touching the stop B (Fig. 91); the lever is pushed forward by means of the handle P, making the bevel. 2nd, the cane is then placed on the wooden socket section upwards, and by pulling the lever backwards the slit is made at the required depth, forming the tongue at the same time.

Many machines have been devised with the idea of helping the making of grafts on the ground, but none have so far proved practical. We may state that grafting by hand has a tendency to be generally adopted, and the number of successful operators is increasing every day. It is almost as difficult to teach operators to use grafting machines properly as to teach them to use grafting knives.

6TH.—LIGATURES AND WAXING.

When grafts are performed on old stumps the joint is generally strong enough, and does not need any binding. Grafts on stocks of smaller diameter should always be performed well enough to be able to do without binding, but it is generally advisable to bind the joints to increase their strength, and to prevent them from getting displaced in case of knocks or wind. String, raffia, rubber, and flexible metal foil are used with this object.

In the South of France string is generally used without any previous preparation. It gives great strength to the joint, and if it is a dry year, it has to be cut away after the knitting has taken place, if not, it might hinder the growth of the plant in diameter. In damper climates, on the contrary, the string must be dipped in sulphate of copper, or tar, so that it will last longer. Raffia (fibre of sagus raphia, of Japan, or raphia tædigera, of Madagascar) is very strong, its flat reedy nature greatly facilitates the operation of binding. It rots quickly when the season is very wet. Champin recommends dipping it in a solution of sulphate of copper, more or less concentrated, in accordance with the desired duration. Vulcanized rubber has even been recommended, used in the shape of tube or rings passed over the graft by means of special tools, or in the shape of fine thongs of about one-fifth inch square section. Rubber tubes have generally been discarded, and the thongs alone are now used. They are more particularly used for grafted cuttings. Their elasticity insures a continuous and regular pressure, never excessive, and forms an excellent ligature. Unfortunately they are rather expensive. The steel ligatures are formed of a flat flexible plate, curved like a kind of collar open on one side. The sides are kept open by means of special pincers, and the collar passed over the cane compresses against the joint as soon as it is released. This system has several disadvantages, and has been very little used.

Cork was recommended some time ago to protect the joint against desiccation, and the action of water. The corks are split in two along their axis, and slightly hollowed in the centre. They are placed on each side of the joint, tightened together by means of special pincers, and kept in position by three ties fastened and tightened with pliers before releasing the pincers (Fig. 93).

The *Cork graft*, as it is commonly termed, has sometimes given very satisfactory knittings, but has generally resulted in failure. The difficulty of execution, and the great care it requires to give good results, greatly restricted its use, and it is only advantageous for grafts made above ground, and in small numbers.

The object of waxing is to cover the section of the grafts, so as to prevent their desiccation, and to protect them against rain-water. It is only necessary in the case of grafts leaving large sections bare, as happens when old stumps are grafted, or when stocks are placed in pebbly, stiff soils where they are liable to dry quickly.

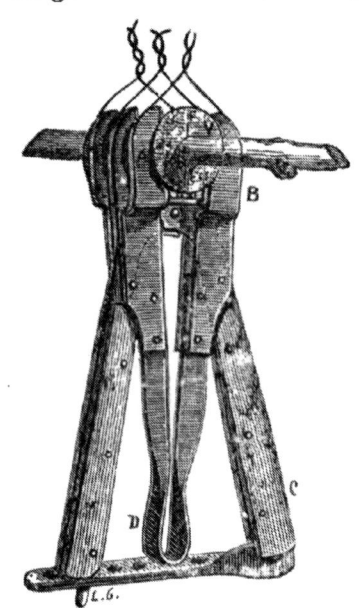

On the contrary, when young stocks are grafted with the whip-tongue, or cleft method, in fresh, mellowed soil not too damp, waxing may be dispensed with, more especially if the ligature is carefully made with raffia or string. The substance which has so far given the best results is clay. It must be pure and form a good paste, not too liquid, and not cracking when worked. It is applied in small quantities on sections.

Tin or lead foils are also used; placed under the ligature they prevent desiccation, and, to a certain extent, root growth. They are especially used with grafted cuttings.

Fig. 93.—Cork Ligature.

Resin putty, such as that of Lhomme-Lefort, gives good results above ground, but has never succeeded under ground.

7TH.—CARE TO BE GIVEN TO GRAFTS.

(A) *Earthing up and protection of grafts.*—As we have shown above, a vine graft can only succeed under ground; however, it is made level with the ground, or slightly above it. Therefore, to place the joint in good condition for growth and to insure knitting, the soil should be heaped around the plant; a mound is formed with well-moulded soil so as to leave only the last eye of the stock visible (Fig. 94). This operation is done with a triangular hoe (Fig. 95), and should be done very carefully, so as not to dislocate the joint. In nurseries the earthing up is done in long ridges following the line.

The considerable development of the young shoots the first year often occasions breakages, or displacement of the joint in windy districts. The best way to avoid this accident is to tie the shoot to a small stake driven near the plant before the mound is formed.

GRAFTING.

(B) *Severing roots from the scion and shoots from the stock.*—The joint should be examined at least once a month during the summer following the operation of grafting, so as to cut away roots growing on the scion and suckers growing from the stock. The success of grafting depends

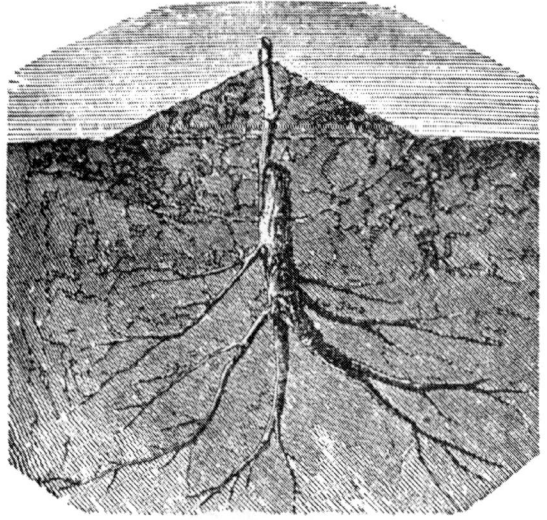

Fig. 94.—Cleft Graft earthed up.

Fig. 95. Triangular Hoe used for covering grafts with soil.

in a great measure on the performance of this operation. When the roots of the scion are left to develop, the vegetation of the stock diminishes, and the growth of the part above ground is more rapid than that under ground. This abnormal increase in size causes the side of the cleft to split, and often results in complete disjointing of a graft. However, even if this accident does not occur, the liberation of the scion is always dangerous, its roots develop at the expense of those of the stock which are not sufficient to nourish the graft. (Fig. 96).

If the suckers are not destroyed they develop at the expense of the shoot of the scion, which often does not knit, or remains sickly, and sometimes withers. At the end of August,* when it is possible to ascertain which grafts have not knitted, the suckers of these are allowed to grow to form grafting wood for the following year. In case these suckers are not strong enough it is always possible to graft lower on the stock, but this weakens the plants in some cases; therefore grafting suckers should be preferred when possible.

8TH.—CONDITIONS OF APPLICATION OF GRAFTING.

(A) *Grafting cuttings.*—The grafting of cuttings gives results varying with the soil and climate. It generally does

---
* February in Victoria.

not succeed well in the dry Mediterranean region, but gives very satisfactory results further north, which is explained very easily, if we remember that the cuttings have not only to knit their scion, but also to grow roots, and that a certain amount

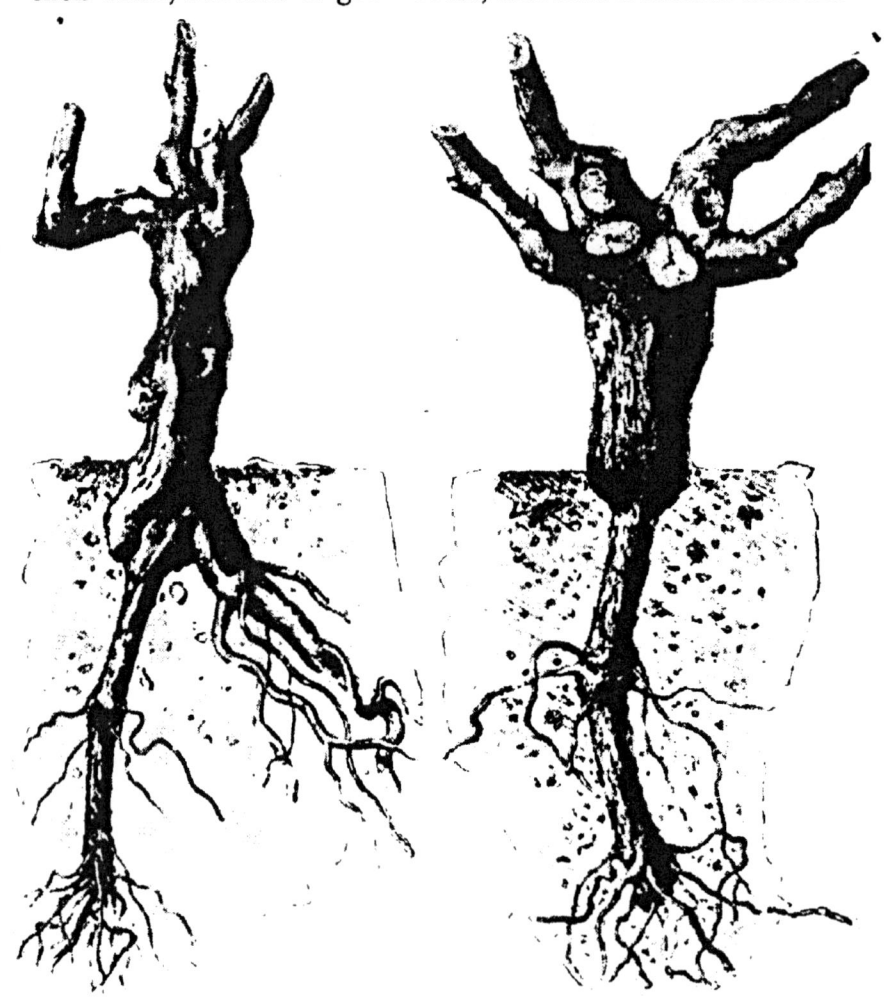

Fig. 96.
A six-year-old vine badly grafted, perishing from phylloxera on roots from scion.

Fig. 97.
Old grafted vine showing almost normal difference between size of stock and scion.

of moisture is necessary for both these phenomena. However, it can be used in dry regions, on the condition that the cuttings are planted in nurseries, well watered, and that certain precautions which we are going to explain are observed; the cuttings, 10 inches in length, are grafted with the whip tongue method with short bevel, the scions having only one bud (Fig. 98); the joint is sometimes bound with lead foil kept in position by raffia; or, better, rubber ligature. Generally the joint is simply bound in raffia over which a light emulsion of clay is brushed, or sometimes it is plunged into the mixture. The cuttings grafted in this manner are planted in parallel trenches. The lines are placed in groups of two, 20 inches apart, with a space of 28 inches between each group, so as to allow the removal of the roots and suckers (Fig. 99). The operation of planting may be organized in the following way which is that of Richter, of Montpellier:—

1st. A trench is opened with a spade along the line, the sides being made almost vertical, and the soil placed on the other side of the line.

2nd. The line is taken away and replaced by a wooden straight-edge 6 feet in length (A B, Fig. 100), divided into two equal parts by a mark, *t*. It is kept in a vertical position by a small piece of wood, B C, screwed in a perpendicular direction.

If the soil is clayey the angle of the trench where the cuttings rest is filled with sand; if, on the contrary, the soil is light it is simply dug at that angle.

Fig. 98.—Whip-tongue Grafted Cutting.

The cuttings are stuck upright in the sand resting against the side of the trench, the eye of the scion level with the edge of the straight-edge, so as to have all the joints at the same depth. (See Figs. 38 to 43, page 79, and Fig. 101.)

3rd. The filling up of the trench is done progressively, as follows:—A workman half-fills the trench with soil, a second workman rams it down with his foot; a third rams it over again with a kind of rammer, and a second group of three workmen finish filling the trench in the same way.

4th. The third group of workmen form the mounds. One man heaps the soil with a little hoe, another compresses it against the scion with his hands, being careful not to shake it; the third man brings the soil over the scion with a rake. A fourth man finishes the mounds and gives them a regular shape.

The plantation should be made in very well mellowed soil, and when it is not too damp. The grafted cuttings must not be brought in large numbers on the ground, for

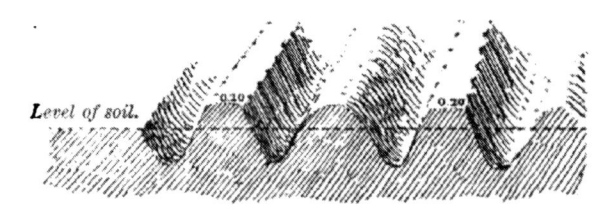

Fig. 99.—Arrangement of Cuttings in nursery rows.

they might become dry and get knocked about. They should be placed in small bundles upright in buckets, the lower parts submerged in water, or covered with a wet rag.

Certain viticulturists incline the cuttings when they plant them so as to allow the stock to be in the more superficial layers of soil which get warmer and promote the growth of roots. Complete covering of the graft prevents the desiccation of short scions. Finally, the system of watering should allow the water to penetrate to the stock without touching

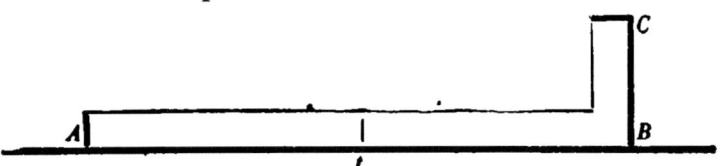

Fig. 100.—Straight-edge for placing cuttings in nursery rows.

the scion, only giving the required quantity of water to avoid the cooling of the soil, which would result from too much water being applied. We know that heat is one of the conditions promoting root growth. This is so very important that Messrs. Grégoire and Co., horticulturists at Denicé (Rhône), place their grafted cuttings, in small bundles, under heated glass-houses, and obtained in this way fine, well-knitted grafts, made in March, ready to plant in May.* The only inconvenience of this method is the difficulty of acclimatisation in the open air of plants obtained under such artificial conditions.

The cultural care to be given to nurseries consists in frequent hoeing and watering when possible. The water should percolate through the soil without flooding it, to prevent caking. With this object ridges are made along the rows of

---

* September and October in Victoria

GRAFTING. 119

Fig. 101.—Nursery of Grafted Cuttings showing method of planting and banking.

vines, and the water allowed to run in the channels formed between the rows (Fig. 101). Watering should be done as seldom as possible with the minimum quantity of water required. An excess of water sometimes prevents knitting, and the cooling of the soil results in some cases in plants which, although well developed, have loose spongy tissues rendering them weak. Finally, under certain circumstances it favours the development of *Dematophora necatrix*, the most dangerous of fungoid diseases. (Fig. 102.) It is preferable to water as late as possible to allow the soil to get warm, which promotes root growth, but this is more particularly useful with grafted cuttings which have to knit at the same time. The soil should always be loosened after watering to prevent it from caking. One should also frequently examine the grafts and sever the young roots which develop very easily in the nursery.

Fig. 102.—White mycelium of *Dematophora necatrix* developed on dead vine.

Nurseries must be carefully protected against mildew on account of the great facility with which the young roots are attacked by this fungus, and of the serious results from the defective lignification caused by it. Notwithstanding the exceptional care which grafted cuttings necessitate, and the smaller percentage of strikes as compared with grafts made on rooted stock, they present certain advantages which will always give them a predominant place in reconstitution. They can be made indoors during the winter, preserved by stratification until the planting season, and vine-growers are enabled to have grafted rootlings after a year in the nursery, and after a few weeks only when frames are used. The improvements made in grafting machines, giving better results, and the decrease in the price of American cuttings, add increased importance to this method of propagation.

The preservation of grafted cuttings by stratification requires certain care. If the sand is too damp the *sclerotia* of a fungus known as the *Sclerotinia Fuckeliana* develops, sometimes inside the cleft of the graft, preventing knitting (Fig. 103). Under these circumstances stratification of grafted cuttings in damp moss was tried as an alternative. Those who used it were unanimous in recommending it.

GRAFTING. 121

In this case grafting should be done a month before planting in the nursery, that is to say, in March or April, in the centre of France. Grafts carefully made so as to have their joints perfectly adjusted are not ligatured, and are joined into bundles of ten to fifteen, lightly bound with raffia. These bundles are put in moss in cases in the following way:—A layer of damp moss, 3 to 4 inches thick, is put on the bottom of the case; the bundles are placed on end one against the other separated by a little moss, the sides of the case being also covered with moss. One must be careful not to leave a space allowing desiccation; finally, a layer of 3 to 4 inches of moss is placed on top of the cuttings.*

The grafted cuttings should be planted as soon as a few roots have started growing at their base; at that time the pads of knitting tissues have united and spread over the sections.

Fig. 103.
Sclerotinia Fuckeliana.

Rougier, who specially studied this method of stratification, points out the following advantages:—1st. It dispenses with ligatures; 2nd. It insures knitting before planting.

* See an interesting article on this subject by F. Richter in *Revue de Viticulture*, vol. ix., pp. 448-453, 189?. (Transls.)

C.—ESTABLISHMENT OF A VINEYARD.

CHAPTER VII.

PREPARATION OF SOIL.

1st.—TRENCHING.

Soils in which American vines are to be planted must be prepared with great care. From the different facts already mentioned in this book, it results that with regard to adaptation to soil the greatest obstacle is, on the one hand, excessive moisture in winter and the cooling of the soil resulting from it, and, on the other hand, considerable loss of water through evaporation in dry summers. The best and the only remedy for both these obstacles is deep and thorough trenching. As a matter of fact, if the excess of water percolates easily through well-divided soil, it also remains longer under these circumstances, for the capillary attraction drawing it towards the surface where it evaporates is less felt than in compact soils. Finally, the roots can penetrate deeper, and find moister surroundings in soils deeply disturbed.

(A) *Depth of trenching.*—Trenching previous to planting is, therefore, essential, but the depth of this cultural operation naturally varies with the nature of the soil. Soils naturally dry and poor must be disturbed deeper than fresh and fertile soils. In the first case the depth should be 24 inches, while in the second 16 or 20 inches might be sufficient. However, if the arable soil is shallow, and rests on permeable limestone subsoil, the latter must not be disturbed, for the roots can naturally penetrate it and get sheltered against drought.

Trenching must be done much deeper when a new vineyard is planted on the site of an old vineyard immediately after it has been uprooted. This is generally the case with American vines. Under these circumstances a depth of 30 to 32 inches is required.

(B) *Mode of execution of trenching.*—Trenching may be done either by hand or with ploughs. The former method is evidently preferable on account of the perfection with which the soil can be loosened, and it is the only possible one in certain rocky soils, but is far more costly than the latter. These can only be applied with efficacy in deep loose soils, unless steam traction is used, which allows considerable obstacles to be overcome, and loosens the soil much better than implements hauled by teams.*

Whatever may be the system adopted, three cases are to be considered—1st, the arable soil is of superior quality to the subsoil, and the latter cannot be improved by the action of the air; 2nd, the subsoil may be usefully modified by atmospheric influences; 3rd, the subsoil may improve the arable soil if mixed with it.

If the work is done by hand one proceeds in the following way:—In the first case part of the men open a trench to the required depth so as to expose the subsoil which other men disturb, leaving it in its place. In the second case the arable soil is thrown into the trench so as to superpose the layers in an inverse order. In the third case narrow vertical slices are cut and mixed together before being modified.

If, on the contrary, draught teams are used, one may go to a certain depth without bringing the subsoil to the surface by ploughing the arable soil with an ordinary plough and following with the subsoiler in the same furrow, disintegrating the subsoil without shifting it.

To completely turn over the soil the best way is to use—1st, a plough of medium strength; 2nd, a Bonnet trenching plough. The first turns over the top layer of arable soil and draws it into the furrow made by the trenching plough; the second draws from the bottom of the furrow opened by the ordinary plough a new slice of soil which it tips over it. In loose light soils these different implements may be replaced by Coëtgreave's trenching plough, which carries them all fixed on the same beam.

(C) *Time most suitable for trenching.*—The most suitable time seems to be the end of autumn or the beginning of winter, for the soils are not too wet and have not become too hard. It is also a slack time in farm work, which enables the use of all the unengaged draught; further, the soil

---

*For further information see *Trenching and Subsoiling for American Vines*, by the present translators, Department of Agriculture, Melbourne, 1901.

disturbed at that time of the year becomes loose and mellowed under the influence of frost; it gets well aerated, and has time to settle down before planting. Further, every thing is in favour of autumn trenching.

2ND.—MANURING.

Manure should be applied before planting, except in the case of soils naturally very rich. This operation is above all necessary when an old vineyard is uprooted and planted again with new vines. All matters must be restituted to the soil (nitrogen, phosphoric acid, potash) which have been abstracted by the old vines. American vines, especially those liable to chlorosis, seem to require these matters more than any others. When a plantation of American vines is made on the site of an old European vineyard in soil of medium fertility 25 to 28 tons per acre of stable manure, or its equivalent, should be applied. Manures or fertilizers decomposing slowly should be preferred, as it gives them time to wait for the roots of the plant and furnishes it with food for a longer period. Bones, leather, residues from glue manufacture, bamboos, box, rock-rose, lentiscus, and other such material may be advantageously used in these cases. Manures of this kind present the advantage of not forcing the vegetation of the young plant, generally too powerful naturally.

Fertilizers should be spread all through the thickness of the ploughed part, without, however, resting on the bottom, where the water would dissolve the matters they contain.

CHAPTER VIII.

PLANTATION.

1st.—Arrangement of Vines.

(A) *Shape of the plantation.*—Plantations in which the whole surface of the soil is covered with vines may be considered as the only ones offering any interest with the actual methods of viticulture. Those in which other plants are cultivated together with vines cannot be considered as having the intensive character of viticulture. But vines may be disposed in different ways, and it is important to study the value of each of these—1st, planting in lines; 2nd, in squares; 3rd, in quincunx.

Planting in lines (Fig. 104) is that in which vines are closer on the lines than the lines are between each other.

This disposition is not favorable to good growth and abundant fructification of vines, the vigour of which diminishes rapidly when their roots come in contact, which happens long before they have grown over the whole surface. Experiments made by H. Marès have shown that the yield under those circumstances is one-fifth smaller than that obtained with vines planted in squares in which each vine occupies the same surface.

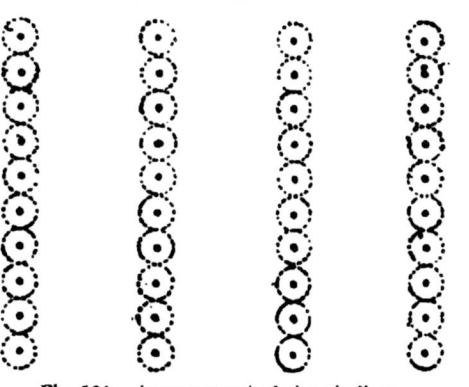

Fig. 104.—Arrangement of vines in lines.

But if this arrangement offers less advantages from this point of view, it offers other advantages, such as allowing ploughing during the whole time of vegetation, even with vines of spreading habit, which means a large saving of labour.

Plantation in squares (Fig. 105) is preferable if the yield alone is concerned, and, further, it renders cross ploughing possible, and if the plant dies it can be replaced by layering a cane from one of the four neighbouring vines.

The arrangement in quincunx (Fig. 106) is that in which the plants occupy in groups of three the angles of an equilateral triangle, and in groups of four those of a lozenge; further, it allows cross ploughing in three directions, the replacing of " misses " with the layers of six neighbouring plants, and finally the planting of a greater number of vines for a given surface, while giving equal space for their development. Therefore, it increases the yield per acre.

The only disadvantage of this system is that the surface of the soil is quickly covered with the canes of the vines, especially of those of spreading habit, preventing the use of teams and ploughs.

To sum up, when vines of an erect habit are planted quincunx or squares should be adopted; when, on the contrary, the vines are of a spreading habit one must ascertain

Fig. 105.
Arrangement of vines in squares.

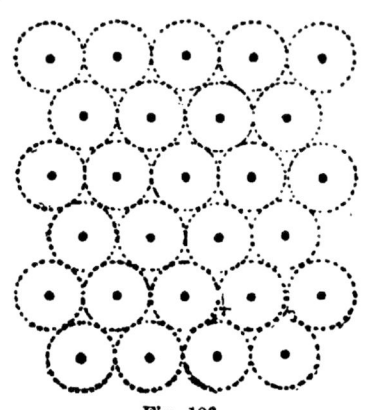

Fig. 106.
Arrangement of vines in quincunx.

if a sufficient number of hands are available to allow the vineyard to be worked by hand in summer, and if the increased cost of this operation will not absorb the benefit of the increased production.

(B) *Distance apart.*—This question need only be considered in the case of direct producers. In the case of graft bearers the conditions remaining similar to those of old plantations, the distance apart should be the same as that proved by experience to have given the best results with European varieties.

(C) *Marking out the land.*—The position of each vine is marked on the land by the intersection of two lines made with strings or traced on the soil with a special implement.

2ND.—GROUPING THE CÉPAGES.

The system of grouping the different cépages in different blocks is generally adopted, and may be considered as far preferable to other systems in which varieties are mixed together. By grouping the varieties more regularity is obtained, as each vine has practically the same vigour and, therefore, cannot live at the expense of another. The maturation of fruit is also more uniform; finally, all the plants have the same habit and can, therefore, be submitted to the same method of treatment.

3RD.—PLANTING.

Planting is done in different ways according to whether cuttings or rootlings are used. In the first case an iron dibble made of round iron, 1 to 1½ inches in diameter, is used; the dibble may be made of square iron ¾ inch in section; it is then called a *Birone*. A wooden handle is fixed on top in a perpendicular direction in the same manner as those of carpenters' augers (Fig. 107). The dibble is sunk down in the ground vertically, drawn out carefully so as to leave an open hole into which the cutting is inserted to the required depth. It is then sunk into the soil again a few inches from the cutting and the earth rammed tightly against it so as to force it to touch the cutting everywhere. One should not be able to pull the cutting out of the ground if the operation has been well conducted. Two free eyes only are left out of the ground, the rest of the cutting being pruned off.

Fig. 107.
Planting Dibble.

When the soil is very pebbly or very rough and lumpy it is advisable to surround the cutting with sand or mellowed soil before ramming. This prevents the contact of the air and therefore desiccation, and places the first root growth under very favorable conditions.

When rootlings are to be planted an iron rod is sunk into the ground in the places marked for planting. A hole 1 foot square is then made on one side of the rod, and when the latter is pulled out a line is marked on one side of the hole in the place where the young rootling is to be planted.

Plants must be removed from the nursery with care, preserving as many roots as possible, as these organs are provided with matters necessary to the first development of the plant. We must only freshen the roots, that is to say, cut the bruised extremities away. The plants are then placed against the side of the hole on the line left by the rod, the roots spread at the bottom and covered with mellowed soil slightly rammed, finishing by filling the rest of the soil loosely.

We have already indicated the most favorable time for planting cuttings when studying propagation by cuttings. It is better in the case of rootlings to plant them before the end of winter, except in very damp and cold soil, to allow the earth to settle in the hole before vegetation starts.

4TH.—CARE TO BE GIVEN TO NEW VINEYARDS.

Frequent ploughing, to keep the surface free from weeds and retain the moisture, must be done during the summer following planting. These operations may be done with hoes or vine scarifiers, and should be completed by hand round the young plants. One must be careful not to shake the young vines which have begun to root. A small stake is often placed near each vine to protect it, or at least at the end of the lines which are more exposed when the teams are turning. At other times five or six buds are left, disbudding the three top ones. This helps at the beginning to show the place occupied by each vine.

The following winter the soil is ploughed away from the vines and the suckers pruned off, "misses" or "weaklings" are replaced with rootlings planted in the nursery for that purpose. The pruning must be done as late as possible on account of the natural tendency of young plants to make an early growth; if the top bud develops vigorously it is cut back to two or three eyes and the shoot borne from the bottom bud removed. If, on the contrary, the top bud does not grow, or is weak, the bottom bud is cut to the required height for the establishment of the crown. A large number of eyes must be left on the young plants to force them to grow many shoots. This prevents them from reaching a large individual development and from getting broken by wind in spring. Finally, the soil is rolled up round the young plant, which is secured to a stake to prevent the wind from breaking it.

The following years the same operations are performed, with the only differences resulting from the degree of rusticity which increases every year.

D.—CULTURE.

CHAPTER IX.

CULTURAL CARE.

Vines require the following cultural operations :—1st, pruning ; 2nd, digging ; 3rd, manuring or fertilizing ; 4th, ploughing. We will study these and indicate how they should be carried out in hot districts, pointing out alterations resulting from the cultivation of American vines.

1st.—PRUNING.

Pruning has such a predominate action on the yield of a vine that everything connected with it deserves to be studied carefully. We will study the following items :—*a*, production of fruit-bearing shoots ; *b*, establishment of vines ; *c*, height of vine ; *d*, time most favorable for pruning ; *e*, pruning tools.

(A.)—Production of Fruit-bearing Shoots.

The vine bears its fruit on shoots of the year resulting from the development of the eyes of the canes of the previous year; therefore, a certain number of these canes must be preserved every year and pruned to a certain length according to circumstances. When two or three eyes only are preserved on the cane the pruning is termed *short*, or *spur pruning*, if, on the contrary, a greater number of eyes are left it is termed *long*, or *rod pruning*.

The choice of either of these systems depends on the special aptitudes of the variety which is to be pruned. Those having their fruit-bearing buds near the base of the cane should be pruned short; those having their fruit-bearing buds at the extremity of the cane should be pruned long ; finally, those which possess fruit-bearing buds all along the cane may be pruned by either of these methods. However, we must not forget that wherever long pruning is possible it always gives the best results.

Most of the old cépages of the South of France only bear crops when pruned short, and their grafting on American stocks cannot modify the systems already adopted. But this does not apply to direct producers of the *Æstivalis* group. Most of these (*Herbemont, Cunningham, Black July*) require long pruning. As for the Jacquez, it bears fruit on all its buds, but long rod pruning seems to suit it better and results in a far greater crop; it should, therefore, be resorted to wherever possible.*

We will study their mode of execution, beginning with short spur pruning. The first element to consider is the choice of the cane furnishing the spur. From the point of view of the yield, medium, healthy, well lignified canes should be preferred. If they are too large they produce wood; if, on the contrary, they are too small, their growth is sickly. It is also necessary to preserve a good shape, and, therefore, to choose a spur on the prolongation of the arm which bears it. In the gooseberry bush system canes radiating from the centre should be selected; they should also be more or less slanting upwards, according to the variety to be cultivated; for varieties of spreading habit the spur should be selected nearer the vertical, for those of erect habit nearer the horizontal, to prevent the foundation wood from closing at the top. Finally, spurs should be selected as close as possible to the parent stem to prevent a too rapid elongation of the arms.

When these canes have been selected all others are pruned away, and these cut down to the required length, that is to say, generally two eyes and a dormant eye (Figs. 108 and 109). It is sometimes advisable to retain a third eye on varieties starting to grow early in the season and growing in regions

Fig. 108.
Spur pruning.

Fig. 109.
Spur after pruning.

---

* From experiments carried out in 1880 at the School of Agriculture, at Montpellier, Jacquez plants, submitted to long pruning, gave 17 lbs. of grapes, and those submitted to short pruning gave only 11½ lbs. All experiments made since seem to corroborate these results.

where spring frosts are to be feared; the dormant eye in this case generally remains so, and may develop in case of accident and furnish some crop, or, at any rate, a good cane for the following year's pruning. A section must be made on the node immediately following the last eye retained, and perpendicular to the axis of the shoot; by doing so a ligneous diaphragm (Fig. 110) is preserved, protecting the pith against atmospheric water, which would rot the eye. As it may be rather difficult to cut exactly through the diaphragm, it is better to make a cut slightly above it, and slanting, so as to destroy the bud which it is not intended to keep.

In some cases if the internodes are very long a slanting section is made a few inches above the retained eye; the slanting disposition prevents water from accumulating in the pith. These general indications apply also to long rod pruning. However, in this case, the long rod having to feed a much greater number of shoots, these shoots do not generally develop enough to furnish replacing wood for the following year; it is therefore indispensable to complete this method by keeping a spur which will furnish more vigorous shoots, better placed, for the following prunings. (Dr. Guyot's method.)

Fig. 110.
Longitudinal section of a vine cane showing diaphragms.

(B.)—ESTABLISHMENT OF VINES.

Vines may be trained in the gooseberry bush, trellis of cordon method. Vines pruned according to the gooseberry bush method consist in a trunk and a crown composed of a variable number of arms radiating from the centre (Fig. 111). This is the method generally adopted in the South of France. It has the advantage of allowing the shoots to spread evenly over the surface of the ground and shelter it to a certain extent, keeping it moist. It is easy with this method to cross-plough, to replace "misses," it does away with stakes and shelters the grapes against the action of the sun's rays, which might roast them, or, at least, diminish their volume.

The number of arms to be left on each stump varies with its vigour; their number must be increased when suckers grow only on the trunk; on the contrary, if a diminution in the vigour of the plant is noticed, the number of arms must be reduced. With this method spurs alone are generally used; however, it is possible to leave a long rod or leader, which is brought down and fastened to the trunk, forming a circle; or two rods may be left and twisted together (*quarante* method modified by Coste-Floret). (Figs. 112 and 118.) We must be careful to select the long rods on different arms every year, on account of the considerable development they promote on that arm. This method gives satisfactory results with *Jacquez, Black July*, and *Herbemont* at the School of Agriculture, Montpellier, and we are of opinion that it is the best for cépages of this character in countries where the gooseberry bush is the rule and where stakes are not used. As a matter of fact, the fruit does not lie on the ground, the fruit-bearing shoots being supported at the same height as the spurs, and spreading in exactly the same way as if short spurs alone were retained. As for European varieties grafted on American stock, we are of opinion that there is no reason in favour of an alteration in the methods usually employed.

Fig. 111.—Gooseberry Bush pruning.

Fig. 112.—Gooseberry Bush with long rod bent in a circle.

The *trellis* method is that in which the arms are divided symmetrically in the same plane (Fig. 113). It is adapted to regions where grapes have to be exposed to the action of the sun's rays to ripen; it is rather more difficult and requires better knowledge and care to keep an even development between the different corresponding parts. In regions necessitating the use of this method we would advise replacing it by the *cordon* method. With this method the plant follows a single direction, which may be horizontal, vertical, or slanting, and is formed by a stem carrying spurs, or spurs and long rods, but no arms (Fig. 114). Under these circumstances we would not be preoccupied in keeping an equilibrium between the different parts of the plant, as the growth always takes place in the same direction.

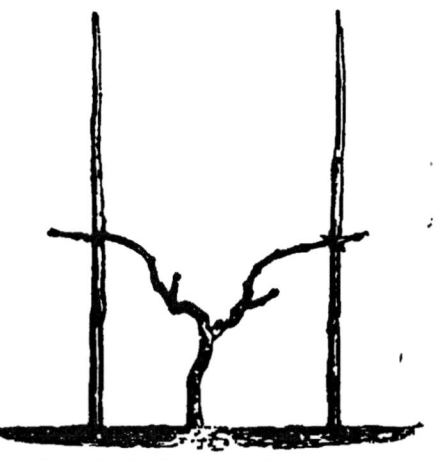

Fig. 113.—Spalier with rods and spurs.

The *chaintre* method used in Touraine is a modification of the trellis. The plants, very far apart, are formed by

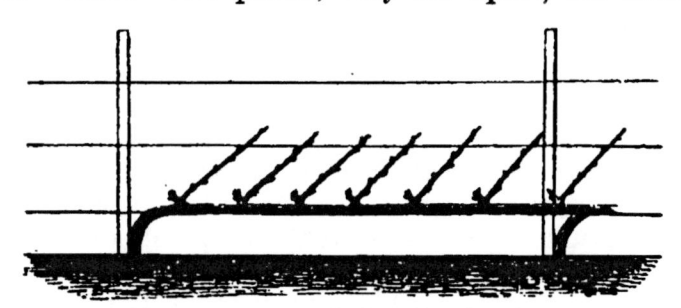

Fig. 114.—Cazenave's Cordon with rods and spurs.

foundation wood, with symmetrical arms extended horizontally above the soil and supported by small wooden forks bearing a long rod (Fig. 115). This system seems to suit Americo-Æstivalis hybrids. If applied to graft-bearers it would have the advantage of diminishing the number of grafts and the number of plants per acre on account of the considerable distance left between each stump. In hot, dry, Mediterranean regions it is inconvenient, as it requires frequent displacement during summer cultivation, which might cause the grapes to roast. In regions where this accident is not to be feared it is preferable to substitute the cordon-chaintre, which is easier to manage.* However, these methods do not allow cross-ploughing.

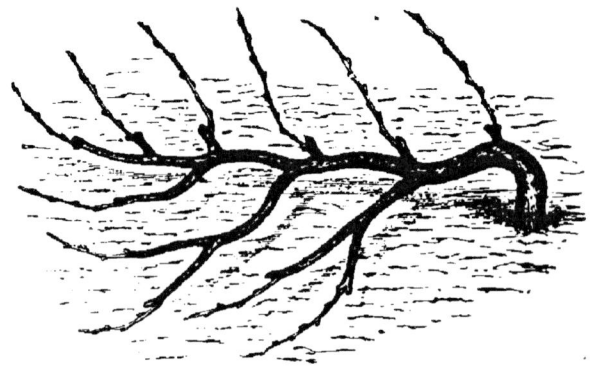

Fig. 115.—Chaintre.

(C.)—Height of Vines.

Vines may be classified as follows with regard to their development:—Low; medium; high.

Low vines are those in which the shoots start near the soil, and the fruit is consequently a few inches from the surface. These give the richest grapes in saccharine matter on account of the proximity to the soil, which reflects the heat and light directly on them. But the action of radiation, which in summer (by an emission during night of the heat absorbed in excess during the day-time by the soil) heats the plant, results on the contrary in spring in reducing the temperature of the soil and the plant often below freezing point. This lowering of temperature results from the loss of heat taking place from the soil towards the atmosphere during clear nights. Low vines are therefore more subject to the influence of spring frosts. This method can therefore only be adopted in warm climates or on hills; but it must always be adopted where possible on account of the superior quality of the fruit. High and medium vines in which the shoots start from a certain height above the soil give musts poor in sugar, and they should only be used when the short method cannot be applied. These two last methods are rarely used in the South of France,

---

* *Culture de la Vigne en chaintre*, by A. Vias, instituteur. Paris, librairie agricole de la Maison rustique, 26 rue Jacob.

but in cases where it would be necessary Jacquez seems to be the cépage better suited, on account of the natural alcoholic richness of its wine.

(D.)—Pruning Methods recently Recommended in the South of France.

Vine-growers have recently tried to increase the yield of their vines in the South by giving them a greater development and by using long-rod methods, which had never been practiced before in that region. The principal methods recommended are—1st, Royat; 2nd, Quarante; 3rd, Quarante modified by Coste-Floret.

(*a*) *Royat method.*—Vines planted in lines 6 to 7 feet apart, and 5 to 6 feet on the line, are trained in cordons, and provided with spurs and long rods as in the Cazenave method; but the long rods, instead of being trained obliquely, are

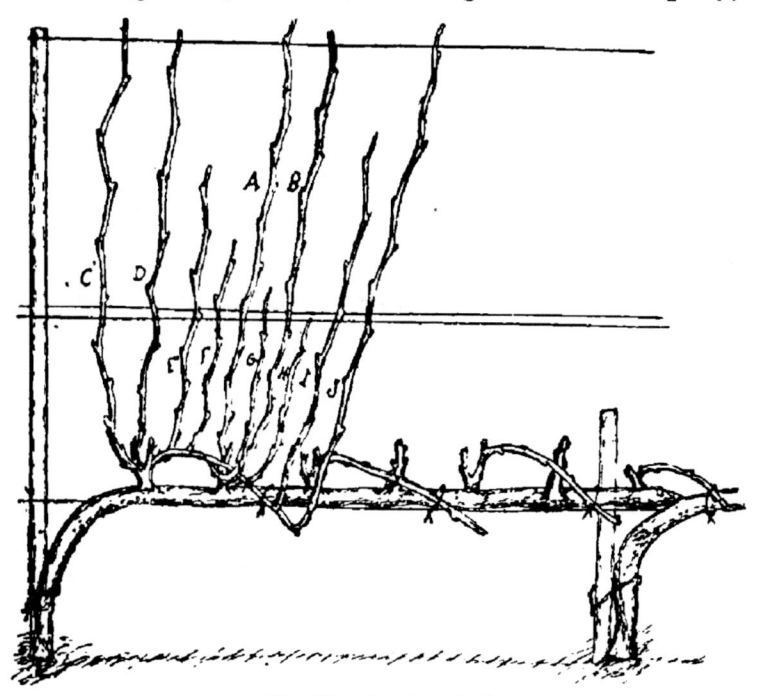

Fig. 116.—Royat method.

inarched (Fig. 116). It has a certain analogy to the Sylvoz system, which differs only from it by the absence of replacement spurs.

The object of inarching is to promote the fructification of the shoots growing on the rod and the development of those borne by the spur. The trellising is done by means of wires, the first row of wire 16 to 20 inches above the surface of the soil carries the cordon, a second double row 12 inches above the first row, and between which the shoots are inserted as they grow; finally, a third row, 28 or 32 inches higher, serves to fasten the extremities of the shoots.

This method, which is very productive in fresh and fertile soils, when applied to vigorous varieties easily standing long pruning, does not give satisfactory results in dry places.

(b) *Quarante's method.*—This method, used in some parts of the Hérault, tends to get generalized. It consists in retaining, on an ordinary low stump, two long rods and two replacement spurs, symmetrically disposed; the two long

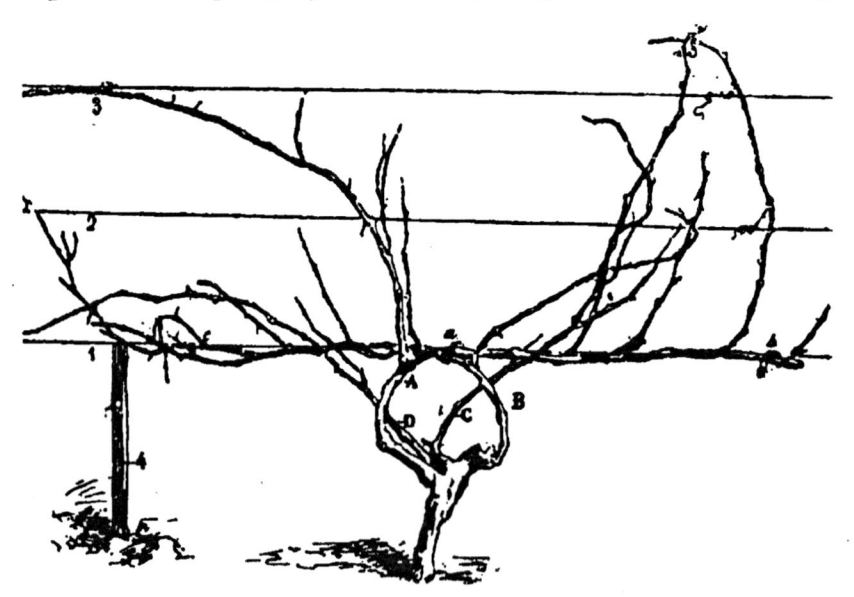

Fig. 117.—Young vine pruned after Coste-Floret's modification of the Quarante method. A, B, long rods; C, D, replacing wood.

rods are twisted together so as to form a loose knot, and the extremities are fastened horizontally on a wire. The eyes of the inarched part of the long rods are cut away or disbudded. Two other wires placed above support the shoots (Fig. 117). This is practically a trellis with spurs and long rods.

Quarante's method seems also to be preferred in fertile soils in which vines grow powerfully, but has the same disadvantage as the above of requiring a great outlay of money for establishing the trellises.

(c) *Quarante's method modified by Coste-Floret.*—Coste-Floret, who appreciated the large production obtainable with this method, and its facility for transforming ordinary gooseberry-bush stumps into Quarante stumps and bringing these back to the gooseberry bush again if required, tried to render

Fig. 118.—Quarante method modified by Coste-Floret.

it more practicable by simplifying the mode of trellising (Fig. 118). He increased also the number of spurs, which he pruned with one free eye only, and dis-budded the crops borne by the spurs.

This modification allows the branches to trail on the soil, and, according to its inventor, would better suit vines planted in rather dry districts.

(E.)—TIME MOST FAVORABLE FOR PRUNING.

Pruning may be done the whole time the vine is without leaves; from the time the canes are well lignified until the vine begins to bleed. However, it is advisable to cease pruning when the weather is very cold and the thermometer below freezing point, for the wood becomes brittle, and the tissues, freshly cut, would be injured by frost. One may be forced to prune late in districts where spring frosts are to be feared, especially with cépages starting to grow early in the season. The object of late pruning is to hold back the vegetation; all the sap which would have acted immediately on a certain number of buds and induced early growth if pruning had been performed will be divided on a greater number of buds, and, therefore, have less influence on each of them.

But, while the canes are not pruned, one cannot proceed with ploughing. Therefore, in such districts the middle course is followed, removing all the canes which are not to furnish spurs, and temporarily pruning the others to a length of 18 inches to 2 feet. Later on, when the frosts are over, they may be pruned back to two eyes.*

(F.)—Pruning Tools.

The tools used for pruning are a strong pruning-knife and secateur. The pruning-knife was for a long time the only tool used, but it is done away with now, especially in districts of large production, and replaced by the secateur. However, it is met with in some places in Bourgogne, Gironde Charentes, and Provence. The pruning-bill of Provence (*poudette*) (Fig. 119) is formed of a blade having a right angled sharp edge on one side and a small straight edge on the opposite side. The cane is pruned with the part *a b*, the cane being held slightly curved outwards, so as to

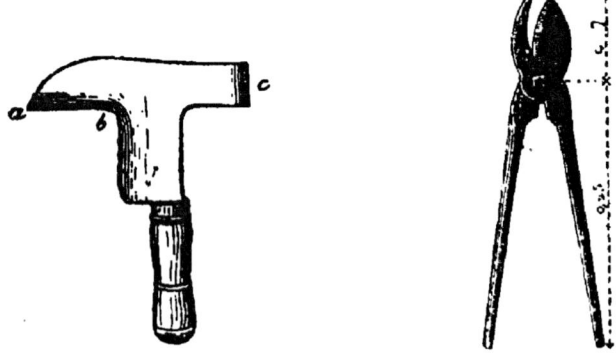

Fig. 119.—Pruning Bill of Provence.   Fig. 120.—Secateur of Languedoc.

cut on the projecting part with a movement similar to that of sawing. The part *c* is used to cut suckers on the old stump. It requires long practice to be able to use this pruning-knife, and this explains why it is replaced by the secateur, with which it is impossible, however, to make such a neat section. The secateur of Languedoc (Fig. 120) consists

---
* This method of pruning vines twice is termed in America "Fall pruning." (Trans.)

of two branches, one bearing a hook against which the cane presses, the other a sharp blade which cuts it. In well-made secateurs the blade and the hook are disposed in such a manner that when they press against the cane the blade does not press normally, but, on the contrary, forms a certain angle with the hook, causing a kind of sawing rather than crushing. The two handles are long, and may be used with both hands; one of them is straight, and ended by a cold chisel used to remove suckers.

Pruners must always be careful to keep the hook above, so that the part of the cane which bears against it, and is always more or less bruised, will be pruned off.

2ND.—DIGGING.

Digging should be done so as to form a basin round the vine (Hérault) or small trenches perpendicular to the line of vines (parts of Bouches-du-Rhône), or in trenches along the rows. In the first case the work is done by hand; in the Languedoc's the basins are made 6 to 8 inches deep, they are wide enough to touch each other. This is considered equivalent to cultivating half the surface; in the second case, the digging is done at the same time as the first ploughing, and may be done by hand (Fig. 121) or with

Fig. 121.—Arrangement of soil after digging.

ploughs. In this case special ploughs are used (see Figs. 92 to 95), and a small ridge left between the vines is dug away by hand. Digging should be done in winter, when heavy frosts are not to be feared any longer, to avoid freezing the trunk. However, it is important not to wait too long, for the efficacy of this operation depends greatly on the length of time the collar of the plant is left exposed to the air.

The object of digging is to completely cultivate round the vine, to destroy weeds which the plough cannot reach, and kill the larvæ or eggs of insects found under the old bark near the collar of the plant. It also helps to destroy suckers or superficial roots, which, in the case of grafts especially, may cause different accidents. It is also often used to bury manures or fertilizers in countries where the custom is to put them round the stumps.

3RD.—MANURING OR FERTILIZING.

(A.)—MANURING.

Vines require nitrogen, phosphoric acid, and potash. The two first matters seem to influence the vegetation only, the third seems to promote the production of sugar in the fruit. All manures containing these three matters in suitable preparations, and in a sufficiently assimilable state, may be used.

According to Müntz, the following are the quantities corresponding to a yield of 1,056 gallons per acre in the Mediterranean regions:—

Nitrogen	121 lbs.
Potash	110 "
Phosphoric acid	88 "

Vine-growers should, therefore, try to furnish their vines annually with the above-mentioned quantities of these fertilizers unless the soil already contains one or more of them accumulated in large quantities. *A chemical analysis of the soil is necessary to ascertain if this is the case.*

Dehérain considers that phosphoric acid will give useful results—1st, in soils containing less than 0·001 of total phosphoric acid; 2nd, in those containing 0·001 of phosphoric acid and only 0·0002 of acid soluble in acetic acid; 3rd, in those containing less than 440 lbs. per acre of phosphoric acid soluble in tartaric acid.

Paul de Gasparin considers that potassic manure does not give good results in soils containing more than 1·25 per cent. of potash. An analysis of the soil is not always sufficient to indicate the matters which have to be added to it. When these are not in an easily assimilable form, they may, although existing in large quantities, have no action on the vegetation, and require the addition of the same matters in a more readily assimilable form.

Cultural experiments are necessary to ascertain these facts. The vineyard to be studied should be divided into plots in squares containing about 100 stumps each, sufficiently far apart for the fertilizers of one square not to influence another. One is used as a check, and does not receive any fertilizer; another receives a complete manure containing sufficient quantities of nitrogen, potash, and phosphoric acid to replace those removed annually by the crop. Three other squares are manured with two of these matters only alternating. The crops are carefully weighed, and if one of the squares with incomplete manure give a crop equivalent to that with complete manure, or if the difference between the value of the crops is less, then the cost of the matter not used in the square considered, we may assume that the soil is in a state to furnish, at least temporarily, the required quantity of this matter, and that it is, therefore, useless to add to the manure.

NO MANURE.	NITROGEN. PHOSPH.AC. POTASH.	NITROGEN. PHOSPH. AC.	NITROGEN. POTASH.	PHOSPH. AC. POTASH.

Fig. 122.—Arrangement of Experiments for ascertaining the relative value of different forms of Manures in a given soil.

Fig. 122 gives an idea of the arrangement of such an experiment; it is easy by a similar method to ascertain the relative value of the different forms under which manures can be applied.

In the South of France the manures used are—Stable manure, sheep manure, night-soil, woollen rags, horns, old boots, marc, bamboos, sea-weed, soot, and, finally, chemical manure.

Stable manure contains per cent:—

Nitrogen	0·4 to 2·5
Phosphoric acid	0·7 ,, 0·8
Potash	0·4 ,, 0·5

Eight to 12 tons are applied per acre for four years; straw is added to it in very cold soils.

Sheep-yard manures contain:—

Nitrogen	0·72
Phosphoric acid	1·52

They are richer than stable manures, and act quicker; that is to say, their effect does not last as long. Six tons are applied per acre every year.

Night-soils vary greatly in composition, and are not generally used for vines, because they are too strong, and cause production of watery must, giving wines lacking in keeping qualities. Their influence does not last more than a year. This disadvantage may be diminished and better effects obtained by mixing with tan, sawdust, peat-moss, or sea-weeds.

Woollen rags contain 10 to 15 per cent. of nitrogen and a certain proportion of phosphoric acid. They give very good results in dry soils in the South of France, where they maintain a certain moisture. Ten to 15 cwt. per acre are applied; their effect lasts four to five years.

Horns containing 14·86 of nitrogen and 46·14 of phosphate of lime and magnesia per cent. have much slower action. The same thing applies to old boots and other waste leather; it is advisable to decompose them beforehand by putting them in lime composts or manure heaps.

Oil cakes contain more especially nitrogen and phosphate of lime. Those mostly used are:—

	Nitrogen. Per cent.	Phosphoric acid. Per cent.
Rape cake, Europe	4·92	2·83
,, ,, Bombay	5·53	1·98
Black Mustard Cake	5·15	1·67
Corn-cole cake	4·46	1·83
Indian poppy seed cake	5·81	2·88
Ravison cake	4·99	1·02
Rough Castor Oil seed cake	3·67	1·62
Decorticated Castor Oil seed cake	7·42	2·26
Black Sesame cake	6·34	2·03
White Sesame cake	5·81	2·07
Variegated Sesame cake*	5·51	1·94

They are used in a quantity of about 13 cwt. per acre, and are entirely absorbed the first year. Their small percentage of potash renders necessary the use of 220 to 440 lbs. of *potassium chloride*, *potassium sulphide*, or *sulphate of potash*. These should also be added when horns or woollen rags are used. Sulphated oil cakes, that is to say, those in which the oil is removed by carbon bi-sulphide are superior, for the oily matters eliminated are without value as fertilizers.

Grape marc contains 1·71 of nitrogen and 0·5 of potash per cent.; it may be used in calcareous soils, on account of its acidity, or may be mixed with lime to neutralize its natural acidity, or with ashes or star phosphate to increase their percentage of phosphate.

Bamboos, sea-weed, box-tree, branches, &c., should be used in stiff soils after having been chopped up, or in light soils after being previously decomposed. These different manures contain the following quantities of nitrogen:—

Box	1·17 per cent.
Bamboos	0·43 ,,
Sea-weed	0·40 to 0·55 per cent

---

* Décugis, *Tourteaux des graines oléagineuses*, Toulon, 1876.

In certain countries green manures are used. Plants with large roots and well-developed tap roots, capable of gathering the ammonia of the air and the mineral matters in the soil should be selected. They generally belong to the leguminous family :—Horse bean, Winter vetch, Clover, and sometimes Winter rape. Some of these plants have the following composition :—

	Nitrogen. Per cent.	Potash. Per cent.	Phosphoric acid. Per cent.
Vetch	0·56	0·43	0·13
Rape	0·46	0·35	0·12
Clover	0·42	0·26	0·08

If we consider the average crop of 4 tons 15 cwt. per acre, when these plants are buried in the ground they furnish the following matters per acre:—

	Yield. Tons cwts.	Nitrogen. Per cent.	Potash. Per cent.	Phosphoric Acid. Per cent.
Vetch	4 15	61·92	51·50	15·60
Rape	4 15	55·20	42·00	14·40
Clover	4 15	51·60	31·20	9·60

The above table shows that in case of necessity these manures might be sufficient for small grape crops, but we must not forget that a part of the nitrogen, and all the mineral matters they contain were derived from the soil which they have to fertilize, consequently they may be considered as a means of transforming rather than enriching the soil.

Soot contains 1·15 per cent. of nitrogen, and has a remarkable effect upon vines planted in calcareous soils. Half to three-quarters ton is used annually per acre.

Different chemical manures, containing *nitrogen*, *phosphoric acid*, and *potash* may be used for completing other manures, or, united in the required proportions, they may sometimes be sufficient for vine requirements.

Georges Ville recently recommended the following formula :—

Superphosphate of lime	...	...	352 lbs. per acre.
Carbonate of potash	...	...	176 〃 〃
Sulphate of lime	...	...	352 〃 〃

It results from what we have already said that the quantities of potash and superphosphate indicated above are too considerable for the requirements of one year (maximum duration of these fertilizers); on the other hand, there is no provision made for nitrogen. An admixture of *carbonate of potash* and *sulphate of lime* may be advantageously replaced by *sulphate of potash*.

In the following table we give an idea of the way of establishing formulæ for chemical manures. They may vary greatly as far as substances are concerned, but they must all represent the same weight of elements:—

Formulæ.	Quantity of—			
	Fertilizer.	Nitrogen.	Potash.	Phosphoric Acid.
1st Formula:—Nitrate of Soda @ 15% Nitrogen	400 kil.	60		
Sulphate of Potash @ 50% Potash	120 ″	...	60	
Superphosphate of Lime @ 16% Phosphoric Acid	100 ″	...	...	16
2nd Formula:—Sulphate of Ammonia @ 20% Nitrogen	300 ″	60		
Sulphate of Potash at 50% Potash	120 ″	...	60	
Superphosphate of Lime @ 16% Phosphoric Acid	100 ″	...	...	16
3rd Formula:—Sulphate of Ammonia @ 20% Nitrogen	300 ″	60		
Potassium Chloride @ 50% Potash	120 ″	...	60	
Superphosphate of Lime @ 16% Phosphoric Acid	100 ″	...	...	16
Sulphate of Iron	150 ″	...		

Superphosphate of lime should be applied at the beginning of winter, and well mixed with the soil; nitrate of soda and sulphate of potash should only be applied in spring.

Other compositions are possible according to the cheapest way matters can be purchased. *Nitrogen* may be derived from *sulphate* and *nitrate of ammonia,* or *nitrates of potash* or *soda.*[*] *Phosphoric acid* may be derived from *mineral phosphates,* star *phosphates, bones, animal black,* and *superphosphates.* Finally, *potash* is to be found in *alkaline salts, sulphate of potash, potassium chloride, potassium sulphide, nitrate* or *carbonate of potash,* &c.

Although cost is the main item in purchasing manures, we must not forget that some act better than others in certain soils. *Potassium chloride* and *sulphide,* and *sulphate of potash,* for instance, seem to give better results than other

---

[*] Nitrogen, in the form of nitrates, seems to promote a greater production of sugar in must than when in the form of organic matters.

potassic salts. *Sulphate of potash* diffuses better than any other, and has so far given the best results in comparative experiments; it promotes better fructification and greater richness in sugar. In calcareous soils we should only use *superphosphates*, as *neutral phosphates* do not produce any effect.

Chemical manures are generally absorbed the first year. It is, therefore, better to alternate their use with stable manure.

Commercial fertilizers are mixtures of different fertilizing matters prepared by manure manufacturers. The variations existing in their composition from the point of view of proportion and the forms under which the matters composing them are found prevents the expression of a general opinion on them. One should always ask for a guarantee of the composition of the fertilizer, specifying the proportion of matters in a soluble state, with the method of analysis used.

(B.)—Means of Improvement.

The means of improving the soil of vineyards are similar to those used for other plants: *drainage*, which is outside the scope of this work; addition of *lime, marl, gypsum*, paring and *burning the sward*, and sometimes the addition of *coal ashes* and *hammerslag*.

Lime (carbonate of lime) and marl help to modify the physical properties of the soil as well as its chemical composition. Their use seems to ameliorate the quality of the wine, giving it a better colour.

Gypsum (sulphate of lime) exerts a more favorable action on the fructification of vines when the soil is naturally rich. Used in quantities of $\frac{1}{2}$ to $1\frac{1}{4}$ tons per acre it increases the yield in a proportion which seems to increase with the quantity used, and which may reach half or more of the usual crop.

Raw gypsum, evenly crushed, or burnt gypsum, are used indifferently. It is applied broadcast in March or April, and ploughed over.

Paring or burning the sward renders clayey soils very permeable, enables them to get warm easily, and, according to Pagézy's experiments, the yield in sugar is increased. This seems due to the transformation of certain mineral salts into a more assimilable form, such, for instance, as potash salts retained in clay in a state of insoluble combination.

(C.)—Time most Favorable for Manuring.

The most favorable time for applying manures is generally the end of winter (January, February, March).* The most soluble manure should be applied last. It is important not to expose fertilizing matters dissolving under the action of rain before vines start to throw spring rootlets, which will absorb them rapidly as they become assimilable. We must not wait, especially in the Mediterranean regions, until the period of drought has begun, as the moisture necessary for the dissolution of salts might not be sufficient in the soil.

(D.)—Methods of Distributing Manures.

Manures may be distributed in three different ways: 1st, in small basins formed round the plant; 2nd, in long trenches between the lines; 3rd, over the whole surface.

Distribution in basins or over the whole surface seems to give similar results, which is easily explained, as the different ploughings spread it from the basins. Distribution in trenches has the disadvantage of destroying, every time the manuring is renewed, the young rootlets developed in the trenches.

Chemical fertilizers, occupying a very small volume (*sulphate of ammonia, nitrate, potash salts*) are placed at the foot of each plant, or simply spread broadcast over the ground, and buried by the ploughs or scarifiers.

(E.)—Ploughing.

Vines require every year a first ploughing to aerate the roots. This may be regarded as the most important and indispensable cultural operation; and a series of scarifyings with the object of keeping the surface loose.

These operations have great analogy in the different countries of Europe with regard to their special character and the order in which they are performed.

1st. *First ploughing.*—The first cultural operation consists in ploughing, with the object of *aerating* the soil; the future growth of the vine depends greatly on the way in which this is performed.

---

* June, July, August in Victoria.

CULTURAL CARE.

This first ploughing should be done at the end of Winter, at such a time that the vegetation may not be influenced by the last frosts and the first spring rains. In low lands exposed to white frosts the first ploughing should not be done too late, for when soil is newly disturbed it favours the production of white frosts. It should not be done too early, for the soil would get covered with weeds before the white frost period, and we know that the presence of weeds equally favours a decrease of temperature.

The first ploughing should be the deepest. In certain countries it is done to a depth of 6 to 8 inches; it should allow the access of air as deeply as possible, and also allow the water to penetrate and be retained in the sub-soil. Some viticulturists however, condemn, in a general way, deep ploughing for vines. They are of opinion that the destruction of superficial roots which play an important part in the nutrition of the plant greatly injures its growth, but we must not forget that in very dry countries, which are those requiring deep ploughing, the superficial root system is not found near the surface, for the amount of humidity there is not sufficient to insure their development, or because, after having grown under the influence of spring rains, they dry and die under the influence of summer drought. Therefore, it is only in climates where soils naturally keep moist that shallow first ploughing can be advocated.

Fig. 123.—Arrangement of soil after first ploughing.

We should try to obtain as high ridges as possible between the rows, so as to increase the surface of soil exposed to the action of the air. To realize this condition we must plough away from the vines, and cover the sods in the centre by digging (Fig. 121). The soil ploughed in this manner (Fig. 123) is termed "saddled" in the Hérault. Workmen perform this with very great skill in Provence, Gironde, and Charente.

The first ploughing is done by hand or with ploughs. In the first case a hoe or a hook is used, sometimes a spade or a fork. Figs. 124 and 125 show the different tools used for this work.

The saddled disposition of the soil in the Hérault may be considered as the best type of aeration ploughing done by hand. A workman follows the diagonal of the squares, so as to obtain as high a relief as possible, and accumulates the soil, forming a high ridge between the lines and a furrow on the line of stumps (Fig. 121). The lumps should not be broken, so as to retain the surface upon which the air can act. When ploughs are used they should be made so as to get as close as possible to the stump without breaking the spurs. The first furrow should be turned in the centre of the lines, turning the sods towards it, and going as close as possible to the vine. The small strip of non-ploughed ground remaining at the foot of the vines is dug by hand. The ploughs most used in the South of France are:—The *cabat* of the Gironde, which is not a very good plough, but serves the purpose very well; the *vigneron* plough of the Aude, which is formed of a

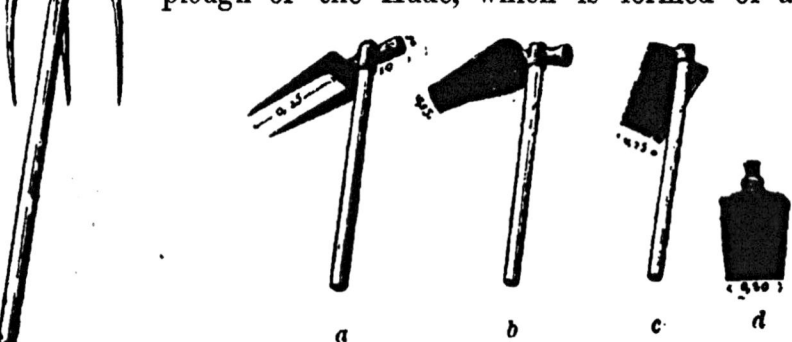

Fig. 124.
Hook used in the Hérault.

Fig. 125.
Different tools used for digging in the Hérault.
(After M. Marès.)

long beam, used as a shaft on one side; on this beam a perpendicular swingle-bar is fixed, to the extremity of which is fastened a trace (Fig. 126). The horse is yoked on the side of the plough beam, so that the body is deflected on the side.

CULTURAL CARE. 149

Vernette's *vigneron's* plough (Fig. 127) has a very low body, carrying a narrow mould-board and a long pointed share; the beam is made of iron, and fits

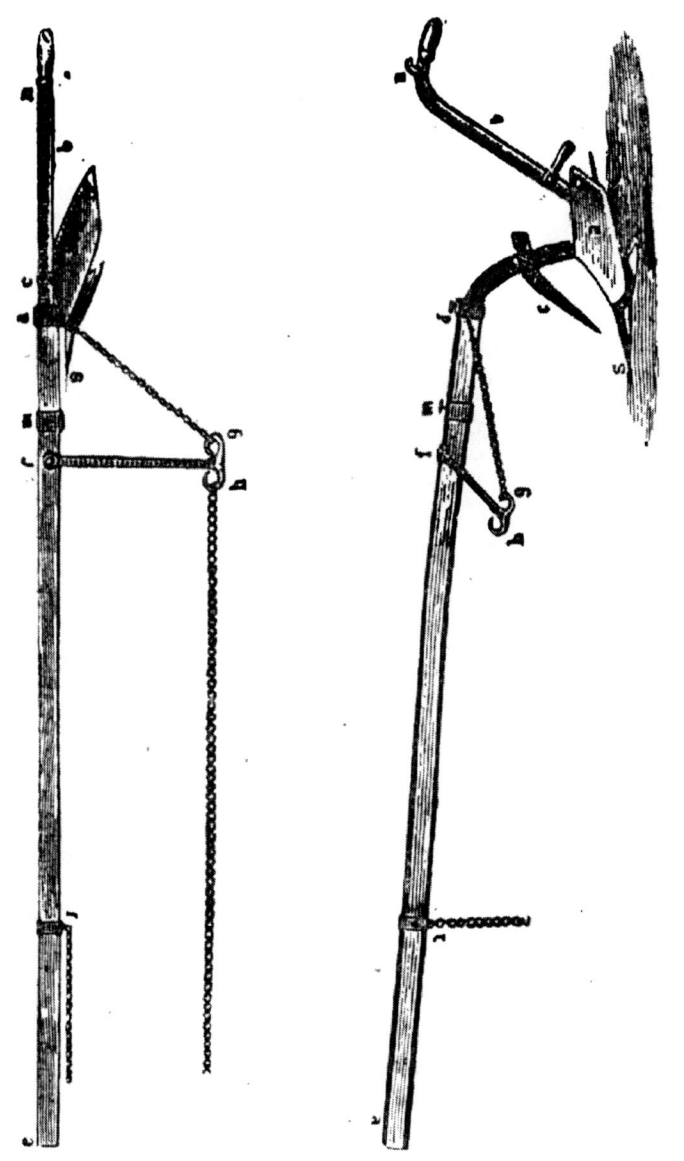

Fig. 126.—Vineyard Plough used in the Aude.

on the end of wooden shafts. This arrangement, common to many vine implements of the Hérault, has the defect of rendering the depth of ploughing irregular,

150   MANUAL OF MODERN VITICULTURE.

on account of the rigidity of the plough in the shafts, transmitting all the oscillations of the horse to the point of the share.

The ploughs which may be considered as most perfect for first ploughing are those of Renault-Goin, of Sainte-Maure, and of Souchu-Pinet, of Langeais.

Fig. 127.—Vernette's Vineyard Plough.

Renault-Goin's implement (Figs. 128 and 129) is a small iron plough, in which the beam is deflected to the right of the

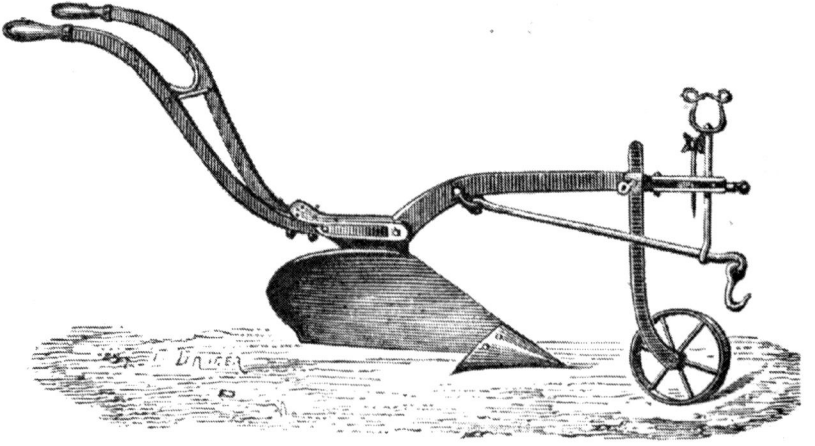

Fig. 128.—Renault-Gouin's Vineyard Plough (elevation).

point of the share; owing to this disposition the body can get much closer to the vines without risk of the beam touching the spurs. The two handles may be inclined at any angle.

Souchu-Pinet's plough (Fig. 130) resembles the former, and has curved stays and movable handles. A special harness is

Fig. 129.—Renault-Gouin's Vineyard Plough (projection).

used for hauling this plough; the swingle-bar is replaced by an iron bow (Fig. 131), upon which a draft chain is hooked.

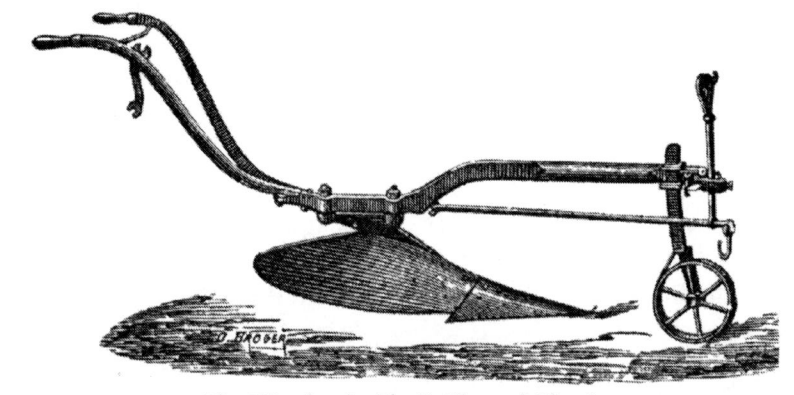

Fig. 130.—Souchu-Pinet's Vineyard Plough.

The old Roman foot plough is still in use in the Bas-Languedoc (Fig. 132). The cross ploughing is done so as to leave undisturbed only the part around the stumps, which has already been dug, as described.

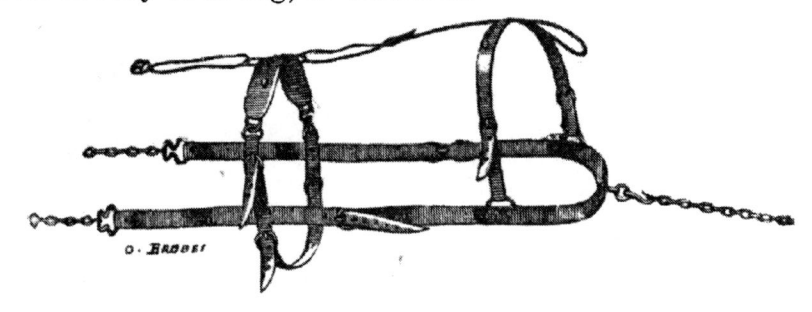

Fig. 131.—Special Harness for vineyard ploughs.

This primitive implement tears the soil instead of turning it over, and leaves it flat instead of rigid; therefore the sooner it is discarded the better.

To sum up, first ploughing has for its object the aeration of the soil, and must be done deeper than any other, and expose as great a surface as possible to the action of the air. It is often crossed.

2nd. *Scarifying or second dressing.*—The object of the following ploughing is to maintain the beneficial effect of

Fig. 132.—Old Roman Foot Plough, still in use in Bas-Languedoc for vineyard ploughing.

the first. These scarifyings are often repeated during the summer in certain districts, while in the Provence only one scarifying is generally done ; in other districts four or five, but usually only two.

(a) *Spring dressing.*—Its object is to destroy weeds grown after the spring rains, and to break up the crust formed on the surface of the land, so as to diminish evaporation.

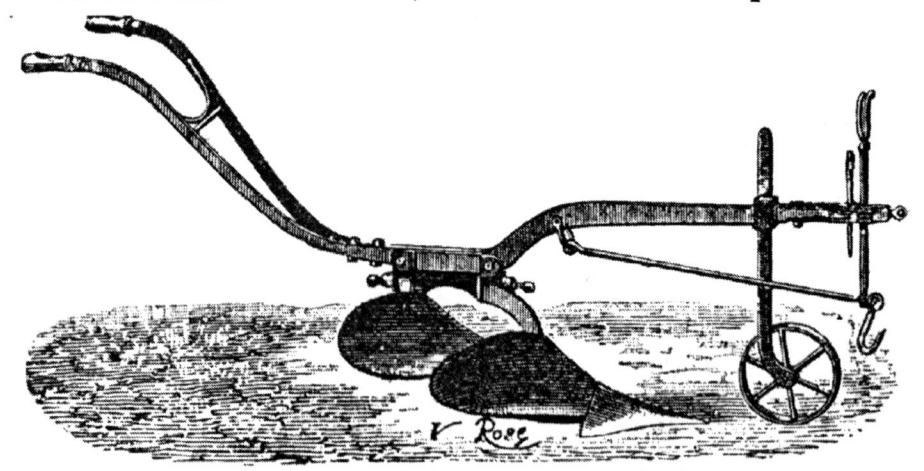

Fig. 133.—Renault-Gouin's Double-furrow Plough.

The rising of the water, replacing surface evaporation is due to capillary attraction; therefore, the more divided the surface the slower the rising. The object of this operation is also to level the surface by ploughing towards the vines, destroying the ridges which in dry climates increase the surface of evaporation. Spring scarifying should be done

shallower than first ploughing, but deeper than the following. It is usually done in May or the beginning of June.*
It should not be done at the flowering season as the decrease of temperature resulting from the active evaporation from the surface of the freshly-disturbed soil would risk bringing about non-setting.

When the distance between the vines or branches spreading over the ground prevents the use of a plough, this may be done by hand; it is cheaper to use draft implements when possible; it also allows the work to be done quicker at the

Fig. 134.—Portal's Scarifier.

right time. In the first case the tools shown in Figs. 124 and 125 are generally used, and, sometimes, but rarely, a spade. In the second case, special ploughs are used with the body deflected on the opposite side to that of the ploughs we have been studying, or scarifiers and cultivators. These implements are preferable to ploughs when the surface is fairly level, because their work is more rapid, cheaper, and leaves the soil more even.

We may mention Renault-Goin's double-furrow plough (Fig. 133), and amongst scarifiers those of Portal, used in the Aude, and that used in the Hérault, which costs £4 (Fig. 134).

(*b*) *Summer dressings.*—The dressings following the spring scarifying, are much shallower. They are generally

---
* November in Victoria.

commenced in June.* We must be careful when scarifying not to touch the grapes or uncover them. This dressing may

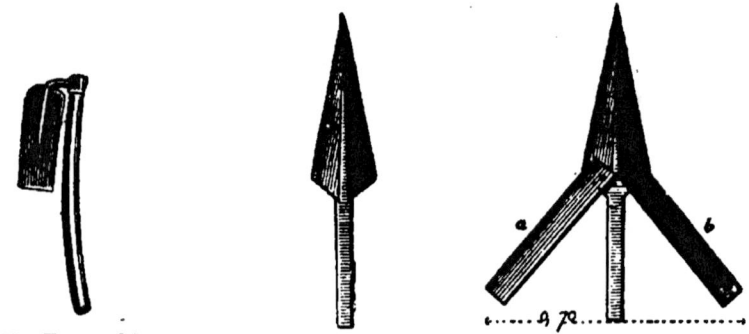

Fig. 135.—Hoe used for summer dressing.

Fig. 136.—Shares of vine cultivators.

be done by hand or with draft implements. In the first case a special hoe (Fig. 135) is used; in the second case special cultivators (Figs. 134 and 136) are used. Pilter-Planet places

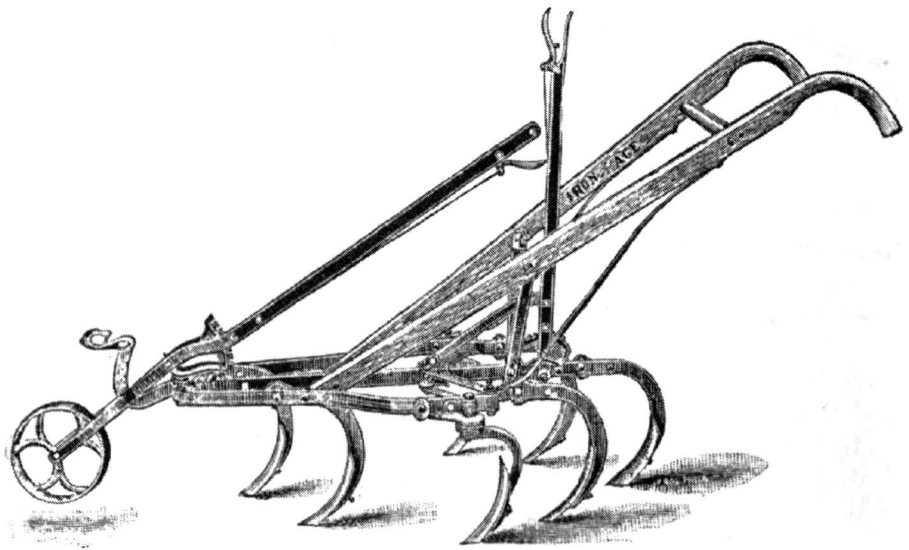

Fig. 137.—Pilter-Planet's Scarifier.

on the market different transformable scarifiers and cultivators, far superior for loose soils, the use of which tends to increase every year (Fig. 137).

The conditions favorable to effective execution of the different dressings of vines are :—1st. Well-drained soil, not hardened, loosening easily without caking; 2nd, dry and warm weather killing weeds quickly.

---

* December in Victoria.

CHAPTER X.

ACCIDENTS, DISEASES, PARASITES.

1st.—ACCIDENTS DUE TO UNFAVORABLE CONDITIONS.

Although vines are generally favoured in the regions where they are cultivated with all the conditions required for the normal development of the different phases of their vegetation, it sometimes happens that modifications in the meteorological circumstances injure the growth of the crop. We will now study these different accidents, their effects, and the means of avoiding them.

(A.)—Frosts.

Vines may be affected by frost in autumn, winter, and spring; but its action differs in each season and does not have the same effects on account of differences of the state of vegetation and in the intensity of the frost.

(*a*) *Autumn frosts.*—These are rarely to be feared in regions where the vine is cultivated. However, they occur sometimes in low-lying lands when heavy rains are followed by north winds. According to Petit-Lafitte this occurs every fourteen years in the Gironde.[*]

Their general effect is to suddenly and prematurely check vegetation and injure the ripening of the canes, which generally dry. If the crop is still on the vine it may suffer seriously, the berries being injured by the action of cold, and always resulting in considerable loss. In countries liable to autumn frosts one may remedy this accident by planting cépages ripening early.

(*b*) *Winter frosts.*—The stoppage of the vegetation in winter enables the vine to withstand low temperatures without being injured. However, when the cold reaches—10° to—15°C. some stumps may die altogether, others are cut down to the level of the soil or lose some of their arms or spurs; at other times with less low temperatures—8°C., but in damp low-lying lands the buds alone are killed, and shoots, generally sterile, grow on the old wood near the surface. This is commonly termed "return of sap."

---

[*] La *Vigne dans le Bordelais*, by Petit-Lafitte, Paris, Rothschild, 1868, page 460.

The damper and lower the soil the more affected the vines will be. Old vines or vines ripening their wood late and imperfectly suffer most. The same thing applies to vines recently dug. If the vines are not pruned they resist cold better.

In countries where winter frosts are frequent the stumps are sheltered by earthing up the soil to the level of the arms, or by burying the stump. This is generally sufficient to prevent them from getting frosted. These methods are used in the Jura, Rhine, Tokay, and Crimea, and the environs of Pekin. In cold regions, such as Beaujolais, it would be advisable to earth up the vines, especially those grafted, for if the plant is cut down to the level of the soil the graft is lost. The cultivation of vines ripening their wood early and late pruning and ploughing are the only remedies.

If a great number of plants have to be cut back the whole vineyard must be uprooted; if a few only have been frosted they should be grafted again or cut level with the soil. But in this case the vine does not give any crop for many years, on account of the great vigour of the shoots born from the old wood which grow wood and no fruit; grafting, on the contrary, enables the vine to produce fruit straight away.

(c) *Spring frosts.*—Spring frosts are much more frequent, and occur at much shorter intervals, even in warm countries. According to Petit-Lafitte, they occur every nine years in the Gironde. Marès states that they occur every three years in Languedoc. They are not so injurious as winter frosts as they do not kill the plant but only affect the crop.

There are two different spring frosts: *black frosts* and *white frosts*. The former result from a general cooling of the atmosphere, the temperature on the ground being much colder than is the case with the latter. They generally occur before the white frosts, at the start of vegetation. When the atmosphere and soil are dry, and the thaw slow and progressive, there is not much harm done; when, on the contrary, the thaw is rapid the shoots dry and the buds die. These frosts often produce swellings (Fig. 138) or excrescences at the base of the spurs or on the roots, known under the name of *Broussins*. The death of the buds often causes the death of the spurs, and sometimes that of the arms. In this case the effects of frost are felt for many years, and the stumps have to be cut back to get them into shape again.

White frosts are produced by the cooling of the soil resulting from the radiation of the heat from the soil towards the sky. The young shoots close to the soil are influenced by this cold and die if it falls below zero. Low and damp sites are generally more exposed to the action of frosts, and it is in April or May,* towards four or five in the morning, that they are most severe. Farmers have noticed that this phenomenon occurs regularly at certain dates. Edouard Roche established in his studies on the climate of Montpellier, resulting from records spreading over 100 years,† that in the Hérault late forests were to be feared towards the 10th or 14th, the 18th or 19th, to the 24th April; from the 2nd to the 4th or 5th, and from the 11th to the 13th of May. Similar observations have been made in other vine-growing countries.

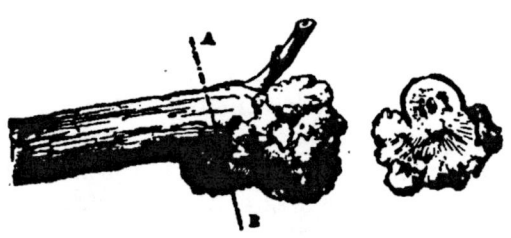

Fig. 138.—Broussin caused by frost.

There is only one means of diminishing the effects of *black frost*, and that is by trying to throw back the bursting of the buds as far as possible, by cultivating special varieties, or by pruning late, as we have already explained (fall pruning, page 137).‡

These prosecutions may also be useful against *white frosts*, but other means may be used. Some are permanent, and result from the way the vines are planted; others are only temporary, and may be repeated every time the frost appears.

Among the first we may mention planting on hills, where the effect of radiation is lessened. This is generally done in the North, Bourgogne, Champagne, &c. The crown may be kept at a certain height above the soil, placing the shoots at a distance from the soil sufficient to diminish the influence of the decrease of temperature. In Savoy vines are trained on high trellises with the object of preventing the action of frosts.

In countries where spring frosts are prevalent one should not build walls or grow hedges about the vineyard, which

---

* October and November in Victoria.

† Edouard Roche. *Les variations périodiques de la temperature dans le cours de l'année à Montpellier.* Messager Agricole du Midi, 10th Mai, 1883.

‡ It has been noticed that sulphate of iron used in concentrated solutions to protect vines against cryptogamic diseases greatly retards the bursting of the buds. It may therefore be used successfully in certain circumstances.

prevent draughts, and, therefore, help the production of this phenomenon; also avoid cultivating between the vines, as it increases the radiating surface.

A temporary means of protecting vines consists in covering them with a screen preventing radiation from the soil towards the sky, and from the vines towards the soil. Dr. J. Guyot* recommends the use of screens made of straw resting on the stakes, which are used with his system of pruning. He indicated an ingenious arrangement allowing the use of these screens as a preventive of non-setting, &c. The disadvantage of this system is the high annual expense, which Guyot estimated at £8 per acre, and further, high winds, which may displace the screens and break a great number of young shoots. These remarks also apply to Du Breuil's system,[†] in which canvas is used, or to Jobard's system, consisting in oiled paper hoods fixed over the vines. An efficient and much cheaper shelter is often attained by tying a handful of straw on the stake, and spreading it so as to form a hood; this diminishes the intensity of the radiation.

Artificial clouds are also used with success to prevent the action of white frosts. These are obtained by burning matters producing an abundant smoke.

The matters most used are manure, green grass, dry leaves, burnt over straw or bushes. The addition of *coal tar or oil, by-product of the manufacture of gas*, which gives a fuliginous flame, increases the smoke. The oil can also be lighted in tins, &c., distributed regularly in the vineyard. When the air is still (which is a necessary condition for the production of white frost) the smoke spreads horizontally, and its thickness prevents the effects of the radiation, forcing the thaw to take place slowly by sheltering the ground from the first rays of the sun. One of the difficulties resides in the fact that it is necessary to obtain constant supervision by the man in charge of the fires, which have to be lighted at opportune times; but electric thermometers have been invented,[‡] which are placed in the vineyard, and by means of an electric battery cause a bell to ring when the thermometer falls to a degree determined beforehand. Lestelle has improved this system by adding an automatic lighter.[§]

---

* Dr. Guyot. *Culture of the Vine and Wine-making.* Translated by L. Marie, pages 24-30 and 40-44. Melbourne, 1865. [Transls.]
† A. du Breuil, *Vineyard Culture*, translated by John A. Warder, pages 263-273, Cincinnati, Ohio, 1867. [Transls.]
‡ Lemaire-Fournier's alarm thermometer has been used successfully at the School of Agriculture, at Montpellier.
§ *Jour. d'agric. prat.*, 1884. Vol. II., page 557.

Heguilus has also devised a very ingenious automatic lighting system.*

It has been noticed that newly-disturbed soil, and soil covered with weeds, are more favorable to the production of white frosts than clean and settled soil; therefore, the first ploughing must be done so as to prevent the realization of these conditions during the period of the first vegetation of the vine.

When a vine has been frosted it should not be abandoned without care during the following year, as certain viticulturists do, arguing that as little as possible should be done to a vineyard which is not going to bear any crop, but, on the contrary, the vegetation should be forwarded as much as possible by ploughing, &c. The crop of the following year generally pays for this work.

(B.)—HAIL.

Hail frequently causes considerable damage in vineyards exposed to its action. Young shoots and grapes are sometimes broken if the hailstones are large enough, but in any case the lesions always compromise the ultimate development of the plant.

When the hailstones come in contact with young herbaceous shoots, during the two first months of their vegetation, they cause such lesions that these remain stunted, and the whole plant has a sickly growth during the following year, and, at the pruning season, the wood left for spurs is in a very bad state. *Under these conditions the best thing to do is generally to prune the green shoots immediately after the frost, as if they were lignified.* The dormant buds, which normally would have developed the following spring, shoot and furnish canes almost as good as those grown normally. They even sometimes give grapes if the soil is good and if the pruning was done early enough.

When the hail falls later on, the canes, better lignified, suffer less, but the crop is compromised; the berries being injured do not reach their normal development, and when the peduncle of the grape is injured, the whole portion below it dries and falls on the ground. No direct remedy is known

---

* *Cours complet de Viticulture*, p. 484, 4th edit. Montpellier. C. Coulet, 1895. See also *Loc. Cit.*, p. 482 and 483, le procédé Schaal et Œschlin.

for this evil. Vignerons must try by numerous ploughings, sulphurings, and by particular care, to increase as much as possible the vegetation of the vines.

Certain regions are particularly liable to hailstorms, and there the losses are very frequent, while in other regions they are unknown. It is this uneven repetition of the damages which has always been an obstacle against the extension of hail insurances. As a matter of fact, only those exposed to hail insured their crops, and the premium required was too considerable to allow the insurance to be of any advantage to them.

Hail guards have often been recommended to protect the crops. These appliances are formed of a pole stuck into the ground, on the top of which a metal point is fixed. They discharge the electricity of the clouds between which the hailstones are formed. Unfortunately, we cannot hope to derive much good from them, for, assuming that they are efficacious, they could only act on the clouds if immediately above them, and it is often very far from the point where they cause damage that hail storms are formed.[*]

(C.)—High Winds.

High winds often cause great damage in vineyards, especially at the beginning of vegetation. They break a great number of shoots when these are young and brittle, if they are not fastened to a stake or lying on the ground. Young vines, and those newly grafted, suffer most on account of the large development of their shoots during the first years. The future of grafted plantations may often be compromised on account of the shaking of the young plants, which breaks the rootlets and disjoints the grafts, the tissues not being properly lignified and hardened. To avoid this accident the young plants must be earthed up and the shoots fastened to pegs or stakes.

The use of cépages with spreading habit cultivated without stakes, as in the Hérault, or with low crowns trellised on wires as in the Médoc, is particularly suitable for regions where strong winds are frequent. The direction of the lines should be such as to be parallel to the direction of the prevailing winds; the vines sheltering each other offer more resistance than if they were struck sideways by the wind.

---

[*] For further information on this matter see V. Vermorel. *Etudes sur la Grêle*. Montpellier. C. Coulet, 1900. [Trans.]

ACCIDENTS, DISEASES, PARASITES.

Sea winds have also a dangerous action on vines planted near the coast when they blow with a certain strength. They carry small particles of salt, which are deposited on the leaves, and disintegrate their margins, which dry off. Plantations made in sand on the sea coast are more specially exposed to this accident. The best means of protecting them is to plant bamboo hedges or make bush fences, which diminish the strength of the winds and arrest the greater part of the salt they carry.

(D.)—NON-SETTING.

The word non-setting applies to abortive flowers which fall before forming a berry. This phenomenon may be the result of three distinct causes—1st. Abnormal constitution of the flowers. 2nd. Excessive vegetation. 3rd. Unfavorable atmospheric conditions.

1st. *Non-setting resulting from abnormal constitution of the flowers.*—The vine flower may be regarded as complete when it is hermaphrodite and has a corolla in the shape of a hood detaching from the base (Fig. 139). These alone can bear fruit. The male flowers (Fig. 140), which are characterized

Fig. 139.—Hermaphrodite vine flower.

Fig. 140.—Male flower.

Fig. 141.—Sterile flowers.

by the abortion of the pistil, the great length of the filaments of the stamens, and a very sweet scent, are naturally sterile; but besides these forms which may be considered as normal, as they are commonly found in wild species, there are abnormal forms which are generally sterile.

These flowers have been studied by Marès and Planchon. They are characterized (Fig. 141) by an indeciduous corolla opening like a star; the stamens are generally found in the petals, which are thick and hollow; the filaments are too short to allow the anther to reach the stigma. Finally, the anthers themselves are imperfectly dehiscent and contain sterile pollen. The pistil is well constituted and may play the part of female flower, be fecundated, and form fruit, but this circumstance occurs very rarely, and it is generally abortive. This abnormal constitution of the flowers is frequent with Terret, and certain wild Riparias.

The flowers of certain varieties, such as *Clairette, Gamay* (V. Vinifera), and *Herbemont* (V. Æstivalis) are sometimes double, this being the result of the transformation of the pistil and the stamens into rudimentary leaves (Figs. 142 and 143). These flowers are naturally sterile. It is generally

Fig. 142.   Fig. 143.

Flowers rendered sterile through the transformation of the pistil and stamens into rudimentary leaves.

in stiff, clayey soils, with damp subsoil, where there is an excess of vigour, that these anomalies take place, but they may get fixed by the use of cuttings taken from canes bearing such flowers. Therefore, the best means of getting rid of non-setting is to carefully eliminate all cuttings from vines naturally liable to it. Another remedy is to graft non-setting vines with scions taken from fertile varieties.

2nd. *Non-setting resulting from an excess of vegetation.*— As we have already seen in studying the general principles of pruning, an excess of vegetation is generally incompatible with abundant fructification. The plant produces wood and leaves rather than flowers, and the scarce flowers which it bears are generally abortive on account of modifications in their reproductive organs. These modifications are generally due to *chloranty* phenomena. They are frequent with *Clairette, Herbemont*, &c., but they are only temporary and cease as soon as the vigour of the plant is diminished. The means of remedying this accident, therefore, consists in diminishing the vegetation of the vine by long pruning, inarching, pinching, and annulary incision.* Experience has fully proved the efficacy of these means.

---

* See Comte de Follenay, *La Couture du Raisin*, Montpellier, 1892. [Transls.]

3rd. *Non-setting resulting from unfavorable atmospheric conditions.*—Non-setting is much more frequently the result of bad weather. In this case the whole vineyard is affected and the harm much greater.

It is generally caused by a sudden fall in the temperature, continuous rains, or dry winds at the period of florescence.

A sudden fall in the temperature prevents fecundation, therefore one must avoid ploughing or disturbing the surface of the soil at the time of florescence, as it causes greater radiation and evaporation, which lowers the temperature. Continuous rains wash away the pollen and cool the atmosphere. Finally, dry winds cause the reproductive organs to dry and therefore prevent fecundation.

In this case the remedies against non-setting are pinching, annulary incision, and sulphuring a few days before florescence. These remedies generally give good results.

(F.)—Millerandage.

Besides non-setting, or complete abortion of flowers, we may sometimes observe that, although the fruit appears to have set properly, differences will be noticeable after a short time between different berries of the same bunch. They do not all assume an even development, so that at vintage time the bunches are loose, formed of uneven berries, some scarcely larger than shot. This is termed *Millerandage* in France; it is caused by *mildew* or other diseases, and often by *chlorosis*, when a cépage is not well adapted to the soil. It also often occurs when cold, damp weather prevails immediately after the setting of the flowers. According to L. de Malafosse these small berries are due to the development of late flowers present in most bunches, which usually abort and are unable to develop on account of the non-setting of some part of the flower. They are not, however, capable of giving normal-sized fruit.

The same remedies as against non-setting may be successfully used in this case.

(G.)—Scorching.

This is the result of intense action of solar radiation on the grapes. Grapes which are not covered with leaves, or those which have been sheltered for a long time and are suddenly left bare, are more particularly liable to this accident. The berries become red, and if they are not fully developed generally dry rapidly. If, on the contrary, they have reached the turning point, and the scorching has not been very severe, their pedicels become flabby, and the berries become red and do not develop completely.*

The danger there is of grapes getting scorched when left unsheltered from the action of the direct rays of the sun, explains the custom in the South of France of leaving the shoots spread over the ground instead of tying them up to a stake. The fruit is sheltered and protected against the rays of the sun, and the last summer scarifying must not be done too late so as not to move the shoots.

Vines with low crowns, having their fruit exposed to the direct reflection of the rays of the sun from the soil, and thus bearing watery fruit with herbaceous peduncles, are particularly liable to scorching. The presence of sulphur seems to favour this phenomenon, therefore we must take care not to sulphur during hot weather unless it is possible, as in certain regions of Algeria, to simply deposit the sulphur on the soil without spreading it over the vines, and still obtain the same results.

Marès indicates as follow the conditions favorable to scorching† :—" When the weather is still and very dry, and if the atmosphere is influenced by currents from the north or north-west, if the temperature in the shade reaches 33° C. (92° Fahr.) the grapes are scorched on the south side wherever they have been struck vertically by the sun's rays."‡ The same author states that scorching not only diminishes the quantity of crop, but also spoils the quality.

(H.)—GRAPE-ROT.

The grapes of cépages bearing watery berries having a thin skin sometimes rot when the autumn is damp and rainy, and when the vineyard is in a low situation. This accident is frequently produced by a fungus, the *Botrytis cinerea*, which seems to cause modifications in the colouring matter to which the *casse* of wine is due. It is generally called *grey-rot*. Low vines are more liable to this fungus. The best remedies are drainage and the formation of a high crown on the vines, and, if these precautions are not sufficient,

---

* Henri Marès; *Des vignes du midi de la France*, Paris, 1863, Loc. Cit., page 353.
† *Id. Loc. Cit.*, page 352.
‡ The directions are, of course, reversed in the Southern Hemisphere. [Transls.]

stripping the leaves a few days before vintage. This operation consists in removing some of the leaves so as to facilitate the circulation of air, stripping in preference the leaves growing under the bunch, and not those above it. The fruit is therefore submitted to the action of air currents and of greater heat reflected by the soil, which helps the completion of maturation, which is generally very imperfect in regions where *grey-rot* is prevalent. Lime may also be spread over the grapes, but, unluckily, the introduction of lime in the vintage constitutes a danger in fermentation.

2ND.—DISEASES DUE TO FUNGI.

The pricipal parasitic fungi attacking vines are :— *Oidum, Anthracnosis, Mildew, Black-rot, Coniothyrium,* and *Pourridié.*

(A.)—OIDIUM. (*O. Tuckeri or Erysiphe Tuckeri.*)

Vines attacked by oidium may be recognised by the following symptoms :—The green parts are covered with a whitish dust; after a while grey spots appear on the places attacked, and if no remedy is applied to the plant the canes seem to become stunted, the leaves fall prematurely, and the berries become cracked and dry, losing all their value. Certain species and varieties of vines seem to be more liable than others to the attacks of this parasite. For instance, while the V. Labrusca is not attacked at all, V. Æstivalis is slightly attacked ; V. Vinifera suffers, on the contrary, greatly, especially certain cépages, such as *Carignane* and *Piquepouls; Grenache, Alicante,* and *Morrastel* resist better.

Hot and damp weather favours the development of oidium. Vines trained on high trellises suffer most, for they arrest better than others the spores of this cryptogam, which are carried by the wind.

Sulphur is generally used to combat oidium. At the beginning sublimed sulphur or flowers of sulphur alone was used. Triturated or bolted sulphur are now used ; they are cheaper, remain more adherent to the leaves, and do not injure the eyes of the workmen to the same extent.

Sulphuring is done by means of different devices :—

1st. A kind of *sand-box* (Fig. 144) made of tin, and having the shape of a cone, the bottom being perforated. The box is filled with sulphur, and the machine shaken over the leaves and the grapes. This contrivance has the disadvantage of using a great quantity of sulphur (three times more than bellows), and spreads it unevenly.

2nd. *Sulphur bellows* (Fig. 145), which is the instrument most used. It is an ordinary bellows without a valve on the bottom part and having on the top an opening provided with a funnel *e*, used for filling it with sulphur; a tube *t*, provided with wire gauze, is used to direct the jet. When the instrument is filled

Fig. 144.—Sulphur-box.

Fig. 145.—Sulphur Bellows.

and the cork G firmly secured, each movement introduces a certain quantity of air into the bellows, which stirs up the sulphur and expels it at the next motion. The sulphur is spread much more evenly with these tubes.

3rd. *Pensard's sulphuring machine* (Fig. 146) is formed of a large tin recipient R, containing from $2\frac{1}{2}$ to $3\frac{1}{3}$ gallons of powdered sulphur. A belt *b* is secured at the back, passing over the shoulder of the operator. The bottom part of the recipient is prolonged by a large rubber tube *c*, connected with a small box

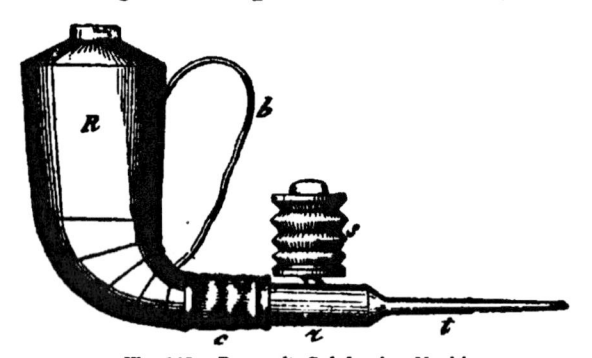

Fig. 146.—Pensard's Sulphuring Machine.

r, surmounted by a cylindrical bellows *s*, and provided with long tubes *t*. A spiral spring, secured on the top part of the recipient R and inside the box *r*, drives the sulphur in the latter at each motion of the rubber tubes.

The machine is worked as follows:—The operator walks along the rows of vines; raises and lowers the tube sharply with his right hand at each step, and expels the sulphur from the machine by compressing the bellows with the left hand. The sulphur is thus spread over the vines in fine clouds.

ACCIDENTS, DISEASES, PARASITES. 167

This machine has the advantage of enabling work to be done very rapidly; one man may sulphur about 5 acres in half a day with it. It also saves the sulphur, as the machine is not filled so often (each filling meaning a certain loss) and distributes the sulphur perfectly.

4th. *Vermorel's torpedo sulphuring machine* (Fig. 147), is a cylindrical tin box, arranged so as to be carried on the back; its shape is very similar to that of the spray-pump used

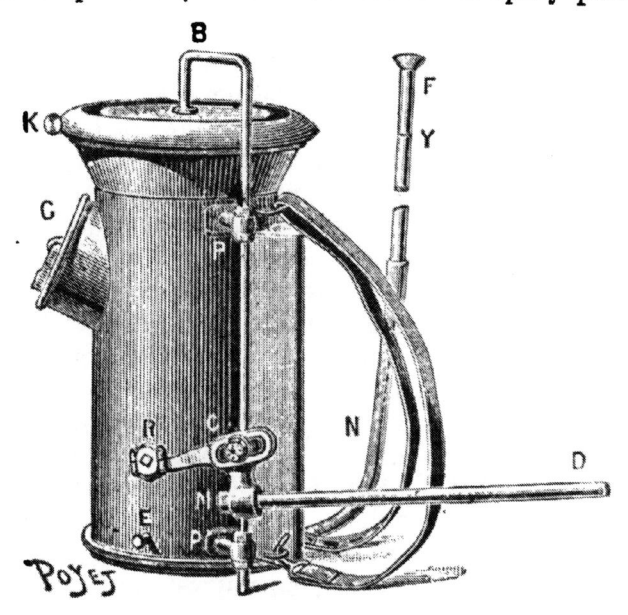

Fig. 147.—Vermorel's Torpedo Sulphuring Machine.

for sulphate of copper solution. The box contains a sulphur reservoir and bellows worked by a lever; a rubber tube connects the bellows with a long tube, at the end of which is a kind of flat plate spreading the sulphur.

This machine has the same advantages as Pensard's and is easier to work.

Three sulphurings are usually applied during the year. The first in May,* at the time of florescence, requires about 13 lbs. of sulphur per acre if the bellows are used; the second, between the 15th and 30th of June,† requires 26 lbs.; and the third, applied in July,‡ requires from 30 to 40 lbs., which makes a total of 70 to 80 lbs. per acre per annum.

---

* November in Victoria. † December in Victoria. ‡ January in Victoria.

The conditions favorable for effective sulphuring are:— Dry and hot weather, leaves perfectly dry, a slight wind facilitating the diffusion of the sulphur, and a temperature reaching from 77° to 86° Fahr.*

(B.)—ANTHRACNOSIS.

This disease is also caused by a microscopical fungus, the *Sphaceloma ampelinum*. It is recognisable by spots or cankers appearing on the green parts of the plants (young shoots, veins, green berries); these spots are areolar and completely black (*punctuated anthracnosis* of Dunal); others are sometimes more or less elongated, irregular, and fringed with black (*maculate anthracnosis* of the same botanist). The spots are small at first and extend little by little, sinking in the tissues (Fig. 148). They may cause the vine to become stunted, and appear as if submitted to strong pinching; the leaves and berries are stopped in their growth (Fig. 149), the leaves being sometimes curled. It generally results in complete destruction of the crop and, perhaps, in other phenomena not yet well known.

Fig. 148.—Shoot attacked by *anthracnosis* (after H. Marès).

It is more especially in damp seasons in low soils and in foggy climates that anthracnosis prevails. The vines most liable to it are:—*Carignane, Alicante-Bouschet, Clairette, Brun Fourca* and *Teoulier* amongst the V. Vinifera; *Pauline*, which has it almost in a chronic state and under a special form; *Jacquez* amongst the V. Æstivalis; and finally, the *Solonis* amongst the V. Riparia.

Fig. 149. Berries attacked by *anthracnosis*.

There are two means of combating anthracnosis: 1st. Preventive treatment; 2nd. Curative treatment.

1st. *Preventive treatment.*—One must avoid planting vines liable to the disease in situations favorable to its development. Drainage may be applied successfully to remove an

---

* See H. Marès (*Soufrage des vignes malades, &c.*—Montpellier, 1856. F. Seguin, libr.-edit.). This book has become classical in the South of France.

excess of humidity, but there is a more efficacious treatment generally applied; this is the swabbing of the stem during the winter, after pruning is done, with a concentrated solution of sulphate of iron. A large number of spores are thus destroyed which would have caused the disease in the following spring.

This solution is prepared in the following manner:—One quart of sulphuric acid is poured over 50 quarts of crushed sulphate of iron, the whole well stirred and then dissolved in 25 gallons of warm water. The solution is applied in February[*] with a mop made of rags tied at the end of a stick, or better, with a special spray pump.

2nd. *Curative treatment.*—The substances which give the best results in arresting the development of anthracnosis are *sulphur* and *lime*, used alone or mixed. Sulphur must be applied as soon as the disease is detected, the applications being repeated as often as possible, once a week for instance, until the development of the cryptogam is stopped. It is probable, according to R. Goethe[†], that the action of the sulphur is greater when the leaves are wet, as the spores germinating on them are more sensitive to outside influence; but, as P. Viala pointed out[‡], the diffusion of sulphur is not as complete when the leaves are covered with dew, and it would be better to apply it directly after the excess of water has evaporated, for it will then come in contact with slightly-developed germs and the above difficulty will be avoided. Mixtures of sulphur and lime seem to have greater efficacy than sulphur or lime used alone.

Sublimed or triturated sulphur is mixed with bolted lime. The first application is done in the following proportions:—

Sulphur 4
Lime 1

The second with:—

Sulphur 3
Lime 2

The third with:—

Sulphur 2
Lime 3

They are thus repeated for eight or ten days until the development of the disease is completely stopped.

---

[*] August in Victoria.
[†] R. Goethe.—*Mittheilungen über den schwarzen Brenner und den Grind der Reben.* [Trans.] Berlin, 1878.
[‡] Pierre Viala.—*Les Maladies de la Vigne.* 3rd edit., pages 239-245. C. Coulet, Montpellier, 1893. [Trans.]

(C.)—Mildew.*

This disease was first discovered in Europe in 1878 by J. E. Planchon. Certain viticulturists thought they had seen it before in many French vineyards, but it was most likely confused with another disease, and they were not able to assert that the disease they witnessed had the characteristics of mildew.

Since Planchon discovered it this disease has been found in a great number of places in France, Italy, Spain, Greece, Algeria, &c. It seems to have spread all over the Mediterranean littoral.

The consequences from a viticultural point of view are very important. Mildewed vines do not ripen their fruit, give weak wines, lacking in colour and keeping qualities; the wood is affected, and does not lignify. It is, therefore, with good reason that European viticulturists are greatly worried at the progress this disease has made.

ASPECT OF MILDEWED VINES.

Leaves and shoots.—On the under faces of the leaves wide spots appear, rather irregular in shape, and resembling a saline efflorescence. Other spots correspond on the upper faces. They have at first a yellowish tint, and gradually assume the colour of dead leaves. They are usually spread over different points, generally limited by the veins, but sometimes joining each other, and may cover the whole surface of the leaves.

The tissues of the parenchyma get destroyed in the places where the spots appear; if the disease lasts any length of time holes soon replace the spots; if the leaf is completely attacked, it may be altogether destroyed and fall prematurely. In some cases, as Prillieux ascertained, the limb becomes detached from the upper part of the petiole. This is due to the mortification of this organ and not to disarticulation.

The white spots may sometimes be seen on the upper face disseminated along the upper veins. Finally, when the under face is much attacked by *erineum*, the upper face often becomes covered with white spots of *mildew*.

Towards the end of the vegetating season the leaves get covered with yellow and brownish spots limited to the under veins, which Cornu compares to tapestry stitches, and, later

---

* Mildew or Downy Mildew has not, up to the present, been identified here. [Transls.]

on, when the leaf dries, some of these spots remain green. If, during this period, the weather is very dry, some of the brown spots fall away, leaving a hole in the leaf.

Mildew also occurs on all the green parts of the vine in the shape of white patches. When on the flowers, it causes non-setting; if on the shoots and grapes, it causes these organs to become brown and fade away, but without ever producing canker.

The bunches of grapes are only attacked by mildew when they are very young, and sometimes, but rarely, at their turning point, when they are completely covered with fructifications of mildew, which entirely stops their development. If they are attacked later on, the skin becomes brown and hard in places; in this case the fructifications of the fungus may not appear outside, but take place inside in the space existing between the seed and the pulp, as Prillieux ascertained. According to some authors the effects of this disease are identical with those of the disease known in America under the names of *gray-rot* and *common-rot*.

The berries attacked by *mildew* sometimes become brown around the pedicle, the alteration gradually reaching the top of the berry. Engelmann pointed out this difference in America, where it is known under the name of *brown-rot* in Missouri. When the peduncle and pedicle are attacked by the disease they may dry and fall away. It was this action of lesions which caused, in 1885, the loss of the greater part of *Jacquez* crop in certain regions of the Hérault.

CÉPAGES MOST LIABLE TO MILDEW.

The cépages of the old world which seem to suffer most from mildew are *Grenache, Carignane, Bobal, Cinsaut, Cot or Malbeck, Opiman, Kawouri, Rosaki, Farrana, Œillade, Mataro*, &c.

Amongst the American vines, according to Meissner,[†] are V. Æstivalis:—*Elsinburgh, Eumelan*, V. Labrusca:—*Adirondac*,

---

* *Mildew* is often confused with *Erineum*, which is the gall of an acarien parasite. (*Phytoptus vitis* or *Phytocoptes vitis*). The leaves attacked by mildew are never bulged, and the erineum always attacks the leaf on the upper face. The parasite punctures the leaf, which develops on the under face a dense felt of hair, coating the gall, always widely open. These hairs are bright white at the beginning, and are often confused with the white efflorescence of mildew. They never have the woolly white appearance of mildew, and are adherent. The part of the leaf bulged by the puncture of the parasite always remains green on the upper face. As the galls become older, the hairs become brownish, the tint increasing in intensity. These stiff hairs are constituted by a few superposed cells with a thick membrane, becoming thinner towards the top, the last one having the shape of a point. They are much stouter than the fructiferous filaments of mildew, and naturally do not bear any reproducing organs.

† Bush and Meissner, *Illustrated descriptive catalogue of American Grape Vines*, St. Louis, 1883. [Transls.]

Cassady, Creveling, Isabella, Iona, Mottled, Maxatawney, Union-Village, Rebecca, Walter; Hybrids:—*Delaware, Agawam, Allen's Hybrid, Aminia, Barry, Black Defiance, Croton, Irving, Massassoit, Merrimack, Salem, Autuchon, Canada, Cornucopia, Othello.*

This disease is caused by the action of a cryptogamic parasite, the *Plasmopara viticola* (Berlese and de Toni)

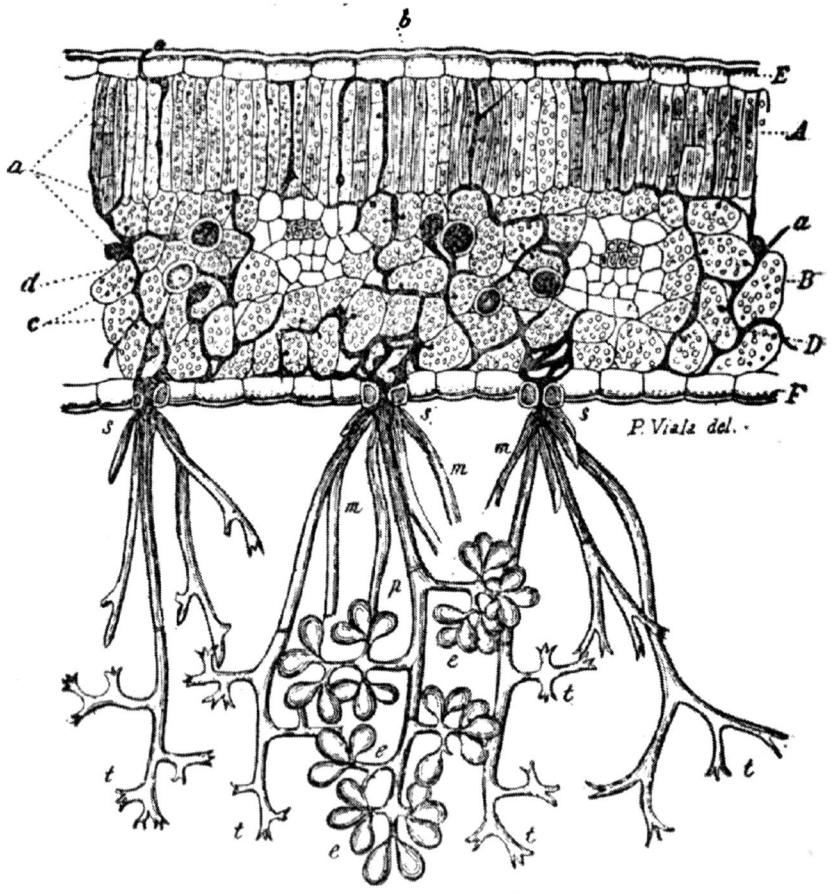

Fig. 150.—Diagram of a vine leaf attacked by *Plasmopara* (after Viala). *A*, Upper face, pallisade parenchyma; *B*, Under-face, spongy parenchyma; *D*, Vein; *E*, Epidermis of the upper-face; *F*, Epidermis of the under-face. *a*, Mycelium of the fungus growing between the cells of the tissues, after entering through the epidermis of the under-face; *b*, Antheridia and oogonium uniting; *s*, Stomatum from which the shoots carrying the conidia emerge; *p*, Fructiferous shoot, with summer spores or conidia, *e, e*; *t, t,* Sterigmata.

closely related to the *Peronospora* of the potato (*Phytophtora Infestans*, of Bary). The name of mildew was given to this disease by the Americans.

If we take a portion of the white efflorescence from a vine leaf attacked by mildew, and examine it under a microscope we soon recognise that it is formed by *fructiferous filaments* covered with *spores*. These filaments come out of the stomata in bunches, and this explains why they are found in great numbers on the under face and only along the veins of the upper face. They are connected with the vegetative part of the fungus, by the mycelium which is ramified between the cells of the parenchyma, from which it derives its food. In certain points swellings takes place, which, after being fecundated, give rise to *winter spores* or *eggs*.

Mycelium:—The vegetative part of the Plasmopara or mycelium corresponds to the white underground part of a large mushroom and lives inside the tissues of the leaf (Fig. 150 *a*). It is a continuous tube without partitions. The mycelium draws all the food necessary to the fungus from the inside of the cells of the leaf by means of spherical suckers, which pierce the cell membrane. At the beginning of spring the mycelium, gorged with nutritive matters, swells in places. Some of these swellings are spherical; others are smaller and irregular, and by their unions they give birth to the reproducing body (*oospore, ova, winter spores*).

The mycelium strongly resists outside agents. Fréchou proved that under certain circumstances it could remain during winter in the dead leaves, and during the following spring grow new fructiferous filaments which would propagate the disease afresh.

Fructiferous filaments[*].—During the winter period of vegetation the mycelium throws out fructiferous filaments from the stomata of the under face of the leaves; these may grow in one night (Fig. 150 *s*). These filaments, projecting from the stomata, number 4 to 8 in each stoma, and are from $\frac{1}{2}$ to $\frac{1}{3}$ mm. in height.

Each ramification bears on its extremity 2 to 4 small short points (*sterigmata*, Fig. 150 *t*), to which is attached the *summer spore*.

---

[*] To examine fructiferous filaments with a scalpel, or better, with a razor; a very small fragment of the whitish fructification is detached from a glabrous leaf tangent to the surface; it is placed on a slide and slightly moistened with methylated spirits. To get rid of all the air interposed between the filaments, a drop of chloride of calcium (50 per cent. solution), or better, a drop of a liquid formed of equal parts of chloride of calcium and glycerine with 50 per cent. of water is placed on it. If only a cursory examination is required the fructifications are immersed in the water after being moistened with methylated spirits.

Summer spore.—Conidia.—The extremities of the fructiferous branches swell and form the summer spores, which become free at complete maturity. New spores are never born again by the same sterigmata. These conidia are pear shaped, generally longer than wide, inserted at the narrow extremity, constituting an agglomeration of fruit on the top of the small tree formed by each filament (Fig. 150 *e*). They have a regular delicate membrane easily detected and are filled with granular matter (*protoplasm*).

Their excessive tenuity and lightness allow them to be carried very rapidly by the wind to great distances. They are from 0·010 mms. to 0·015 mms. in width and 0·015 to 0·30 mms. in length. On young vines they are smaller and more spherical in shape. Towards the end of the vegetative season they are rather larger and filled with granular protoplasm, the membrane being less distinguishable.

The conidia propagate the parasite during the whole summer. Their vitality is not very great; in dry climates they become wrinkled and burst, completely discharging the contents, as we have been able to ascertain from personal experiments in the field.

If they fall into a drop of water they germinate rapidly at a temperature of 77° to 86° Fahr. The contents of the conidia then become divided by dark lines into 5 to 8 fragments or zoospores; the membrane of the conidia becomes softer, generally opposite its point of insertion, and, within half-an-hour to an hour, gives birth to these fragments of protoplasm, deprived of membrane.

They have an irregular shape, and are provided with two cilia, inserted near a light spot which are usually detected when the zoospore is about to attach itself to the cuticle of a vine leaf. Helped by those two cilia they travel through the liquid, whence their name of *zoospore* and the name of *zoosporangium* given to the conidia or bag which contains them. After they have attached themselves to the cuticle of their host they become invested by a delicate, transparent membrane and throw out a tube (mycelium) which permeates the intercellular spaces of the parenchyma.

Winter spores.—Ovæ.—(Fig. 150 *d, b*):—Spherical, large swellings are formed on the mycelium inside the tissue of the leaf, in which the protoplasm accumulates. This spherical body, full of protoplasm, is the origin of the female organ, and is named oogonium. The protoplasm, coating the inside membrane of the *oogonium,* contracts after a partition membrane has been formed between the oogonium and the mycelium, and produces a small spherical body inside the oogonium which is termed *oosphere.*

Side by side, generally on another branch of mycelium, a small body is formed rather irregular in shape, and filled with granular protoplasm. It is limited by the partition of the tube which bears it; this is the male organ or *antheridia.* The antheridia gets separated from the mycelium, and, through a special mechanism, which has not been studied in detail for the *Plasmopara viticola,* the antheridia comes in contact with the oogonium. Its protoplasma passes through the membrane of the oogonium and blends with that of the oosphere without the volume of the latter increasing. After being fertilized in this way the oosphere becomes covered with a cell membrane and develops gradually into an oospore or simply Winter spore, which may grow into a new plant similar to the parent.

The germination of the spores of mildew is not known, and has not up the present been definitely studied. In the Peronospora family to which the *Plasmopara* belongs, the spores of these plants germinate like the conidia, and throw out *hyphae* bearing *sporangia* or *summer spores.*

MOST FAVORABLE CONDITIONS FOR THE DEVELOPMENT OF MILDEW.

In spring, when the maximum temperature reaches 77° to 86° Fahr. and the moisture is sufficient, mildew starts growing. It is more particularly noticeable in places where mildewed leaves have been buried. Although the germination of winter spores has not yet been definitely studied, and consequently the exact conditions required for that germination are not yet known, it is probable that the first germs of the disease come from them. Millardet[*] thinks that they attach themselves to young seedlings growing accidentally in vineyards. They would develop on these, and after completing the fructification of conidia, the latter, scattered by the winds, would spread the disease to all the old stumps.

Although our experiments seem to confirm those upon which Millardet based his hypothesis, the fact does not seem to be constant. We have often found *plasmopara* on

---

[*] A. Millardet, *Nouvelles Recherches sur le Développement et le Traitement du Mildiou et de l'Anthracnose*—Bordeaux, 1887. [Transls.]

seedlings growing in soils where mildewed leaves had been buried in Autumn, we have also found it in other isolated parts where mildewed leaves had been buried, but where no seedlings had grown.

After the invasion has started, the disease is propagated by the *conidia* during the whole summer if the atmospherical conditions are favorable. The only two conditions necessary for the development of *mildew* are moisture and heat.

Light showers followed by warm weather, abundant dew followed by a bright sunny day, sea winds, greatly increase the growth of conidiferous filaments, and are the main causes of the germination of these conidia in the drops of water suspended on the leaves. The importance of these causes has been proved by well-established facts. Vines have been completely invaded in 24 hours after foggy weather or heavy dew, so much so that vignerons have often attributed the cause of the destruction of their vines to this excess of humidity, which is called *nèble* in the South of France, *melin* in Mèdoc, *sun scald* in the state of Missouri, and *mehl-thau* (flour dew) by the Germans. Finally, it has been noticed that on vines planted under the shelter of trees preventing radiation and, therefore, dew which always follows it, the mildew does not develop. Low vines are more attacked than high-crowned vines, and suffer most.

The temperature most favorable to the germination of conidia is 77° to 86° Fahr. When the temperature falls below 77° the germination takes place more slowly; for instance, at 62° it takes place irregularly, and only after two or three days when the conditions of humidity are favorable and constant. The germination may even be completely stopped by a temperature of 57° Fahr. However, below this temperature the conidia do not always lose their germinating power. Conidia submitted to a temperature of 32° Fahr. have even germinated when progressively brought up to a temperature of 73° to 77° Fahr.

In dry surroundings germination does not take place, and the spores die. This explains the beneficial effects of northwest winds in the South of France and siroccos in Algeria.

The disease is propagated from one year to another by means of winter spores or oospores, which are formed, as we have seen, inside the leaf. These oospores are very resistant to the action of outside agencies. They withstand the lowest temperatures reached in regions where the vine grows; drought and excessive humidity do not deprive them of their germinating power; they have been found in sheep's excrement, and, after passing through the digestive organs of these animals, do not seem to lose their vitality; finally, some have germinated after having been preserved for over a year. This remarkable vitality is one of the great obstacles against the efforts made to combat *mildew*.*

MEANS RECOMMENDED TO COMBAT MILDEW.

None of the curative means used so far have given any results against mildew; these failures are not surprising if we remember that the *mycelium* of this *cryptogam* offers very great resistance to the action of outside agencies, and further, it is difficult to reach it inside the leaf, where it is spread, without destroying the leaf. Experiments have, therefore, been made with the object of finding preventive remedies. The following were at first recommended:—

(*a*) *Use of cépages resisting mildew.*—The first means proposed was to plant or graft only cépages resisting mildew, amongst which the following attracted the attention of vine-growers—*Persan* or *Etraire de l'Adui, Durif, Grapput* of Dordogne or *Prolongeau, Pignon* of Médoc or *Pardotte, Sauvignon, Semillon*, &c., amongst V. Vinifera; and *Cynthiana, Elvira, Noah, Montefiore, Missouri-Riesling, Herbemont*, amongst Americans.

Unfortunately, the resistance of these different cépages to mildew is not constant; it varies with the year. It probably depends on the state of the tissues of the leaf at the time the disease appears; the above-mentioned cépages, although suffering less than others from this parasite may, however, be attacked by it. Further, the use of such means is only possible for new plantations; even in this case it has the disadvantage of restricting the choice of types to be multiplied.

(*b*) *Use of copper salts.*—Since the invasion of mildew in the Gironde, it was noticed that vines planted on the side of roads, where it was the custom to spray the grapes with a mixture of lime and Paris green, or lime and blue-stone, to prevent them being stolen, preserved all their leaves perfectly, while those further from the road which had not been thus treated, lost them when attacked by the disease. This treatment was, therefore, applied to whole vineyards, and the results

---

* The above remarks have been extracted for the greater part from G. Foëx and P. Viala, *Le Mildiou ou Peronospora de la vigne.* Montpellier, 1884.

were very satifactory. Ultimate researches enabled experimenters to ascertain that the active substance in this mixture was the copper, and that traces of compounds of this metal in water were sufficient to prevent the germination of Plasmopara conidia. Different cupric compounds adhering to the leaves were therefore tried, with the object of forming a deposit which would furnish the drops of water resulting from dew or fogs (and in which the spores of the disease germinate), with traces of copper. The principal matters recommended were:—

A.—Liquid matters—
  1. Bordeaux mixture.
  2. Blue water.
  3. Copper ammoniacal solution.
  4. Mixture of Dauphinée.
  5. Verdet gris.
  6. Copper sucrate.

B.—Pulverized solid matters—
  1. Mixture of sulphur and sulphate of copper.
  2. Sulpho-steatite.
  3. Skawinski powder and sulphur.

(a).—*Liquid Matters.*

1st. *Bordeaux mixture.*—This is a mixture of quick lime and sulphate of copper. If freshly-slacked lime is poured into a solution of sulphate of copper a light blue precipitate is obtained, remaining a certain time in suspension in the liquid, which is a hydrated oxide of copper surrounded with a little sulphate of lime and free lime, the latter soon becomes carbonate of lime. Under this form copper adheres strongly to the parts of the plant upon which it is applied, and dissolves in small quantities in rain water or dew containing carbonate of ammonia or carbonic acid.

The Bordeaux mixture is prepared in the following manner:—6 lbs. of sulphate of copper is added to a gallon of warm water; after the crystals have dissolved the solution is poured into about 100 gallons of water; on the other hand, 4 lbs. of freshly-slacked lime (milk of lime) are added to 2 gallons of water, and the milk of lime thus obtained slowly poured into the copper solution, stirring the whole time so as to mix it thoroughly and assist combination. The mixture should be prepared in a wooden vessel on account of the action of copper salts on common metals. It should be well stirred before use. The quantities necessary in the South of France are 18 gallons per acre for the first treatment, 27 for the second, and 36 for the third, which are applied when the leaves are fully developed.

Bordeaux mixture is the remedy most generally used against *mildew, black-rot* and *Coniothyrium*. Its general use is due to its effectiveness and fairly good adherence to the leaves, its small cost, and facility of preparation. We will later on study the methods used for applying this and other liquid mixtures.

2nd. *Blue water.*—Audoynaud, formerly Professor of Chemistry at the School of Agriculture, Montpellier, recommended some years ago the replacing of the Bordeaux mixture (the adherence of which he considered was not sufficient, because the proportion of lime was too great) by blue water. This compound is prepared in the following manner:—1lb. of sulphate of copper is dissolved in $2\frac{1}{2}$ pints of warm water contained in a wooden vessel; when the dissolution is complete and the liquid quite cool, $1\frac{1}{4}$ pints of ammonia, of 22° Baumé density, is poured into it. The liquid becomes of a bright blue colour; it is diluted in 10 or 20 gallons of water according to whether we require a solution at $\frac{1}{2}$ or 1 per cent. This liquid contains sulphate of ammonia, which is useless, and *hydrated oxide of copper*, which is of a colloid nature, and adheres strongly to the leaves when dry. It forms a cupric deposit on the leaves which furnishes the drops of rain, or dew, with the quantity of copper necessary to kill the spores, and it resists the dissolving action of rain for a long time.

Blue water has effectively protected vines treated with it, and has the advantage over the Bordeaux mixture in being more lasting; it may be used without previously stirring, and without risk of choking the spray pumps, as the solid matters it contains are dissolved, and not in suspension. The only disadvantage is that if it contains ammonia in excess it is liable to burn the leaves, but it is easy to remedy this by preparing the mixture some time in advance and leaving it exposed to the air, when the free ammonia will evaporate. However, the accidents resulting from its use induced vine-growers to discard it.

3rd. *Ammonical solution of copper.*—This liquid was first recommended to vine-growers by Bellot des Minières, who obtained remarkable results with it in his vineyard of Haut-Bailly (Gironde). It is obtained by combining ordinary ammonia with copper turnings, or copper oxide, in the presence of air. The blue liquid thus obtained is diluted with water, so as to bring the proportion of copper to 1 or 3 per cent. Its adherence is equal to that of blue water, its qualities are similar, and it has the advantage of never burning the leaves. The high cost alone prevents its general use.

4th. *Mixture of Dauphinée.*—Masson, Professor at the School of Viticulture of Beaune, and Dr. Patrigeon[*] proposed *hydrocarbonate of copper* as a substitute for blue water. It is obtained by the action of carbonate of soda or potash (commercial) on sulphate of copper. According to the authors, it has the following advantages:—

1st. The carbonates are much cheaper than liquid ammonia.

2nd. The liquid resulting from their combination with sulphate of copper is easier to handle than blue water.

3rd. The greenish white, or greenish-blue spots left on the leaves allow the proprietor of a vineyard to check the work done by his workmen.

4th. The colloidal precipitate of hydrocarbonate of copper is very adherent to the leaves, and plays the same part as the hydrate precipitate of blue water.

5th. This precipitate remains a long time in suspension in the liquid, and does not choke the machines.

6th. There is no formation of acid sulphate liable to burn the leaves, as in the case of blue water, the acid remaining constantly neutralized.

Masson gives the following practical formula for preparing this mixture:—

Water	...	...	100 parts
Sulphate of copper	...	...	1 "
Carbonate of soda	...	...	2 "

If the copper percentage is increased the quantity of carbonate of soda should be increased in the same proportion.

Dr. Patrigeon uses the following mixture:—

Sulphate of copper	...	...	...	4 parts
Carbonate of soda (commercial)	...	...	6 "
Water	...	...	...	...	100 "

The mixture of Dauphinée has given good results wherever it has been properly applied. It has more adherence than the Bordeaux mixture, but is rather more expensive.

---

[*] Dr. J. P. G. Patrigeon, *Le Mildiou, peronospora viticola*, Paris, 1887. [Transls.]

5th. *Verdet gris.*—Georges Bencker*, of Montpellier, recently recommended the use of verdet gris or *bibasic acetate of copper* against mildew, used in the proportion of 1 part per 100 parts of water. According to the author, the solution should be prepared in the following manner:—

About 50 parts of dry granulated verdet gris are dissolved in 500 parts of water three or four days before using, and the mixture stirred as often as possible during this interval.

The day the treatment is to be applied 20 parts of this preparation are poured through a copper sieve into 200 parts of water. These 200 parts of water contain 2 parts of verdet, therefore the solution contains 1 per cent. This liquid is applied with spray-pumps in the ordinary way.

Experiments made at the School of Agriculture, Montpellier, with *verdet gris* constantly gave results equal to those obtained with Bordeaux mixture, and it proved to be more adherent.

6th. *Sucrate of copper.*—Copper forms with sugar a compound capable of preventing the development of mildew. Michel Perret proposed adding molasses to *hydrocarbonate of copper*, and originated the following mixture:—

"Two parts of sulphate of copper are dissolved in 15 parts of water; 3 parts of commercial soda are added to this solution. After the precipitation is completed one-fifth to one-half part of molasses are added, and the mixture left for twelve hours, after which 100 parts of water are added.

"The mixture thus obtained is of a deep-green colour, easily detected and very adherent; the part dissolved by the sugar acts directly when applied. The part precipitated prolongs the action of the mixture by dissolving in drops of rain or dew.

"Experiments proved this year (1889) that this new mixture was more effective on grapes than those used so far."

Experiments made with *sucrate of copper* in 1890 at the School of Agriculture, Montpellier, did not allow us to ascertain its action on mildew, as this disease did not appear in the experimental plots; but the mixture did not remain on the leaves as long as the mixture of Dauphinée or verdet gris. It appears desirable, therefore, to wait for other trials before expressing a definite opinion on the subject.

Mode of application of cupric compounds.—Cupric compounds prevent the germination of the conidia or spores

---

* Georges Bencker was the first to suggest the use of verdet gris in 1886.—See *Progrès Agricole*, Montpellier, vol. xii, page 90, 1889; vol. xiv, page 510, 1890; and vol. xxvii, page 212, 1897. [Transls.]

which propagate mildew in summer; they should, therefore, be used before the disease has made its appearance; that is to say, towards the 15th of May in the Mediterranean regions.* But, as new leaves develop in course of time, it is necessary, to protect them, to further treat the vines. The second treatment should be made at the beginning of July, and a third towards the 15th of August. It may even be necessary

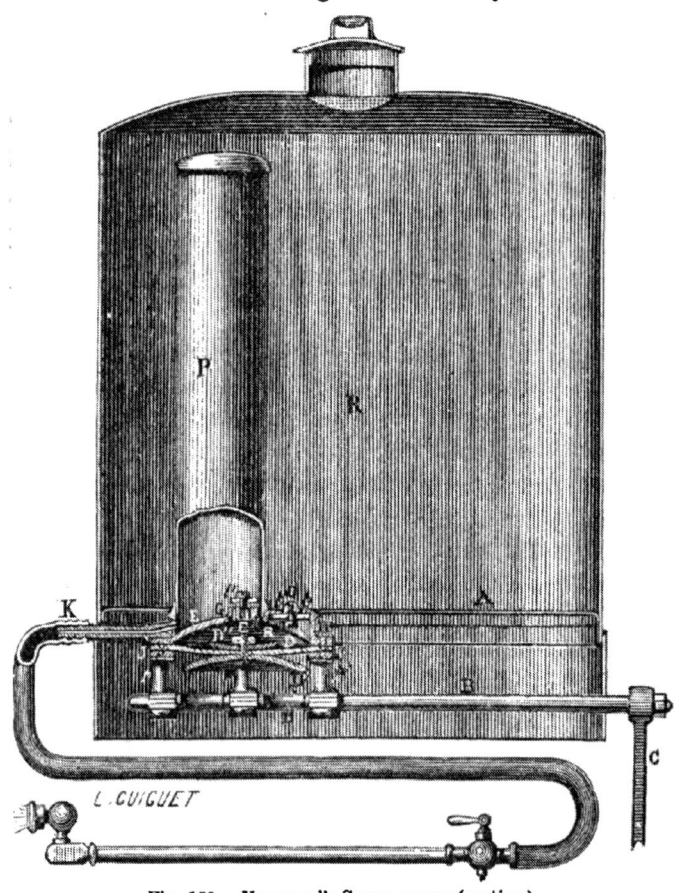

Fig. 151.—Vermorel's Spray-pump (section).

to give a fourth treatment after the vintage, so as to enable the wood to ripen normally. However, vine-growers must be guided by the atmospherical conditions being more or less favorable to the development of the disease.

The liquids should be finely sprayed, as the object is not to accumulate a large quantity of copper on a certain spot, but to spread it everywhere; that is to say, on every part of the plant where drops of dew may be formed. Spray-pumps

---

* Towards the middle of November in Victoria.

(*pulverizers*) give the best results, and large numbers have been invented. The best known are those of Vermorel (Fig. 151), Vigouroux, Japy Bros., Albrand, Messrs. Lasmolles, Fréchou, and R. de La Faye.

These instruments have been thoroughly described by Ferrouillat.*

(b.)—*Pulverized Solid Matters.*

1st. *Mixtures of sulphur and sulphate of copper.*—The necessity of sulphuring vines against *oidium* induced viticulturists to use sulphur as a vehicle for sulphate of copper by mixing the copper salt with sulphur in a finely triturated state. These mixtures are generally made in the following proportion:—

Sulphate of copper	5 to 10 parts
Sulphur	100 ″

This powder has sometimes given satisfactory results when the mildew does not develop much, but is quite useless when the disease reaches a certain intensity. It has the disadvantage of not adhering to the leaves, and, if it does not rain, the wind carries it away, while it is dissolved and washed off by heavy rains.

2nd. *Sulpho-steatite of copper.*—With the object of increasing its adhering power, Baron de Chefdebien added pulverized steatite (a variety of talc) to the mixture. He obtained better results, but not yet quite perfect in bad years. It is impossible to obtain the lasting effect of hydrated oxides in a colloidal state; and, further, the sulphate, being easily soluble, is always washed away by rain.

3rd. *Skawinski powders.*—Skawinski Bros. used, in the Médoc, mixtures of sulphur, sulphate of copper, with different powders and pulverized coal. They recommend the two following formulæ:—

1st Mixture—
Sulphur	50 parts
Sulphate of copper	10 ″
Lime	3 ″
Powdered coal	29 ″
Calcined and powdered alluvial soil	50 ″

2nd Mixture—
Sulphate of copper	10 parts
Lime	3 ″
Powdered coal	72 ″
Calcined and powdered alluvial soil	15 ″

---

* *Manuel pratique pour le traitement des maladies de la vigne*, by P. Viala and P. Ferrouillat, Montpellier, 1888.

These mixtures have the same disadvantages as those above studied. The first, however, should be preferred to ordinary mixtures of sulphur and sulphate of copper, as far as oidium is concerned, in countries where solar radiation is not intense. The black colour due to the coal favours the absorption of heat, and therefore the heating of the sulphur and the disengagement of *sulphurous acid*, which acts as a fungicide.

These powders are applied with the machine used for sulphuring (Fig. 152). They should be applied in the morning when the leaves are covered with dew, to help their adherence (Fig. 153).

Nobody doubts the efficacy of copper salts against mildew, but many people are alarmed at the idea that their application might introduce into wine an element dangerous

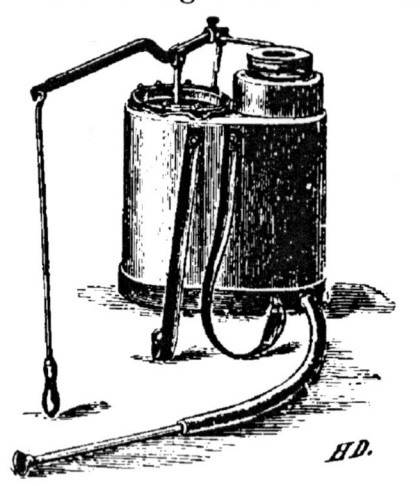

Fig. 152.—Vermorel's Torpedo Sulphuring Machine.

Fig. 153.—Woman working a Torpedo Sulphuring Machine.

to public health. Experiments made in many places prove that the copper is precipitated in an insoluble state in the marc, and that the wines resulting from treated vines do not contain measurable quantities of this metal. Sugar wines and piquettes seem to realize the same conditions. Even the consumption of table grapes treated with these mixtures does not seem to have resulted in any accident. The treatment of vines with copper salts must therefore be considered as completely harmless to consumers.

It results from the above studies that pulverized mixtures do not give the same guarantee of success against mildew as liquid compounds ; therefore, notwithstanding the great facility of their mode of application, they must only be used as a supplement, *and should never be substituted for the latter.* Their action against *oidium*, which is sufficient when they contain sulphur, enables vine-growers to substitute them for pure sulphur, and to obtain a double object without greatly increasing the cost.

The *Bordeaux mixture,* which has been successfully experimented upon, and is the most generally used, should always be preferred. One may use the mixture of Dauphinée and the verdet gris with equal chances of success in districts where high winds and frequent rains would wash away the particles of copper quickly.

(D.)—BLACK-ROT.

The *black-rot* was introduced into Europe from America, where it was first found by B. Batheam, in 1848, in the south of the Ohio State*. Many American authors have mentioned it since. It was first discovered in Europe in 1885, by Ricard, manager of the Valmarie vineyard, near Ganges (Hérault). It was immediately examined and identified by Viala and Ravaz as similar to the type known in America. Inspection made that year proved that the disease was limited to a small part of the valley of the Hérault. Subsequently, it was detected further south at Cournonterral in 1887, and Lunel in 1888. The disease has actually spread along the valley of the Rhône, and has disappeared from the places where it was first discovered.

According to Viala and Ravaz the disease presents the following characters :—" A small bluish-red spot is first seen on the berries, rapidly increasing in width and depth, surrounding the whole fruit, which is completely altered in two days. It then becomes brown-red, soft, spongy ; the berries drying in three or four days, the colour becoming dark-black, the skin adhering to the pips, the whole surface being covered with small, black, prominent spots. These spots make their first appearance when the berry begins to dry, and are formed by two different fructifications— organs of the fungus, which cause black-rot : *Phoma uvicola* (Berk. and Curt.)."

* B. Batheam and Nicholas Longworth were the first to mention the disease. English readers will find studies on the subject in—R. Buchanan, *The Culture of the Grape and Wine Making,* Cincinnati, 1865 ; Andrew Fuller, *The Grape Culturist,* page 206, New York, 1867 ; Dr. G. Engelmann, *In Journal of proceeding Transactions of the Acad. of Sc.,* St. Louis (Missouri), page 265, September, 1861 ; Berkeley and Curtis, *Grevillea,* vol. ii., page 82, 1873 [Transls.]

"Black-rot has only exceptionally been detected on the canes, petioles, and veins of the leaves. At first it has the appearance of a large, black stain; the fungus penetrates inside the tissues and over the surface; blisters, characterizing the disease, may be seen. Finally, black-rot develops but rarely on the parenchyma of young leaves. In this case it is characterized by small stains, in two days both faces of the leaf dry, leaving the fructifications of the fungus apparent. The harm done on the leaves may be overlooked."[*]

The fungus is formed by the mycelium penetrating the soft tissues, upon which it develops a series of *conceptacles* (*pycnidia, spermogonia, perithecia*), which contain the reproductive bodies serving to propagate it.

The disease appears to develop naturally in very damp situations, and seems to more readily attack cépages with juicy berries. The Aramon amongst the vines of the South was most attacked, and some years ago over half the crop was lost through it (1885).

Black-rot requires a high temperature and a great amount of moisture to develop. This explains why it is only found in the damp districts of the south and south-west of France.

Means of combating the disease.—The means used to combat mildew have generally proved successful in preventing black-rot from developing, but to get good results Bordeaux mixture of 3 per cent. strength should be used, sprayed in such a way as to cover all parts of the plant up to the extremities of the shoots.

The first treatment should be applied as far as possible a few days before the disease makes its appearance. This means that we have to guess the right time, and sometimes if the first appearance of the disease does not take place as early as expected the treatment must be repeated. For ultimate infections the maximum of action of copper salts takes places two to five days after the acute period of infection, that is to say, five to eight days after the appearance of the first stains. It is therefore between these two limits that the treatment should be applied, and viticulturists should follow very closely the development of the fungus in order not to miss the right time.

The removal of stained leaves as soon as the disease is detected greatly retards the infection of the vineyard. This

---

[*] P. Viala and L. Ravaz.—*Le Black-Rot Américain dans les Vignobles Français.* Compt. Rendus, 1886.

also applies to the removal of tendrils remaining attached in winter to the wires of a trellis if the vine was attacked by black-rot the previous summer. The leaves and tendrils should be burnt on the spot.

Heaps of old canes from diseased vines should not be left near the vineyard, but should be burnt or removed as soon as possible.

If these different precautions are followed, and if the applications of Bordeaux mixture are made carefully and at the right time, the vineyard should be protected, in most cases with four or five successive treatments.

(E.)—CONIOTHYRIUM DIPLODIELLA OR WHITE-ROT.

When grapes are affected by this disease, some of the parts are covered with greyish-blue stains. These stains increase rapidly in size, and the whole berry is very soon affected. As the disease progresses numerous small blisters, salmon coloured, appear on the surface; they are formed by the fructification (*pycnidia*) of the *Coniothyrium diplodiella* (*Phoma diplodiella*; *Phoma Briosii*, Sacc.). Soon after the berries dry away and assume the aspect of shagreen, resulting from the high relief of the blisters. Similar alterations take place on the peduncle and the pedicles of the grape, and later on, on the berries. Their colour turns a deeper brown, rapidly extending on the whole surrounding tissues, reaching the berries which are first affected at their point of insertion with the pedicle.

The lesions of the peduncle are frequently so deep that they cause the grape to fall to the ground, especially when cépages with soft stalks, such as the Aramon, are attacked. In any case they cause the grapes or the berries to dry. Certain vineyards planted with Aramon in the alluvial soils of Vidourle, near the Sommières (Gard), and in the plains of the Ganges (Hérault), completely lost their crop; the whole ground was covered with grapes as if they had been cut purposely. The alteration to the peduncle seems to be the main cause of the damage.

In two vineyards at Bollène (Vaucluse), and at Landun and Bagnols (Gard), the same lesions were observed on canes. They seem to attack canes which are not yet lignified; therefore *Grenache*, which ripens its wood late in the season, is the most affected, while *Clairette* and *Carignane* are seldom attacked. The disease rarely affects the internodes. In some cases it starts from the peduncle and travels towards the point of insertion on the cane. It spreads rapidly over all the surrounding parts, and sometimes extends regularly round the cane, sometimes in the shape of a long, narrow strip. In the first case a thick pad of healing tissue is formed above the affected part, the leaves become reddish in colour, fall away, and the cane dries. The affected tissues are black at first, but the blisters we have mentioned very soon cover the black stains, which become of a deep-grey colour. The blisters develop on the surface of the bark and sometimes on the affected parts of the wood; in this case the bark detaches in long strips.

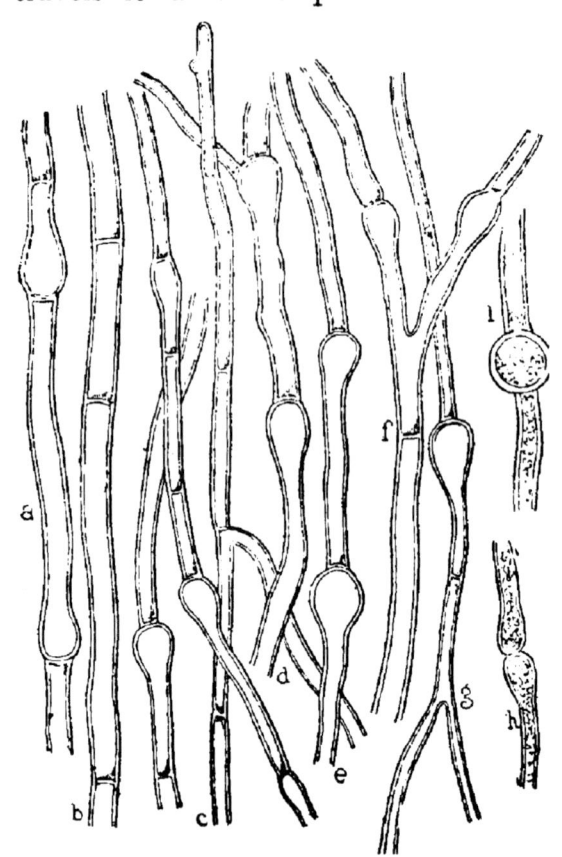

Fig. 154.—Brown Mycelium Filaments of *Dematophora Necatrix* (after P. Viala).

Coniothyrium diplodiella was first observed in 1878 in Italy by Spegazzini; Viala and Ravaz discovered it in the Isère in 1885; Prillieux and Marsais found it in Vendée in 1886. It extends over a considerable area in the South of France in certain seasons. It was found in 1887 in the *départements* of Aude, Hérault, Gard, Vaucluse, Ardèche, Drôme, Isère, Rhône, Ain, and in Switzerland in the cantons of Geneva and Vaud. It was found in the same year in Italy and Vendée, and many departments of the south-west. Further, Viala discovered it during the course of his mission in America in 1889. He found it on the boundary of the

Indian Territory and the Missouri State, and on a few vines in the Wyandotte district. The existence of this fungus in the latter district where European vines were never imported would prove, according to Viala, that the disease is of American origin. It has never been found in the northern and southern states of the Union where European vines are frequently imported. The disease is called *white-rot* in America, and Viala suggested the retention of this name in France. This disease is not as dangerous as *black-rot*, and the damage caused by it was located to a few vineyards only of the Gard and Hérault.

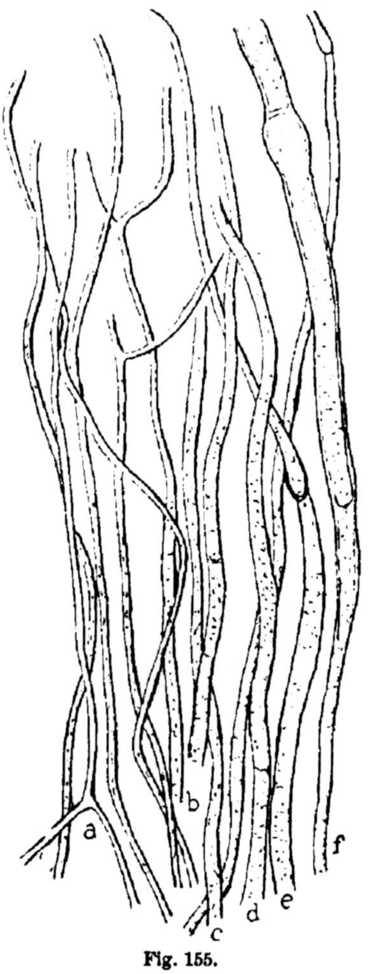

Coniothyrium is formed, like the black-rot, by a mycelium penetrating the tissues of the portion of the plant upon which the pycnidia germinate. These pycnidia, or conceptacles, contain spores (*stylospores*). This is, therefore, also a fungus living in the shelter of the organs destroyed by it, and preventive means only are effective. The liquid cupric compounds used against mildew and black-rot gave satisfactory results, and it would appear that the almost complete disappearance of this fungus since 1887 is due to the treatment against mildew.*

Fig. 155.
Transparent Colourless Mycelium Filaments of *Dematophora Necatrix* (after Viala).

(F.)—Pourridié.

Pourridié has been known in Europe for a very long time. Fruit and forest trees are affected by it. Affected

---

* *Mémoire sur le Coniothyrium diplodiella*, in *Annales de l'Ecole Nationale d'Agriculture de Montpellier*, Vol III., p. 304.

vines, like those having damaged roots, show general signs of weakness; their fructification increases at first suddenly, the shoots become stunted, the leaves small, although remaining green; the stump affects the shape of a cabbage, and can be easily pulled out of the

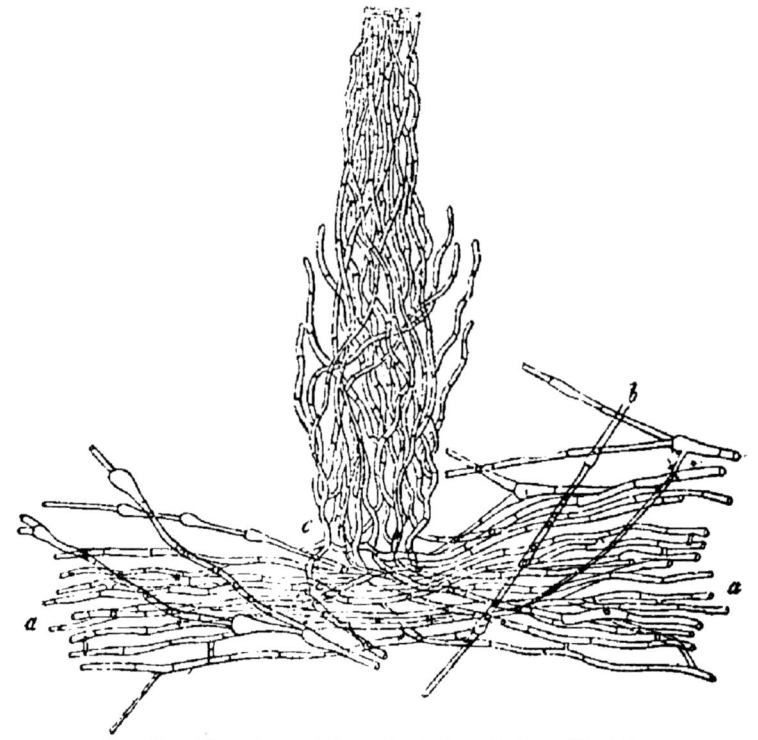

Fig. 156.—Fructiferous Filaments of *Dematophora Necatrix*.

ground. The roots are decayed (whence its name, "*pourries*" the French for "*decay*"). They are brown in colour, saturated with water, which exudes when they are cut; the trunk alone remains healthy.

Vines attacked by this disease present the same external symptoms as those attacked by phylloxera or larvæ of other insects. The course of the disease is very similar; it spreads like a blot of oil on a sheet of paper. Under ordinary circumstances affected vines in the South of France succumb after fifteen or eighteen months. In certain situations where pourridié acquires a large development the harm done may be considerable.

The condition which seems to induce the growth of pourridié is excessive moisture. Soils resting on an impermeable

ACCIDENTS, DISEASES, PARASITES.

subsoil, forming basins in which water remains stagnant, are those where the disease develops with the greatest intensity. Heat seems to play a secondary part.

Pourridié is due to the development of the roots of fungi of different species; *Dematophora necatrix* (R. Hartig),

Fig. 157.—*Dematophora Necatrix.*
a, Mass of white filaments.

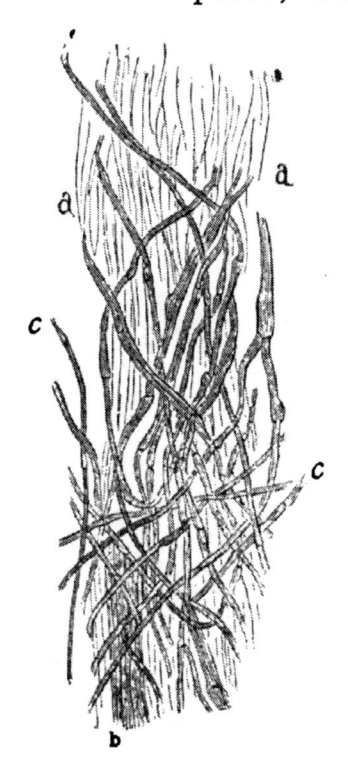

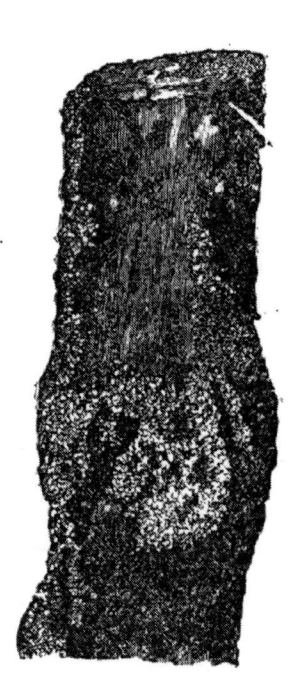

Fig. 158.—Fructifications of *Dematophora Necatrix.*

Agaricus melleus (L.) and *Rœsleria hypogæa* (Thum. and Pass). These often grow on parts of the tissues already injured.

Dematophora Necatrix.—The roots of vines affected by *Dematophora necatrix* (Figs. 154 to 158) show, between the bark and the wood, felty patches of mycelium penetrating the medullary rays, or stuck against the bark. If the conditions of humidity are suitable the fungus will develop white fluffy filaments round the roots, assuming later on a felt-like appearance penetrating the whole soil. These filaments become mouse-grey, and, later on, brown. If the surrounding soil is saturated with water, abundant fructifications appear (Fig. 159), giving a special velvety appearance to the parts attacked.

192   MANUAL OF MODERN VITICULTURE.

Agaricus Melleus.—The mycelium of Agaricus melleus forms roots travelling through the soil. They are like those of the *Dematophora*, brown inside and white outside;

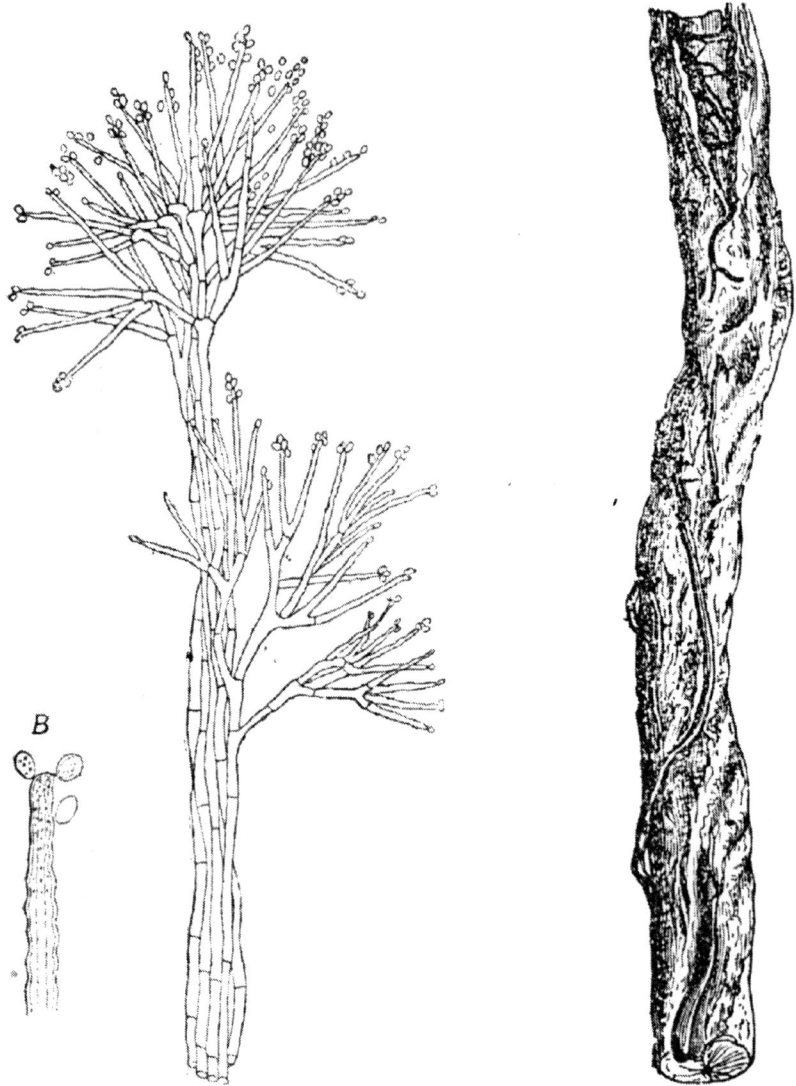

Fig. 159.—Extremity of Fructiferous Filament of *Dematophora Necatrix.*

Fig. 160.—Vine Root covered with *Agaricus Melleus* (after Millardet).

they can only be distinguished by microscopical examination of the filaments composing them. These cords of mycelium travel along the roots of the vine (Fig. 160), insert themselves between the bark, and form white patches (Fig. 163), phosphorescent at night.

Rœsleria hypogæa.—Has the aspect of small white beads, greyish in colour, 5 to 6 mms. in height (Fig. 164). The mycelium, which is very delicate, lives inside the tissues of the plant (Fig. 167). The underground development

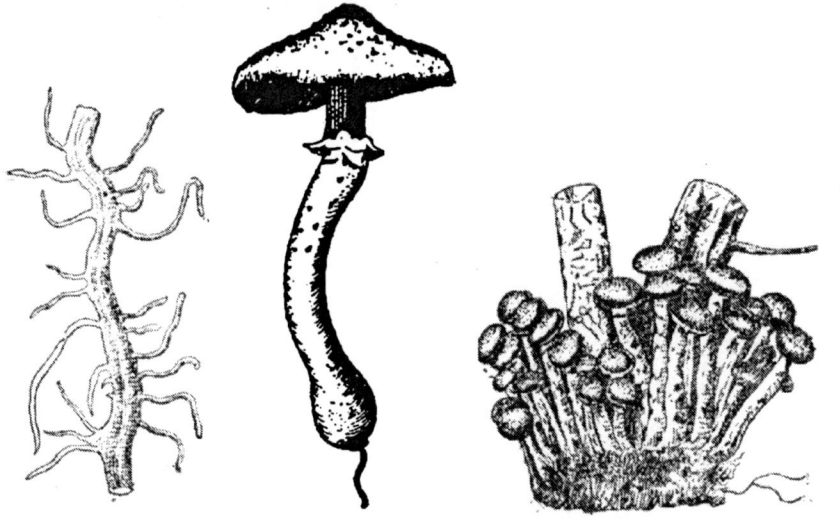

Fig. 161.—Mycelium of *Agaricus Melleus*, var. *subterranea* (after R. Hartig).

Fig. 162.—*Agaricus Melleus*.

Fig. 163.—Bunch of same at foot of a vine.

of the organs of the plant affected by *pourridié*, and the fact that the mycelium of this cryptogam develops inside the tissues of the roots, prevents the plant from being

Fig. 164.—*Rœsleria Hypogæa* on vine root.

Fig. 165.—Fructification of *Rœsleria*.

Fig. 166.—Section of same (after E. Prillieux).

cured. We can only practically modify the constitution of the soil so as to prevent the start of this disease or stop its propagation if it has started to develop. The first result may be obtained by deep cultivation and drainage, which removes the excess of water, and renders the soil unfit for the development of the disease.* To clean the soil one must carefully remove all the roots and burn them on the spot so as to avoid the diffusion of the spores, which might take place if the roots were carried away. The affected spot is surrounded by a trench 18 inches deep, the soil being thrown inwards, and a treatment of bisulphide of carbon at the rate of 600 lbs. per acre applied. All the fragments of roots and fungi in the ground are killed. A few days after the soil may be planted again.

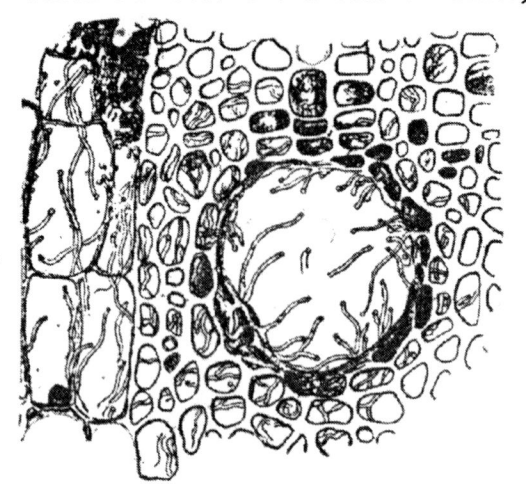

Fig. 167.—Section of a Vine Root attacked by *Rœsleria* (after E. Prillieux).

3RD. MALADIES.

Chlorosis.—Vines affected by chlorosis become yellow on account of the insufficient formation of chlorophyl.

Most American vines are much more sensitive than European vines to the action of this malady; however, we have seen (page 55) that some species are not affected.

The grafting of European vines on American stocks generally causes an increase in chlorosis, although sometimes, but very rarely, it diminishes it. We may often notice *Riparias* becoming yellow after grafting, although they remain green when not grafted. On the other hand chlorosed *Herbemont* were endowed with a fine vegetation after being grafted with European vines. Amongst our Southern cépages, those which seem to improve the conditions of existence of varieties upon which they are grafted are *Clairette* and *Carignane*.

The chlorosis of American vines is generally due to the presence of limestone in the soil; this was studied when

---

* See introduction to *Trenching and Subsoiling for American Vines*, by R. Dubois and W. Percy Wilkinson. Melbourne, 1901.

speaking of adaptation to soil (page 55); and it was shown that it is possible to obtain good graft-bearers resisting chlorosis in calcareous soils. But it is possible, however, to efficiently combat this malady on vines established under bad conditions, from the point of view of their adaptation, by using Dr. Rassiguier's process.

This process consists in painting the sections after pruning with a solution of sulphate of iron, of 30 per cent. strength. The sooner the pruning is done the greater efficiency the remedy seems to have, therefore it should be applied as soon as the vine begins to shed its leaves. If spring frosts are feared the pruning may be done twice, leaving the spurs 1 foot or 18 inches long, and painting the sections directly after the first pruning. The action of the liquid is the same in this case as if it had been applied at the definitive pruning.

The results obtained by this process are excellent, and enable us to recommend it.

PART II.

SUBMERSION OF VINEYARDS.

Submersion consists in flooding the whole surface of a vineyard with water for a period sufficient to kill phylloxera. This method can only be applied to vineyards established in certain special conditions which we shall now study, together with the installation necessary in practice and the special cultural care necessitated.

CHAPTER I.

CONDITIONS NECESSARY TO THE SUCCESS OF SUBMERSION.

These conditions are :—

1st. Possibility of procuring a sufficient quantity of water at the right time without considerably increasing the cost.

2nd. Application of water in regular sheets to soils capable of retaining it.

3rd. Use of varieties not suffering from this treatment.

1ST.—WATER.

(A.) *Quantity required.*—Submersion requires, as a rule, very large quantities of water, varying according to the permeability of the soil and the duration of the operation. Formerly Faucon considered that 123,500 cubic feet per acre were sufficient, but this figure must be considered as a minimum, and it is greatly exceeded in most cases. We must reckon upon 353,000 to 530,000 cubic feet per acre, and under some circumstances even 1,000,000 cubic feet per acre. A part of this water must be delivered in a constant flow to recuperate the loss by evaporation and imbibition.

(B.) *Quality of water.*—Waters containing air, such as those pumped by centrifugal machines or collected from natural water-falls, are considered as less efficacious from an insecticidal point of view, for the presence of a small number of air bubbles is sufficient to enable phylloxera to live. Those completely deficient in fertilizing matters would exhaust permeable soils during percolation through them.

But this fact is only of secondary importance from a practical point of view, and one should not discard submersion if the only reason against it is that water does not contain fertilizing matters.

2ND.—SOIL.

(A.) *Permeability.*—Soils to which submersion is to be applied must not be too permeable. The permeability of the soil is not only an obstacle on account of the large quantities of water required and the washing resulting from the current taking place through the soil, but it also fixes in the subsoil a number of small air bubbles on account of the downward movement of the water. These bubbles, as we have seen, enable phylloxera to live. Clayey-calcareous and clayey-siliceous compact subsoils are those which generally realize the best conditions. Those containing pebbles or formed of disintegrated rock have, on the contrary, often resulted in failure.

(B.) *The contour of the land.*—Land to be submerged must be horizontal or only have a slope of 2 to 3 per cent. Greater slopes render necessary the establishment of a large number of banks. This is expensive, and has the disadvantage of diminishing the area of the basins. Further, the surface of the soil must be regular so as to have an even depth of water right through.

3RD.—ADAPTATION OF CÉPAGES TO SUBMERSION.

No cépage to which submersion has been applied so far seems to have suffered directly from its effects, but many have been affected in a more or less acute way by certain accidents to which they were predisposed by nature.

Clairette and *Carignane*, for instance, which are sensitive to *anthracnosis*, are often largely affected by this disease when submerged.[*] *Grenache* and *Alicante*, which ripen their wood late in the season, suffer greatly from the check submersion gives to their vegetation, especially when it is applied rather early in the season.

Aramon, Mataro, Tinto, Malbeck, Cabernet, Shiraz, and *Chasselas* may be submerged without detriment.

---

[*] This is probably the result of the special situation of the vineyard rather than of submersion itself.

CHAPTER II.

ESTABLISHMENT OF SUBMERSION PLANT.

1st.—Sources of Water Supply.

Water used for submersion may be taken from a river, channel, lake, dam, spring, artesian well, or even drainage channel. It may be carried to the vineyard by channels, elevating machines, or sometimes by temporarily blocking drainage channels.

(A.) *Channels.*—This is evidently the simplest means, and should be used every time the water can be taken from a level higher than that of the vineyard, the only expense being the making of small channels.

(B.) *Raising water by mechanical means.**—The above method, unfortunately, cannot be applied in every case. It is not always possible to make weirs through certain rivers and small differences of level necessitate water being taken from a great distance to travel through neighbouring properties; the intermittence of the rate of flow of certain channels often renders necessary the use of the second system. The elevating machines generally used are *centrifugal pumps* (Fig. 169) or *rouets* (Fig. 171), invented by Dellon, engineer, at Montpellier, and built by Bergeron, of Nimes.

Fig. 169.—Centrifugal Pump.

---

* The centrifugal pumps made by Neut and Dumont, and those of Gwyne, yield 22 gallons per second, and require 1·20 H.P. per 3 feet of elevation. The consumption of coal is about 4½ to 6¼ lbs. per hour and per H.P. When the coal is not of very good quality the quantity reaches 9 lbs. and more.

The rouet seems to give better yield for a difference of level under 16 feet, but it cannot be shifted about like the centrifugal pump, and cannot be used in certain properties where the blocks of vines are far apart. Norias and chain pumps have also been used, but they do not give such good results as the above machines.

These various elevating machines are generally worked by steam, this being the cheapest and the handiest means of working. The cost of the operation varies between 24s. and

Fig. 170.—Gwyne's Centrifugal Pump.

32s. per acre when the water has not to be raised over 16 feet. This should be the maximum limit in practice. The machinery is sometimes established in a fixed position (Fig. 172) on the highest point of the vineyard to allow the water to run all over the surface through small channels made for the purpose. In other cases the machinery is portable and may be shifted from one block to another (Figs. 170 and 173). The system of fixed machinery should be preferred whenever possible; it is cheaper, works better, and lasts longer. It also saves time and enables the water to be distributed more regularly over the whole vineyard.

It is possible, in some cases, to use water power derived from rivers or channels from which the water for submersion is taken; in this case turbines or water wheels are used. The work is done very economically. Wind power, although very variable, can be used in conjunction with water power or steam.

Whatever power is used to raise the water, the latter is brought to the machine by means of sluices made a little below the lowest level of the river, and provided with sluice doors for stopping the water when required. This does away with embankments, always necessary when machines are established near the river. When possible the drainage reticulations should bring the water back to the pumping machine.

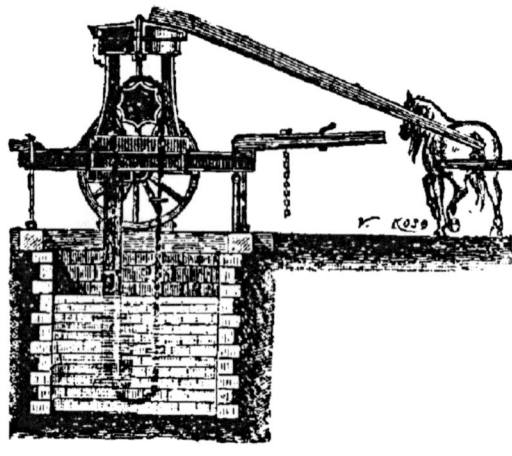

Fig. 171.—Dellon's Rouet.

(C.) *Stopping drainage pipes.*—Old reclaimed swamps may sometimes be used for submersion by throwing them into their primitive state. The soil must be first levelled so as to have an even depth of water, and the lowest point through which the drainage water is taken away should be stopped by means of sluice boxes placed for that purpose, and if drainage pipes exist they must be stopped at their lowest point during the whole operation. When the submersion is finished the pipes are opened again to allow the soil to dry. Many applications of this system, which has the advantage of being very economical and of great efficiency, have been successfully carried out.

2ND.—FORMATION OF SUBMERSION BASINS, OR BED-WORK SYSTEM.

In this system the water is kept on the soil by means of small banks forming a bed-work.

(A.) *Shape of beds.*—Beds should be made rectangular whenever possible, for they render ploughing easier and

Fig. 172.—Pumping Station placed in a fixed position on the highest point of the Vineyard.

Fig. 173.—Movable Pumping Station.

correspond to the systems of plantation in use. On horizontal lands where large beds can be made it is preferable to give them a square shape, as a greater area can be surrounded with the same length of bank, and as it allows cross ploughing. If the land is slightly sloped it is necessary to make rectangular beds following the mean line of profile, so as not to increase the height of the lowest bank.

(B.). *Size of beds.*—From the point of view of the destruction of phylloxera the larger the bed the better. As a matter of fact the area of the banks is small if compared to the whole surface, and we know that the roots of vines growing under the banks always harbour living insects and become a centre of infection, which must be diminished as much as possible.

But is it generally impossible in practice to apply this principle to its last limit, which would be that of making a single bed of the whole vineyard, surrounding it by a single bank. The reasons preventing it are—1st, that the soils are not horizontal, thus compelling the slope to be divided in sections to avoid making too high a bank on the lowest side; 2nd, the impossibility of having a sufficient quantity of water to fill it; 3rd, the danger of having the banks washed away by the small waves formed by the wind if the surface is too large; 4th, the large loss which would result from the bank breaking in one point and emptying the whole basin. To sum up, the size which seems to be the most practical is from 7 to 25 acres.

The beds should be arranged so as to allow the water to overflow from the top into the lower basins; for that purpose small sluice boxes are placed in suitable positions, these being also fed from the main channel and emptying automatically. Finally, drains must be established to enable the soil to be drained quickly after the operation.

(C.) *Banks.*—The banks should be prism-shaped, with slopes at 45°. This shape insures greater strength, and enables them to be used as paths during the operation. The width on the top depends on the depth of the water. It varies between 18 inches for a height of 18 inches, which is the minimum, and 3 feet for a height of 18 inches to 3 feet. If very large beds are made the banks should be large enough to enable them to be used as roads during the vintage. There is no danger in making banks as high as 3 feet, but above this limit the stumps would be completely covered with water, which is injurious. In any case the banks must allow a constant depth of 10 inches of water all over the bed, and be made 6 to 8 higher to stop the waves formed by the wind. Further, the banks must be built 10 per cent. higher than the required height, on account of the subsidence of the earth.

The banks should be built before planting, so as not to injure the young plants and to leave time for the soil to settle before the water is spread over it; trenching and levelling should be done before. The soil for forming the banks may be taken on the spot from either side, but it is preferable to take it on the lowest side to equalize the level.

It is advisable to strengthen the banks by covering them with grass, but care should be taken not to use any grass detrimental to the vineyard; *trifolium repens* seems to give the best results. It grows well in very dry or very damp soil, and forms a kind of dense felt all over the soil. In vineyards exposed to the winds, and if the beds are very large, it is advisable to cover the banks with rushes or bamboos to prevent the erosion caused by the waves.

CHAPTER III.

1st.—MOST FAVORABLE TIME FOR SUBMERGING VINEYARDS.

Faucon* noticed that phylloxera is very sensitive to the action of water during the most active period of its life, from the 15th of April to the 15th of October, and sometimes later. During winter, on the contrary, when the insect is hibernating, it does not suffer much from the action of water; therefore, if it were only necessary to take into account the efficacy of this treatment against phylloxera it should be done during the summer; but we must also take into account the life of the vine and its culture, which would suffer from a long submersion during the summer, and would become unworkable at certain times when it is most necessary. During the winter, on the contrary, water does not injure the plant, and the field work being stopped the vines can be inundated without inconvenience. *Water can be used without danger directly the canes are completely lignified, and the sooner it is applied after that time the better.* Most of our southern varieties ripen their wood towards the 1st of November.† *Grenache, Alicante,* and *Carignane,* however, are generally not sufficiently lignified by that time, and submersion must be done later on for vineyards in which they are planted. Frequent failures resulted from not taking this fact into consideration with regard to *Grenache.*

2nd.—DURATION OF SUBMERSION.

It varies according to climate, nature of soil, and seasons.

(A.) *Influence of climate.*—Experience has proved that in our northern districts the duration of submersion may be reduced to 25 or 30 days, while it must last 35 to 40 days in the Hérault and Gard (south of France). This fact is explained by the poor multiplication of phylloxera in cold climates, which enables a relatively large quantity of insects to be left living without much detriment resulting. Altitude has probably a similar influence, and in high lands of the southern regions the duration of submersion may be reduced.

---

* Louis Faucon, *Guérison des Vignes phylloxérées—Instructions pratiques sur le procédé de la submersion,* Montpellier, 1874. [Trans.]
† End of May in Victoria.

(B.) *Influence of soil.*—Compact soils with an impermeable subsoil do not require such long submersion and such a large amount of water as those having a certain permeability and resting on a pebbly subsoil. As a matter of fact, the former get rid of the air they contain quicker than the latter, and, therefore, the insect dies sooner.

(C.) *Influence of season.*—The season has also an influence on the duration of the operation, for phylloxera, as we have already seen, is more sensitive to the action of water when its life is most active. In autumn it is still laying eggs in the southern climates, and will therefore be killed quicker than in winter, when it is in a state of complete torpor. Therefore the submersion must last 35 to 40 days in autumn, and 40 to 50 in winter.

To sum up, the duration of submersion is, acccording to circumstances, from 30 to 60 days. A depth of 8 to 10 inches of water should cover the whole surface of the soil throughout the operation. A large number of failures, or accidents, resulted from not following the above rule, which had been pointed out from the very beginning by Faucon;* the slightest interruption is sufficient to allow air to penetrate in the soil, and enable the phylloxera to prolong its existence until the operation is finished.

One should, therefore, always ascertain before starting submerging that the water course or channel will be able to furnish water at a regular and even rate during the whole operation.

3RD.—AGE AT WHICH VINES MAY BE SUBMERGED.

When new vines are planted in soil, or near vineyards already attacked by phylloxera, they should be submerged as early as possible during the first year, or better, the land should be inundated before plantation, so as to destroy the insect, which would attack a large number of young plants' as soon as they throw roots, and would cause great damage. When, on the contrary, vines are planted in soils free from phylloxera, it is preferable to wait until the second year. A careful examination of the roots, however, will help to fix the date at which the first operation should be performed; one must start without hesitation, directly the slightest indication of the disease is detected.

---
* In work mentioned above. [Trans.]

4th.—PERIODICITY OF SUBMERSION.

Submersion should be repeated every year. Although this treatment may be considered as the most perfect insecticide, if well applied under proper conditions, and although it is often impossible to detect a single insect on the roots of treated vines in spring, they are always attacked afresh every summer, as proved by Faucon, by the aptrous form travelling over the soil, and by the winged forms carried by the winds from neighbouring vineyards. It becomes necessary, therefore, to destroy every winter the insects which arrived during the summer, to prevent their multiplication, which might cause great damage.

CHAPTER IV.

PLANTING AND CULTIVATION.

The planting and cultivation of submerged vines are in a general way governed by the same rules as those set forth for American vines. We will point out a few special precautions necessary in this case.

1st.—Planting.

Vines planted with the object of submerging them should not be mixed, as it is necessary to have the whole vineyard completely lignified before water is applied. It is impossible to fulfil these conditions if a block is planted with different varieties, but this object can be reached if we group the several varieties in different blocks, which may be submerged at different times. We must also avoid planting too close to the banks, for the roots penetrating under them, not being affected by the water, would remain covered with phylloxera, and constitute a danger for the rest of the block during the summer multiplication.

2nd.—Cultivation.

(A.) *Pruning.*—Late pruning is above all necessary for submerged vines, to prevent them from being destroyed by white frosts. Spurs should be left 1 to 2 feet long, and pruned finally after the buds have started bursting.

(B.) *Manures.*—It has been stated that submersion exhausts soils by washing away the soluble matters they contain. This assertion, which seems groundless as far as impermeability is concerned, may be true in a certain measure for those which are permeable. It is therefore advisable to furnish vines with manures, containing in an easily assimilable form matters necessary for their nourishment during one year, and renew it every year. The following formula, used by Faucon, answers very well:—

Rape cake	90 per cent.
Sulphate of Potash, Stassfurt (containing 38 per cent. of potash)	10 ,,

Eight ounces of this mixture are spread around each stump. The mixture indicated on page 144 can also be used with advantage.

(C.) *Ploughing.*—Ploughings should be frequent, and great care should be taken in their performance, on account of the settling resulting from the long duration of the flooding. We must avoid ploughing when white frosts are feared, on acount of the generally low and damp situations of vineyards submitted to submersion.

Numerous sulphurings and sulphatings should be done to prevent non-setting and to combat oidium, mildew, and anthracnosis, which are frequent in such vineyards.

These indications may be considered as summing up the experiences of submersionists.

PART III.

PLANTING IN SAND.

Sea sand protects vines from phylloxera. Considerable areas of downs have been planted with vines during the last few years in the environs of Aiguesmortes (Gard) with the object of utilizing this remarkable property. Although the methods of planting and culture used under these conditions are almost similar to those in ordinary vineyards, there are frequently slight differences of detail necessitated by the special conditions of their application. We shall study these, and also indicate the soils in which such plantations have succeeded.

CHAPTER I.

SELECTION OF SOIL AND CÉPAGES.—PLANTING.—CULTURE.

1st.—Selection of Soil.

We will examine this first question from the points of view—1st, of the indemnity the soil may insure to vines; 2nd, the influence it may have upon the development of the vines.

(A.) *Indemnity.*—All sandy soils, that is to say, those in which the physical properties of sand are predominant, have a more or less marked action on the prolongation of the life of vines, but they only endow them with perfect immunity in *sea sand containing more than* 60 *per cent. of silica.** Calcareous sands do not have the same action as siliceous sands. They seem to agglomerate more easily, and immunity increases with the state of division of the soil up to a certain limit. A subsoil composed of siliceous sands of suitable nature, where portion of the vine roots may

---

* The insecticide power of sand is due to two different causes:—
1st. The tenuity and mobility of its particles prevents the penetration of the insect into the soil, and therefore its multiplication underground.
2nd. The capillary power of sand retains the water which reaches it by imbibition or infiltration. This water surrounding the insects and their eggs prevent them from respiring and developing. [Transls.]

develop, is sufficient to insure the life of the plantation; the roots living in the soil are attacked and destroyed, but those penetrating in the subsoil are protected.

(B.) *Conditions favorable to the success of vines.*—Vines seem to grow well in almost all the sea sands of Aiguesmortes, even in the soils containing decomposed pines and briars, which are generally considered as injurious.

Of all the sea sands now planted with vines those where madder was formerly cultivated seem to have given the best results; they are richer, and they have been ploughed for a great number of years. They have yielded up to the enormous quantity of 5,500 gallons per acre. The accumulation of organic matters in such soils does not seem to have diminished their insecticide power.

Soils situated near the sea are less favorable. The yield is much smaller, and the vineyards are subject to many accidents.

2ND.—SELECTION OF CÉPAGES.

Aramon, Petit-Bouschet, Cinsaut, Chasselas, and *Carignane* have succeeded more or less in sea sand. *Cinsaut* seems to be best adapted for pure sands near the sea. *Carignane,* on the contrary, which is easily attacked by anthracnosis, suffers very much from the action of winds blowing from the sea. *Aramon, Petit-Bouschet,* and *Chasselas* succeed very well if they are furnished with the necessary quantity of fertilizing matter to recuperate their enormous yield, and if they are sheltered against the wind.

3RD.—PLANTING.

(A.) *Preparation of soil.*—Sandy soils being naturally very loose, it seems at first useless to trench them deeply. However, experience has proved that trenching exerts an important influence on the future of vines planted in sand. This influence may be easily explained, if we remember how great is the importance of dividing the soil, from the point of view of its resistance and its aeration, and the assimilation of fertilizing matter, more particularly phosphates, which it already contains.

Sands must therefore be deeply disturbed with trenching ploughs followed by sub-soilers. This operation is not very expensive in such soils; it should therefore be performed with the greatest care.

(B.) *Planting in sand.*—We may plant rather long cuttings (which grow very well when there is not too much salt in the soil), or sometimes rootlings.

The quincunx method seems best adapted to the conditions of sea sands, because it enables the shoots to cover the whole surface of the soil, and prevents the sand from being blown away by the wind.

4TH.—CULTURAL CARE.

(A.) *Manuring.*—Care must be taken to avoid, as far as possible, introducing in sandy soil matters which would modify its physical properties, for it may lose its resisting qualities, which, as we have seen, are the result of its mobility. The use of suitable manures even in large quantities does not seem to alter its physical composition, but the accumulation of such matters during a great number of years might have a dangerous influence. Chemical manures and oil cakes seem to be best adapted to these conditions.

(B.) *Summer ploughing.*—The small number of weeds growing in sea sand does not necessitate numerous ploughings, and the action of the wind carrying the sand away when it is dry renders ploughing dangerous at certain times. On account of these considerations one ploughing only is given at the end of winter. After this operation rushes, or straw, or marsh plants are spread over the whole surface, and slighly buried with shovels or sharp discs. The object of this is to fix the soil until the autumn rains fall. If, after very heavy rains, weeds grow during the summer, they are pulled out by hand without using a hoe.

Sulphuring and spraying should be done very thoroughly, on account of the considerable development of cryptogamic diseases resulting from the enormous amount of moisture.

APPENDIX.

BENCH-GRAFTING RESISTANT VINES.
By F. T. Bioletti and A. M. dal Piaz.

Bulletin No. 127, University of California, 1900.

The conviction that the vineyardist has to deal with the phylloxera as a factor in the success or failure of his business becomes stronger every day. This applies both to the

Fig. 174.—1. Solonis. 2. Rupestris du Lot.
3. Riparia Gloire de Montpellier.

grape-grower who already has bearing vines and to the intended grape-grower who is engaged in planting his vines. Each succeeding year sees new vineyards and new localities attacked, and the grape-growers who believed their vines safe on account of the richness or sandy nature of their soils, the practice of irrigation, or the isolation of their vineyards are gradually being forced to change their belief by the sad fact of the death of their vines. Yet there are still many who fail to realize the true nature of this disease, and even now there are growers who are planting varieties of Vinifera on their own roots in localities adjacent to infected districts, and even in the infected districts themselves.

Even those who are thoroughly persuaded of the necessity of establishing their vines upon resistant roots are in doubt as to what species or variety to choose.

When the phylloxera first invaded the lower parts of the Sonoma and Napa valleys, over twenty years ago, the vineyardists were completely unprepared for it, and unable to combat it in any way, so most of them allowed the insect to have undisputed sway, with the result that the vineyards disappeared. A few of the more intelligent growers, however, tried the method, first practised in France, of planting resistant stocks. The principal varieties planted were Riparia and Lenoir. Other varieties were planted in small quantities by a few growers, but most of them are at present of little interest. The results varied widely. Though a certain number of vineyards were fairly or even perfectly successful, the majority were total or partial failures. This lack of general success was due to three principal causes:—

1. Many of the soils and locations were unsuitable for the growth of either Riparia or Lenoir.
2. The Riparia cuttings used were not of one variety, some being very small growers, unable to support a large Vinifera.
3. The Lenoir is not sufficiently resistant in all soils, and therefore failed to give full crops on any but the best soils.

To these should be added, in many cases, ignorance of the methods of planting and grafting resistant stocks.

Ten or fifteen years later the coast valleys south of San Francisco, which the vine-growers had hitherto considered immune for some mysterious reason, were attacked. They were just as unprepared as the vine-growers of Napa and

Sonoma had been when their vineyards were attacked. It is in order to prevent any further unpreparedness and consequent costly mistakes that vine-growers of uninfected locations are earnestly advised to commence now to test the most promising resistant stocks on their own places, in order to determine which of these is most suitable for the conditions of the soil, climate, and moisture that exist there. This is especially true of such localities as Fresno and others in the lower San Joaquin valley, where there are large stretches of contiguous vineyards as yet uninfected.

The phylloxera is as menacing a foe to the "raisin-grower" as to the "wine-grower," and it would be well worth while for every vineyardist in California, not only to test various resistants, but also to learn the methods of bench or cutting, grafting, and all the various processes of establishing a vineyard on resistant roots. Then, when the insect enters his own or his neighbour's vineyard he will know exactly what to plant and how to plant it, and not be obliged to experiment for three or four years or trust to the experience of some one else whose conditions may differ in some way from his, and thus run the risk of making costly failures.

The work of the Experiment Station in this line for the last two or three years has been to establish some general principles to guide the individual grower in his own attempts and to narrow the scope of his experiments in order that he may not waste his time on methods and varieties which have already been proved valueless. Our conclusions have been based on observations of our own experiments, and also of the successes and failures of grape-growers in various parts of the State. These observations have so far been directed principally to:—

1. The adaptability of various resistant varieties to different conditions of soil, climate, and moisture.
2. The best method of grafting for various varieties and conditions.
3. The growth of various Vinifera varieties upon various resistant stocks.

The problems presented by the phylloxera were studied by Professor E. W. Hilgard very early at this Station, and a certain amount of attention has been given by the Station since then to methods of extermination of the insect and to resistant stock. The results of this work having already been published, the present article deals only with the work done during and since 1896. In that year Professor A. P.

Hayne, of this department, imported the following resistant varieties, which were recommended as the best in France for soils similar to our California soils:—*Rupestris du Lot, Riparia Gloire de Montpellier, Riparia Grand Glabre, Rupestris Martin.* These varieties were as widely distributed over the various vineyard districts as possible, and particular satisfaction was given by the first two mentioned.

In 1897 the Station continued this work of distribution, and put upon its "Distribution List" *Rupestris du Lot, Riparia Gloire de Montpellier, Riparia Grand Glabre,* and *Solonis.* A more limited distribution was also made of *Rupestris Martin, Rupestris Mission, Rupestris Ganzin, Champini,* and of three hybrids of Rupestris crossed with Riparia, viz., *Rup.* × *Rip.* 101–14, *Rup.* × *Rip.* 3306, *Rup.* × *Rip.* 3309.

In the same year the station published an appendix to the Viticultural Report of 1896, entitled "Resistant Vines," by Professor Hayne, in which was given a summary of what is known in France of the practical selection and adaptation of resistant vines, and also of the methods of grafting adapted to these vines. During the years 1898 and 1899 the two varieties which seemed to have given the most general satisfaction, and for which there was the most demand, were again placed upon the "Distribution List." These varieties were *Rupestris du Lot* and *Riparia Gloire de Montpellier.*

In 1898 the station decided to make a series of practical experiments with these recently imported resistants, and on various methods of grafting, in order to bring the matter before the vine-growers of California in a practical form, and also to throw light on some doubtful points. This it was enabled to do by the public spirit of Mr. J. K. Moffitt of the First National Bank of San Francisco, who kindly allowed us to use a portion of his vineyard at St. Helena, Napa County, for our experiments.

These experiments were planned on a somewhat elaborate scale, but unfortunately were almost a complete failure, on account of the bad condition of the resistant cuttings when they arrived from France. There were imported 9,300 cuttings of various varieties, and of these about 85 per cent. were completely spoiled. They were packed with the greatest care, but had somewhere been exposed to too much heat (probably on the steamer) and had suffered a fermentation which had completely blackened the pith and inner bark. These were planted out in the nursery without grafting, but failed to grow. The remainder were a little better, but were full of dark streaks, showing that they also had suffered from the heat but in a less degree. These were grafted, and the ill-success of the grafts was undoubtedly due to this bad condition of the stocks. This showed the danger of importing large quantities of cuttings from so distant a place, and it was determined for the next year's experiments to use only cuttings grown in California.

Adaptability of various Varieties of Vinifera to various Resistant Stocks.—One of the principal experiments made was to test the adaptability of certain Vinifera varieties for different stocks, that is to say, to test on which resistant stocks certain varieties did best. The negative results (the cases in which there was very poor or no growth) of course taught nothing, as it was impossible to tell whether the failure was due to lack of affinity of the scion for the stock, or simply to the bad condition of the stock. The positive results, where there was good growth and good unions, are however worth chronicling.

The varieties which grew well and made good unions on *Riparia Gloire de Montpellier* were :—

- Aramon
- Blue Portuguese
- Chardonay
- Folle Blanche
- Gros Mansenc
- Kleinberger
- Marsanne
- Peruno
- Petit Bouschet
- Seedless Sultana
- Semillon
- Valdepeñas.

Those which did well on *Riparia Grand Glabre* were :—

- Aramon
- Cabernet Sauvignon
- Chardonay
- Cornichon
- Fresa
- Gros Mansenc
- Huasco
- Marsanne
- Mataro
- Mourisco Preto
- Semillon
- Sultanina
- Verdot
- Vernaccia.

Those which did well on *Rupestris du Lot* were :—

- Barbera
- Beba
- Cornichon
- Franken Riesling
- Kleinberger
- Mantuo de Pilas
- Marsanne.
- Palomino
- Peruno
- Petit Bouschet
- Seedless Sultana
- Valdepeñas
- Vernaccia

All these made good growth, and the unions were all apparently strong and well formed. They were planted out in the spring of 1899 in three rows of 25 vines each, in order to watch their future development. Besides these were also planted out two rows of 25 vines each as follows:—One row of *Mondeuse*, grafted on *Riparia Grand Glabre;* one row of *Mondeuse*, grafted on *Rupestris du Lot;* and one vine of *Mondeuse*, grafted on *Rupestris × Riparia* 3306.

Eleven other rows of ungrafted varieties were planted as follows:—One row each of *Pinot*, *Cabernet du Lac*, and *Hybrid Franc;* two rows each of *Rupestris Martin*, *Rupestris × Riparia* 101-14, *Rupestris × Riparia* 3309, and *Rupestris du Lot;* one row each of *Vialla* and *Rupestris Mission*.

On 29th December, 1899, the following notes were taken on the foregoing vines:—

Varieties Grafted on Riparia Gloire de Montpellier.

Blue Portuguese.—Strong growth, canes 3 feet long, but not very ripened.
Chardonay.—Medium growth   One dead.
Fresa.—Poor growth.
Folle Blanche.—Medium growth.
Gros Mansenc.—Good strong growth, canes 3 feet long.
Kleinberger.—Medium growth.
Marsanne.—Good strong growth, 3 feet long. One graft dead.
Peruno.—Medium growth, shoots still green except at the base.
Petit-Bouschet.—Medium growth.
Seedless Sultana.—Medium growth, and wood still green except at the base.
Semillon.—Medium growth.
Valdepeñas.—Good growth of thoroughly ripened wood.
Vernaccia.—Medium to poor growth.

Varieties Grafted on Riparia Grand Glabre.

Aramon.—Growth poor, about 1 foot.
Cabernet Sauvignon.—Growth good.
Chardonay.—Good growth, some shoots 3 feet long.
Cornichon.—Medium growth, about 2 feet.
Fresa.—Medium growth, about 2 feet.
Gros Mansenc.—Growth about 1 foot.
Huasco.—Good growth, shoots about 3 feet long, but still green at the tips.
Marsanne.—Excellent growth of ripe wood.
Maturo.—From 1 to 2 feet of growth.
Mourisco Preto.—Good growth.
Semillon.—Growth about 2 feet. One graft dead.
Sultanina.—Many shoots, but green at the tips.
Verdot.—Poor growth. One graft dead.
Vernaccia.—Poor growth; thin shoots 2 feet long.

VARIETIES GRAFTED ON RUPESTRIS DU LOT.

Barbera.—Medium growth.
Beba.—Fine growth.
Cornichon.—Medium growth.
Franken Riesling.—Long growth; tips still green.
Kleinberger.—Long thin canes.
Mantuo de Pilas.—Poor growth.
Marsanne.—Small growth.
Palomino.—Very vigorous growth of eight or nine canes to a vine.
Peruno.—Strong growth.
Petit-Bouschet.—Vigorous growth, strong canes.
Sultana.—Good growth.
Valdepeñas.—Good growth.
Vernaccia.—Medium growth.

The one graft of *Mondeuse* on *Rupestris* × *Riparia 3309* had made a very good growth.

The row of *Mondeuse* grafted on *Riparia Grand Glabre* had grown well, with the exception of one graft, which was dead.

The row of *Mondeuse* grafted on *Rupestris du Lot* was more irregular. Two vines were dead and five had lost the Mondeuse scion, and the Rupestris was growing from suckers. Where the Mondeuse was growing, however, it was on the whole more vigorous than in the last row.

VARIETIES ON THEIR OWN ROOTS.

Pinot Cabernet du Lac.—This variety made very poor growth. Most of the vines lived, but the canes were only a few inches long. The soil, which was black adobe, was evidently unsuited to this vine.

Hybrid Franc.—The growth of this variety was more irregular than that of the last, and no stronger. A few vines had made medium growth, but many were dead and the majority were very poor.

Rupestris Martin.—This resistant made a fair growth; in some cases the canes were 4 to 5 feet long, but not thick.

Rupestris × *Riparia 101–14.*—Fair growth of 2 to 3 feet.

Rupestris × *Riparia 3309.*—Fair growth, somewhat longer and stronger than the last.

Rupestris du Lot.—Growth good to very good; many canes to each vine.

Vialla.—Good growth of shoots 2 to 3 feet long.

Rupestris Mission.—Good growth, but the canes were rather thin.

EXPERIMENTS MADE IN 1899.

The experiments carried out this year consisted chiefly of tests of various methods of grafting and of planting in the nursery.

The cuttings used as stock in these experiments were—

1. Rupestris du Lot, 3,000 from Beringer Bros., St. Helena.
2. Riparia Gloire de Montpellier, 100 from John Swett and Son, Martinez.
3. Lenoir, 96 from G. Husmann, Napa.
4. American Ruländer, 26 from G. Husmann, Napa.
5. Herbemont, 21 from G. Husmann, Napa.
6. Cunningham, 27 from G. Husmann, Napa.
7. America, 10 (rooted, one year old) from W. B. Munson, Texas.
8. Champini, 10 (rooted, one year old) from W. B. Munson, Texas.
9. Elvicand, 7 (rooted, one year old) from W. B. Munson, Texas.
10. Munson, 13 (rooted, 1 year old) from W. B. Munson, Texas.

The following varieties were used as scions:—

11. Zinfandel, from J. K. Moffit, St. Helena.
12. Mondeuse, from J. K. Moffit, St. Helena.
13. Tokay, from John Swett and Son, Martinez.
14. Ferrara, from John Swett and Son, Martinez.

The following varieties were used for rooting experiments:—

15. Rupestris du Lot, from Beringer Bros., St. Helena.
16. Riparia Gloire de Montpellier, from John Swett and Son, Martinez.
17. Solonis, from John Swett and Son, Martinez.

The main objects of this series of experiments were to ascertain the relative value of:—

(a) The English graft and the Champin graft.
(b) Leaving two eyes on the scions, and leaving only one.
(c) Preliminary callusing in sand, and planting out in the nursery immediately after grafting.
(d) Callusing in sand alone, and in straw covered with sand.
(e) *Rupestris du Lot, Riparia Gloire de Montpellier, Lenoir, Herbemont, Cunningham,* and *American Ruländer* as regards root formation when bench-grafted.
(f) *Rupestris du Lot, Riparia, Gloire de Montpellier,* and *Solonis* as regards rooting when not grafted.

Light was thrown on other points, such as the possibility of grafting successfully various varieties of different habit, such as the small-growing *Zinfandel* and the large-growing *Ferrara,* upon *Rupestris du Lot.*

Grafting.

Preparation of Cuttings for Grafting.—The Rupestris du Lot cuttings used for grafting stock were in excellent condition at the beginning of the grafting season, as they were kept under cover in moist sand during the winter. The cuttings were less than 2 feet long, rather short jointed, and generally too thick at the lower end and too thin at the upper for grafting. This was doubtless due to the dry summer, which resulted in a short growth, and it was rarely possible to obtain more than one graft from a cutting. The sizes used for grafting varied from $\frac{1}{4}$ to $\frac{1}{2}$ inch in diameter. The thin tips which could not be used for grafting were put out in the nursery for rooting.

The cuttings were all treated in the same way for the various experiments as follows:—They were cut into sections of from 6 to 9 inches; the lower cut was made through the knot of the bud; the last internode of the upper end was left as long as possible, as the internodes were of rather short length, sometimes scarcely long enough for the grafting cut. Special care was given to the perfect removal of all of the buds of the stock, a deep cut being made in order to remove not only the main bud but also the small adventitious or dormant buds which surround its base, and which often grow out when not carefully excised and form suckers, which grow at the expense of the graft. The cuttings thus prepared were sorted into three sizes according to their thickness, put up in bundles, and placed vertically in a tub of water, so that the lower end was covered with water; the cuttings thus remained fresh and sappy, which facilitated greatly the making of cuts. The cuttings remained in the water until they were needed for grafting, that is to say, from six to eighteen hours.

The washing and placing in water had also the object of cleaning the cuttings from all adhering dirt and sand, which would blunt the edge of the sharpest grafting knife in a short time.

The scions were prepared in a similar way, with the exception, of course, that the eyes were left. Two kinds of scions were needed for the experiments; one with the one eye, the other with two eyes. The first kind was cut through the second knot so as to leave the eye protected by a closed internode, which on the one hand prevented penetration of moisture and of fungi, and on the other hand drying out of the part above the eye. Scions of the second kind (with two eyes) were treated differently in order not to make them too long, the upper cut being made about an inch above the second eye.

The scions were also sorted into three sizes corresponding with those of the stock, tied up in bundles, and put in water to keep them fresh and sappy.

Methods of Grafting.—Before grafting, the cuttings of both stock and scion having been carefully sorted into three sizes, and the eyes of those of the stock cut out deeply with a sharp knife in order to prevent the production of suckers, the greatest care was taken to prevent the slightest drying out of the cuttings and afterwards of the grafts.

The raffia used for binding the grafts was soaked in a 3 per cent. solution of bluestone (copper sulphate) for one day and then hung up to dry. Before using it was thoroughly washed in running water to remove the superfluous bluestone. The raffia was cut into short pieces of 10 to 12 inches, and then kept in a box, moist and ready for use.

The grafting knife was not of the pattern generally used in California, but was one especially constructed for Champin and English tongue grafting; it had a wooden handle 4½ inches long to give the hand a firm grasp, a straight and very thin blade of excellent steel which was easy to sharpen, and which kept its edge for a considerable time. A good hone and a razor strop were used for sharpening the knife.

The object of the experiment in methods of grafting was to ascertain the advantages and disadvantages of the two most commonly practised methods, viz., the English graft

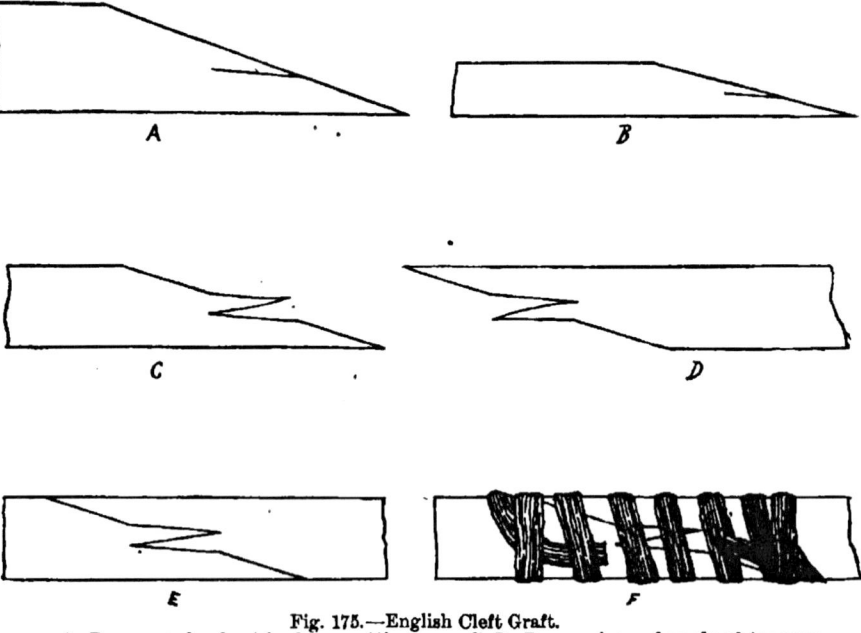

Fig. 175.—English Cleft Graft.
A. Proper angle of cut for large cuttings.   C, D. Proper size and angle of tongues.
B. Proper angle of cut for small cuttings.   E, F. Method of uniting and tying graft.

and a modification of the old Champin graft; the first is universally used in European vine nurseries, the latter is less practised there, but is frequently used in California.

English Cleft or Whip Grafting.—This method was applied in the usual way as shown in Fig. 175. The stock and scion were chosen of equal size, and were cut at the same angle. The length of the cut surface, in cuttings of solid texture and full size, was about three times the diameter of the cuttings, that is to say, the cut was made at an angle of about 19°. This may be taken as the maximum angle that can be used practically. For smaller cuttings the length of the cut was relatively somewhat greater, being about four times the diameter or about 14°, which may be taken as the minimum angle which should be adopted. The tongues were made by a longitudinal cut, care being taken *not to split* the wood, and usually commenced at about one-third the distance from the sharp end of the cutting, and to a depth about equal to the diameter. Thus when the two cuttings were placed together the sharp end of one corresponded exactly to the thick end of the other, so that no portion of the cut surface was exposed, and the maximum contact was obtained. The object of the grafter in making his cuts is to make them as straight as possible, but it will be found that a cut made by the most skilful hand is slightly concave. This is, however, no objection, as this extremely slight concavity is useful in allowing for the slight swelling in the middle due to the insertion of the tongues. This is probably one of the reasons why hand-grafting is generally more successful than grafting with a machine, as a machine makes a cut which is absolutely straight, and the ends have thus a tendency to be drawn away from the cut surface of the other cutting. The cut for the tongue is not made quite parallel to the grain of the wood in order to minimize the danger of splitting.

Champin Graft.—Perhaps the commonest method of grafting used in California for small vines or cuttings is a modification of the Champin method. The Champin graft is made as shown in Fig. II. below. The modified method is a compromise between the true Champin graft and the English tongue graft. It is made in a way similar to that described for the latter, but the tongue is made much deeper and the end of the point (see Fig. 176, No. 12) projecting over the cut of the opposite cutting is cut off.

The Champin graft is based on the theoretical principle that the greater the surface of contact between the two cuttings the greater the chances of union. Thus in the English graft the amount of possible contact is theoretically only about half that of the Champin. The latter is apparently twice as great as the former. In practice, however, it is found that the contact in the English graft can be made so much more perfect than in the Champin graft that the actual contact is usually greater in the former than in the latter. Moreover, the strip of bark on the long tongue of

Fig. 176. End-to-End and Champin Graft.
1, 2. Method of making the End-to-End Graft.
3, 4. Cross-section through the union of the above graft, showing how completely the stock unites with the scion on all sides.
5. Union of End-to-End Graft.
–12. Method of making Champin Graft.

the Champin graft is more likely to become detached or injured than the well-supported bark on the English graft; and, finally, the exposed cut at the end of the scion is almost sure to emit strong roots, while that on the stock prevents the complete and thorough union which is possible with the English graft. The tongue, therefore, should be reduced to the minimum, that is to say, should be as short as possible, while giving solidity to the graft until union takes place. For purposes of comparison, parallel experiments were made with both methods.

Another method, new and not thoroughly tested as yet, was tried with a few Rupestris St. George cuttings, Mondeuse being used for scions. This method originated in France, and is called "End to end" grafting. Its nature is shown in Fig. 176. The ends of stock are cut at an angle of about 70°, and are held together by a piece of galvanized-iron wire which is pushed into the pith of each piece. The number of successful grafts was low, but those which did unite made such excellent unions that the method seems worthy of further trial. It is especially promising for machine grafting.

Binding Grafts.—Raffia, treated as explained on page 222, was used for binding the grafts. The raffia seemed to have deteriorated somewhat during the twelve months it had been allowed to hang in an open shed. It was weaker than usual, and some of it rather brittle. It was cut into lengths of about 12 inches.

It has been shown that the grafts would do better without any binding, but for two reasons, first, because it is difficult to handle unbound grafts without disturbing the union; and second, because the callus does not form simultaneously on all parts of the union, and the first formed tends to push apart the stock and scion, thus making it difficult or impossible for all parts to unite. The object then in binding is to use as little raffia as is compatible with the thorough firmness of the union. The free ends of both scion and stock should be made firm with about two turns of the raffia, and the rest with wide spiral turns, which leaves as much of the union in direct contact with the sand as possible. The sand, while keeping the union sufficiently moist, does not completely exclude the air, which is necessary to the formation of healing tissue. A somewhat closer tying than this was adopted in these experiments, on account of the weakness of the raffia used.

The grafts were tied in bundles of ten, and then treated in various ways to aid their uniting.

METHODS OF AIDING CALLUSING.—The main reason for callusing the grafts before they are put in the nursery is that we can have more perfect control of the conditions which favour the formation of callus. Those conditions are an even and not too low temperature, and a moisture content of the soil in which the grafts are callused, not exceeding 10 per cent., and not falling below 5 per cent.

Two methods of obtaining those conditions were tried.

1st. *Callusing in Sand.*—The sand used was taken from Napa Creek, and was very suitable for the purpose. The grafts were put in the sand nearly vertically in bundles of ten, in rows. The sand was moistened sufficiently to give it the compactness necessary for making the piles. The location of the sand pile was chosen on the south side of a building, which protected the sand from the north winds, and rendered it possible to give the grafts the maximum amount of sun. A layer of about 4 inches of sand was put on the bottom, and then the grafts were put in vertically, and covered up as soon as they came from the grafting bench. The tops of the grafts were covered with a thin layer of sand (about 2 inches). The whole pile of sand with the grafts was then covered with a waterproof cloth, in order to protect the grafts from excessive moisture, and to maintain the even temperature of the sand during cold weather and at night. This cover was easily removable in order to facilitate watering, if necessary, and to make it possible to warm the pile on sunny days. This arrangement, somewhat improved, is shown in Fig. 177.

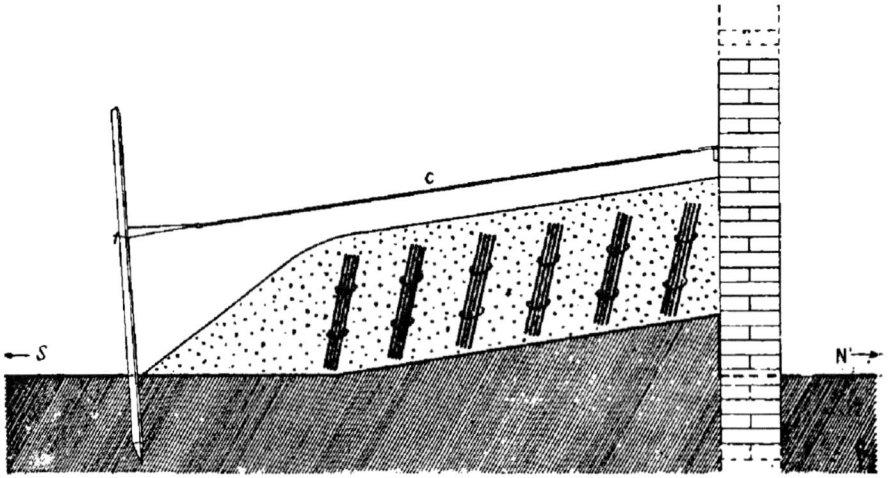

Fig. 177.—Callusing Bed.

The grafts were put in the sand from 7th March to 18th March, the time of grafting.

2nd. *Callusing in Straw or Moss.*—To test this method, 360 grafts were placed in straw, moss not being obtainable at the time. Moss is considered somewhat better, on account of its hygroscopic power. The method of layering the grafts in straw was as follows:—A large box without cover was laid on its side, a layer of about 2 inches of chopped straw was placed on the lower side, and then a single layer of grafts. This was repeated until the box was full. The grafts were so placed that the scion was nearest the bottom of the box, which was then turned upright, and still more straw pushed in between the layers of grafts until they were tightly packed. The box was then placed in the sand pile, 2 inches of straw placed on top, and the whole covered with sand, 1 inch of sand being placed over the top layer of straw. The straw was moistened before being used for layering the grafts.

All the grafts were left from six to eight weeks to callus, and then planted out in the nursery during the first week in May.

Planting Grafts in the Nursery.

Planting immediately after Grafting.—There is no doubt about the disadvantage of planting freshly grafted vine cuttings out in the open nursery, as we have there no practical means of sufficiently controlling temperature and moisture. But, in order to have definite data in regard to this method in comparison with a preliminary callusing with more or less perfect control of temperature and moisture, the following experiment was tried:—360 grafted cuttings were planted out in the nursery directly after they were grafted. The soil of the nursery was in good condition. In planting, a trench was dug about 18 inches deep and 15 inches wide. The bottom of the trench was then filled in for a few inches, with well-pulverized top soil, in order to facilitate the penetration of the roots. The grafts were placed 4 inches apart nearly vertically, in two rows (one on each side of the trench), sand being previously placed on each side in order that the bases of the stock should be in favorable condition for root formation and growth. The trench was then completely filled by putting in soil and sand alternately in such a manner as to surround the grafts completely with sand. The point of union of scion and stock was placed at a level with the surface of the soil, and was also carefully surrounded with sand. Sand was then heaped completely over the scions, and the rest filled in with soil, thus making a bank, which covered the grafts to a depth of about 2 inches, as shown in Fig. 178.

The reason for completely covering with sand was to prevent the scions from being dried out by the wind.

Fig. 178.—Method of Planting in Nursery.

Planting the Grafts after previous Callusing.—The grafts were planted in the nursery after they had been from six to to eight weeks in the callusing bed.

When the grafts were taken out of the callusing pile it was noticed that the unions of those which had been buried on the south side were much more complete than those buried on the north side, showing the effect of heat in promoting the formation of healing tissue. In the warmer parts of the pile the buds of the scions had started, a disadvantage which was, however, more than counterbalanced by the good callusing, as was proved by their subsequent better growth. The only other difference noted was that the Riparia stock had developed more rootlets than the Rupestris at this time.

The grafts were planted out in the nursery in trenches about 18 inches deep and 14 to 15 inches wide, as already described. The grafts were planted in a manner similar to that described on page 227, with a few modifications which were found to be necessary. The grafts first planted were put in the soil so as to bring the unions just level with the soil surface. But the loose soil soon settled about 2 inches, so that the unions became actually deeper. The grafts planted later were placed with the unions about 2 inches above the surface to offset this settling. Moreover, some further precautionary measures had to be taken to prevent the soil from drying out too much near the grafts. It was found best to make the bank of piled-up earth wider by putting more soil at the sides so as to preserve the moisture of the soil.

The soil was moist enough when the grafts were planted, but the sand had to be moistened before putting into the trenches. A thorough ploughing and harrowing were given the hard soil between the rows in order to prevent excessive evaporation.

The nursery received but little care after the grafts had been planted. The soil received the same cultivation as that of the neighbouring vineyard, was weeded once, and the grafts were irrigated in July.

Removal of scion-roots and suckers from the stock.— About the middle of July the earth was carefully removed by means of a shovel, and then the sand was taken away from the unions, partly by means of a trowel, partly with the hands, as circumstances required. The smallest rootlets were still soft, and could be rubbed off by the hand; the older and firmer roots had to be cut with a sharp knife. Great care was taken not to disturb the unions of the grafts, as they were still very brittle.

Few suckers were found, as the eyes of the stock had been carefully cut out before grafting. In cases where the suckers came from the deepest eye, it was found necessary to dig down to the base of the whole graft in order to cut the shoot at its base as well as to properly remove the dormant eyes. The removal of roots was done without injury to the grafts, as they were covered up before they had a chance to dry out, and the soil was irrigated immediately after; so that the grafts looked as fresh as ever the next morning.

The soil was found dry to a depth of from 5 to 6 inches, but the soil below this had preserved sufficient moisture to keep the unions of the graft from drying, as they were all in the moist region. The sand on the surface became very much heated in the middle of the day, which may account for the many tender young shoots and leaves which were found dry and withered. The second eye at the base of the scion had in most of these cases developed new shoots, so that the injury done was only in retarding the vegetation of the burnt plants.

A thorough irrigation was found necessary at this time in order to prevent injury from the drought and heat of summer. The water was run in little ditches about 1 foot from the grafts, and so applied that the soil around the unions was never thoroughly water-soaked, which experience has shown to be deleterious to the graft. The soil was cultivated as soon as dry enough after irrigation. The raffia in many cases was rotten already.

Condition when scion and suckers were cut.—The following observations were made during 14th to 18th July, when the roots of the scions and the suckers were cut:—

English grafts with scions of two eyes; 180 Zinfandel on Rupestris du Lot. Almost all the grafts had started to grow; about 50 per cent. of the grafts showed roots on the scions; 162 grafts had started, that is 90 per cent.

English grafts with scions of one eye; 180 Zinfandel on Rupestris du Lot. A lower percentage than of the above had developed shoots (78 per cent.), but the roots on the scions were less developed and fewer in number.

Champin grafts with scions of two eyes; 180 Zinfandel on Rupestris du Lot. The scions had well developed shoots, but also a good many strong roots on the bases of the scions. Of the 180 grafts, 165 were growing, that is about 92 per cent.

Champin grafts with scions of one eye; 180 Zinfandel on Rupestris du Lot. This lot was better developed than that with two eyes left on the scions; less strong roots were found on the scions, but only 150 were growing, that is about 83 per cent.

Champin grafts with scions of one eye; 180 Zinfandel on Rupestris du Lot; *planted out immediately after grafting.* The unions of the grafts that were growing seemed to have joined very well; the soil near to the scions was dry, so that but few roots had developed, the 75 grafts growing made but a low percentage of the whole, about 42 per cent.

Champin grafts with scions of two eyes; 180 Zinfandel on Rupestris du Lot; *planted out immediately after grafting.* The grafts were in about the same condition, but showed a higher percentage of growing grafts; of the 180 grafts, 98 were growing, that is about 54 per cent.

Champin grafts with scions of one eye; 180 Zinfandel on Rupestris du Lot; *grafts callused in the straw.* The scions showed small and few roots, and the number of growing grafts was 154, that is about 85 per cent.

Champin grafts with scions of two eyes; 180 Zinfandel on Rupestris du Lot; *grafts callused in the straw.* The grafts of this and the foregoing experiment (callusing in straw) looked the best of all the grafts made, and had very well developed shoots, with an average length of 10 inches; the proportion of growing grafts was 90 per cent.

America grafted with Zinfandel; English graft with scions of two eyes on one-year-old rooted stock. The grafts showed good growth; six grafts of the ten had started, that is about 60 per cent.

Munson grafted with Zinfandel; one-year-old rooted stock, scions of two eyes, English graft. The grafts showed good growth; a few only showed small rootlets on the scions; eleven, or 85 per cent., were growing.

Champini grafted with Zinfandel; one-year-old rooted stock, scions of two eyes, English graft. The scions did not take in most cases, the proportion being about 30 per cent.

Elvicand grafted with Zinfandel, one-year-old rooted stock, scions of two eyes, English graft. The grafts showed very poor growth, and only about 29 per cent. growing at all.

Mondeuse on Rupestris St. George; Champin graft, scions of two eyes. The shoots were found to be short, about 5 or 6 inches long. Only a few rootlets were found on the scions, and many of them were dead already. The proportion of growing grafts was about 63 per cent. Altogether the Mondeuse were growing less vigorously on Rupestris St. George than the Zinfandel.

Lenoir grafted with Zinfandel; English graft, scions of two eyes. Many of the grafts did not grow, they were found dry and dead; the few growing were backward in development; the nourishment came apparently from the reserve food in the cuttings, as there were few or no roots on the stock. Only 28 per cent. were growing.

American Rulander grafted with Zinfandel; English graft, scions of two eyes. Neither scions nor stock had developed roots; a few were growing somewhat by means of reserve food; in all 19 per cent.

Herbemont grafted with Zinfandel; English graft, scions of two eyes. A few started to grow (about 24 per cent.), but no roots were found on the scions or the stock.

Cunningham grafted with Zinfandel; English graft, scions of two eyes. No roots had formed on the scions. The growth was small, and only 26 per cent. showed any.

Riparia Gloire de Montpellier grafted with Zinfandel; Champin graft, scions of two eyes. The green shoots were 5 to 6 inches long, some even smaller (that is, shorter) than those on Rupestris St. George. But few rootlets were found on the scions. The proportion of growing grafts was 58 per cent.

Tokay on Rupestris du Lot; Champin graft, scions of two eyes. The grafts were very well developed, showing abundant foliage. Not many roots were found on the scions, and 87 per cent. were growing.

Ferrara on Rupestris du Lot; Champin graft, scions of two eyes. The grafts showed very good growth; but many roots were found on the scions, and most of them were already well developed. The proportion growing was 96 per cent., which is higher than in any of the other experiments.

Condition when raffia was cut.—The following observations were made from the 28th to the 30th of August, when the raffia was cut:—

In the case of many of the grafts the raffia should have been cut earlier (two or three weeks), the raffia having prevented the proper development of the covered unions. In all these cases where the raffia had prevented the proper enlargement of the union, though the parts below and above the raffia showed good development, the scions had developed strong roots. These roots favoured in some cases an unusually heavy growth of the green parts, often as much as 2 to 3 feet. In these extreme cases when the raffia was cut and the roots of the scions removed, the thin, undeveloped union was unable to support the heavy top, and broke off at a touch of the spade or a puff of wind. In the first row worked there was a loss of about 3 per cent. from this cause. It was found before the other rows were touched, however, that this loss could be avoided by a heavy pruning-back of the green shoots. This not only lessened the weight of the top, thus preventing breaking, but diminished the evaporating surface of leaves, which was too great for the roots of the stock after those of the scion had been removed.

The raffia on many grafts (about 20 per cent.) was quite rotten, and cutting was not needed; very good unions could be observed in all these cases. In other cases the raffia did not show any sign of decaying, and was strong enough to prevent the development of good unions, and was therefore cut. The raffia of the grafts which were planted out immediately after grafting, was, contrary to all expectations, still strong, apparently because nearer to the surface and therefore drier. Undoubtedly the raffia should have been cut at least a month earlier on these.

Conditions when grafts were removed from nursery.—The following observations were made from the 26th to the

30th of December, when the grafts were taken out of the nursery:—

English grafts with scions of two eyes: 180 Zinfandel on Rupestris du Lot. Most of the unions were very well joined. The average length of the shoots was from 1 to 2½ feet; the wood was mature. The roots were well developed and grew mostly straight down to a depth of 3 feet, the fine rootlets even deeper, 4 or 5 feet; 83 grafts had made good unions, that is 46 per cent.; eleven grafts showed imperfect unions.

English grafts with scions of one eye: 180 Zinfandel on Rupestris du Lot. The difference in the development of the grafts with two eyes and with one on the scion was very slightly in favour of the first, and the shoots as well as the roots of the successful grafts looked nearly alike; 51 grafts had developed fine unions, that is 28 per cent.; twelve grafts made imperfect unions. This experiment shows clearly the advantage of using scions of two eyes for grafting, as 20 per cent. of grafts were lost by using scions with one eye only.

Champin grafts with scions of two eyes; 180 Zinfandel on Rupestris du Lot. The unions with this method of grafting did not develop so well as those of the English graft, and though the number of passable unions was 116, they were not of so perfect a character as those of the first experiment, and the number of imperfect unions was greater; the growth of the shoots was short when compared with the parallel experiment with English grafting. The root system of the stock was well developed, the main roots always going down, with the smaller rootlets mostly horizontal. The main roots had an average length of 3 to 4 feet, the shoots a length of about 2 feet. There was 64 per cent. of good unions.

Champin grafts with scions of one eye; 180 Zinfandel on Rupestris du Lot. The unions in this experiment were somewhat inferior to those of the last. A good many roots had formed; all were of smaller diameter than those mentioned above; but, like them, going straight down with an average length of 3 feet. The roots were, as a whole, less developed than those of the foregoing experiment. The quality of the unions in this case was decidedly inferior to the parallel experiment with English grafts; 58 per cent. of the grafts made sufficiently good unions.

Champin grafts with scions of two eyes and one eye, as in the last two experiments, but planted out immediately after grafting without previous callusing in sand; 360 Zinfandel on Rupestris du Lot. The unions of the grafts in this experiment were of medium quality, and an especially high amount of second-class grafts were noticed in the lot of 180 grafts with two eyes. The grafts with scions of one eye did, in this experiment, comparatively better than in other parallel experiments, as there was less difference in the percentage of unions; 28 per cent. of the grafts with two eyes left on the scions had made good unions, and 24 per cent. of the grafts with one eye, while in the first case there were found 17 per cent. of grafts with imperfect unions, and in the other only 9 per cent.

Champin grafts with scions of two eyes and one eye, as in last two experiments, but callused in straw; 360 Zinfandel on Rupestris du Lot. The unions of the grafts in this experiment were in every respect inferior to those of the grafts callused in sand, though the shoots were well developed (average length 2 feet), and the roots proportionately. There was very little difference in the general appearance of the grafts with two-eye scions and of those with the one-eye scions. The percentage of grown and well-developed grafts of the two kinds are also close together— 88 grafts grew of the first kind with two eyes, that is at the rate of 49 per cent.; and 76 grew of the second kind, that is 43 per cent. The second-class grafts with imperfect unions grew at the rate of 17 per cent. and 8 per cent. respectively.

America grafted with Zinfandel; ten-year-old roots, scions of two eyes, English graft. Only three grafts had started, and showed imperfect unions and poorly developed shoots.

Munson grafted with Zinfandel; thirteen one-year-old roots, scions of two eyes, English graft; nine of the thirteen grafts grew, that is 69 per cent. The unions were mostly good and strong. The grafts showed a strong root system, but the shoots did not show a proportionate growth.

Champini grafted with Zinfandel; ten one-year-old roots, scions of two eyes, English graft. Only a few showed growth, and the unions were very imperfect.

Elvicand grafted with Zinfandel; seven one-year-old roots, scions of two eyes, English graft. None had made a good union.

Mondeuse on Rupestris du Lot; 910 Champin graft, scions of two eyes. The unions of this kind formed better than those of Zinfandel on Rupestris du Lot; most of them were well formed and strong. The shoots were well developed, and the roots more numerous than those of the grafts of Zinfandel on Rupestris du Lot with the same kind of treatment. The water level at the time of digging was at a depth of 3 feet, so that the roots could only be followed to a depth of about 4 feet, but they undoubtedly went deeper. It was also observed here that the roots of the Rupestris du Lot penetrated the soil vertically through alternating layers of compact soil and layers of coarse but fertile sandy soil without the slightest deviation, and sent out an equal growth of secondary rootlets into all layers, except that most of the finer rootlets and roothairs were formed on the lower parts of the main roots, 3 or more feet deep; 452 grafts made first-class unions, that is a total of 54 per cent. Moreover, about 10 per cent. made unions that were more or less imperfect.

Lenoir grafted with Zinfandel; 96 English grafts, scions of two eyes. Most of the grafts had formed no roots, and only three had started growth, one of which was a strong, good graft, with long, thick roots.

American Rulander grafted with Zinfandel; 26 English grafts, scions of two eyes. The grafts were all dead.

Herbemont grafted with Zinfandel; 21 English grafts, scions of two eyes. The grafts were all dead.

Cunningham grafted with Zinfandel—27 English grafts, scions of two eyes. Two grafts showed good unions. They had a well-developed root system with thick roots, which grew horizontally at first and then straight down. Only 7 per cent. grew in all.

Riparia Gloire de Montpellier grafted with Zinfandel—100 Champin grafts, scions of two eyes. The unions were not of very good quality. The shoots were short and thin and altogether of scanty growth. The roots were mostly thin and branching, but often very long; most of the main roots did not penetrate the soil, but grew more or less horizontally, and scarcely deeper than $1\frac{1}{2}$ feet below the surface. It was noticeable that the roots of the Riparia Gloire de Montpellier followed the softer layers and streaks in the soil and lacked the penetrating power of the Rupestris St.

George. Only 15 per cent. of the grafts had made good unions, and 12 per cent. of them showed imperfect unions.

Tokay on Rupestris St. George—100 Champin grafts, scions of two eyes. The unions were nearly all good and strong. The average length of the shoots was 3 feet. The grafts showed a finely-developed root system with strong penetrating roots, which went directly down into the subsoil. The percentage of well-developed grafts was 60, which is better than the Zinfandel and Mondeuse with the same kind of treatment. There were found only 6 per cent. of imperfect grafts.

Ferrara on Rupestris St. George—100 Champin grafts, scions of two eyes. The unions of this lot were nearly always found to be well formed, and they were really the best unions in the whole plot. All the shoots were more than 2 feet long, many 3 feet, and a few even 4 feet. The root system showed the same fine development and was fully proportionate to the upper development of the grafts. 75 per cent. of the grafts made perfect unions, and 9 per cent. made imperfect unions.

Tabular Review of Grafting Experiments.

Nature of Experiments.	1st Class. Per cent.	2nd Class. Per cent.	Remarks.
Champin grafts	44	11	
English cleft grafts	37	6	Unions very complete.
Scions with two eyes	46	13	
Scions with one eye	38	7	
Grafts callused in sand	61	7	
Grafts callused in straw	46	12	Unions weak.
Grafts not callused	26	13	Growth rather short.
Zinfandel on Rupestris du Lot	64	11	Good growth.
Mondeuse on Rupestris du Lot	54	10	Good growth.
Ferrara on Rupestris du Lot	75	9	Very strong growth.
Tokay on Rupestris du Lot	60	6	Strong growth.
Rupestris du Lot as stock	64	11	
Riparia Gloire de Montpellier as stock	15	12	Small growth.
Herbemont	0	0	
Lenoir	1	2	
Cunningham	7	4	
American Rulander	0	0	
Munson, rooted vines	69	0	Good growth.
America, rooted vines	0	30	
Champini, rooted vines	0	0	
Elvicand, rooted vines	0	0	

The figures in the above table must not be taken as representing the exact relative values of the various methods and varieties compared, but taken in connexion with the following remarks they may be considered as valuable indications.

A word of explanation is perhaps necessary with regard to certain figures. The 44 per cent. of successful grafts given as the average for Champin grafts and the 37 per cent. for the English cleft grafts are somewhat low, on account of the fact that they include various experiments, some of which were comparative failures, and made only for the sake of comparison and not to attain the maximum number of good grafts.

The proportion of successful Champin grafts, as shown by the table, is slightly greater than that of the English cleft. The successful English cleft grafts, however, were considerably superior to the other in the matter of completeness and strength of the union. The lower percentage is probably due to the fact that the English cleft grafts were placed in the northerly end of the callusing sand heap, where the temperature was too low. (See page 226.)

The experiments with two-eye and one-eye scions on the whole were in favour of the use of two eyes. The additional chance of success given by two eyes, when the first eye is injured by frost or other cause, no doubt accounts for the higher percentage of success in this case. In the case of the grafts planted out immediately after grafting, the one-eye scions made on the whole the strongest growth. This seems, however, to be due to the fact that the upper eye of the two-eye scions started and broke through the sand early enough to be killed by the spring frosts, while the one-eye scions, being more deeply buried, were later in emerging and escaped the frost. This gave the latter an earlier start, and therefore a longer period of growth, for there was a check of growth and an interval of waste time in the former case between the killing of the upper bud and the starting of the lower. The remedy here, therefore, if this explanation be true, is a deeper layer of sand over the scions, and not the use of only one eye.

The difference between previously callusing the grafts in sand and planting them directly in the nursery as soon as made is very striking. Those previously callused produced 61 per cent. of good unions, while the others produced but

26 per cent. There was also a difference in the growth of the grafts in favour of those callused in sand. The grafts callused in straw were a disappointment, for, though when planted out they seemed to have callused more successfully than those in sand, they produced only 46 per cent. of sufficiently good unions, and these were weaker than those of the grafts callused in sand. The cause of this was probably the growth of moulds and wood-rot fungi around and in the unions while they were in straw.

The influence of scions of different varieties on the growth of the grafts is well shown by the four varieties tested. The Mondeuse, though quite satisfactory, gave a smaller percentage of successful grafts than any of the others. They started later than the Zinfandel, and though the growth and root system were somewhat stronger the wood was not quite so well matured. The Zinfandel did very well, giving 64 per cent. of good grafts, and making good growth. The black Ferrara, however, made almost phenomenal growth, and yielded 75 per cent. of first-class unions. The growth of the Tokay was almost equal to that of the Ferrara, but the number of successful grafts rather less—60 per cent. Fig. 179 shows an average Zinfandel graft upon Rupestris St. George in comparison with an average Tokay upon the same stock. It will be noticed that the larger growth of top is accompanied by a corresponding development of the root system. This dispels the doubt that our very heavy growing varieties, especially table and shipping grapes, would succeed upon resistant vines, at least as regards Rupestris du Lot.

The greater adaptability of Rupestris du Lot for bench-grafting than of Riparia Gloire de Montpellier is well shown in these experiments. Where the Rupestris du Lot gave 64 per cent. of first-class grafts, the Riparia Gloire de Montpellier gave only 15 per cent. This is due in great measure to the difference in texture in the wood of the two species. The Rupestris has thick firm wood, with short joints and small pith, while the wood of the Riparia is softer, more pithy, and longer jointed. In consequence of this difference, it is much easier to make a well-fitting firm union with the Rupestris than with the Riparia. It would appear from this experiment that grafting in the vineyard when the Riparia is two or three years old would be the best method for varieties of this species.

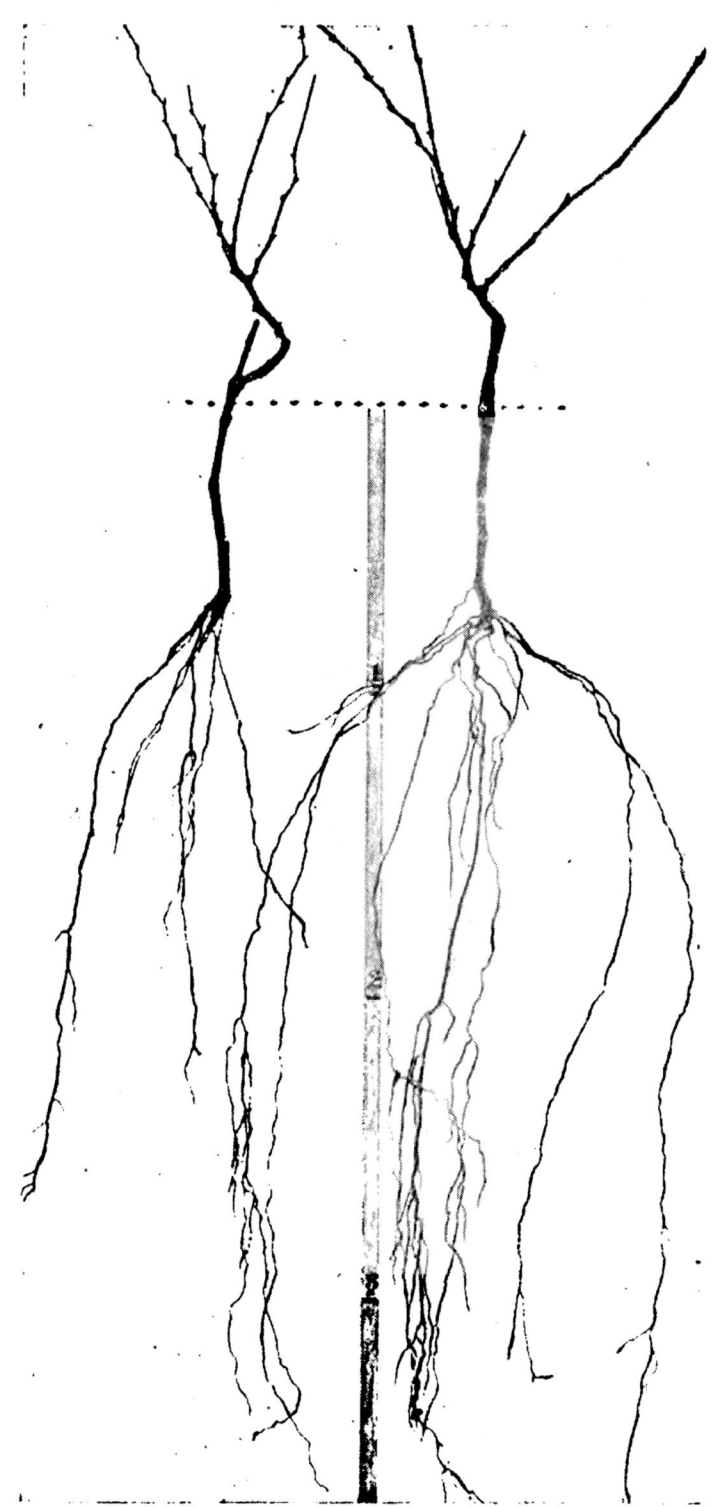

Fig 179.—Vine on left, an average graft of Zinfandel on Rupestris du Lot;
Vine on right, an average graft of Flame Tokay on Rupestris du Lot.

Of the other stock tested, including Lenoir, it is plain, with the possible exception of Munson, that they are unadapted to this method of grafting. This is to a great extent due to the difficulty of making roots with many of these varieties, and their consequent failure to properly feed the scion. The Munson not only gave a high percentage of first-class grafts, but the unions were particularly good. As this variety's resistance to phylloxera has not been thoroughly tested, however, this success in grafting must not be construed as a proof of its utility as a resistant stock.

The effect of failing to cut the raffia or other binding material early enough in the season is well shown by the middle graft of Fig. 180. The graft, as can be seen, had

Fig. 180.—Effect of Black-Knot and of failure to cut the Raffia.

made a perfect union, but the raffia had been imperfectly removed, one or two turns having been left uncut. This is of course an unusual case, as when the raffia is cut in one place it is usually loosened completely. The same thing occurs, however, when the raffia is not cut at all except that the constricted part is longer, as is the case with the two outer vines. The swelling of the vine above the constriction is due to the difficulty which the food, elaborated by the leaves, finds in passing the part where the bark is compressed by the raffia. The large swellings on the two outer vines below the raffia are due to another cause. They are doubtless indicative of disease, and resemble very closely the black-knot which attacks older vines, especially in wet soils. The nature of this disease is not well understood, but as it usually accompanies an excess of water in the soil it was doubtless due in this case to heavy rains in late spring after the grafts were planted.

The accumulation of food material above a constriction of the bark and the consequent starvation of the lower part and root system are similar to what occurs when a vine is girdled. Fig. 181 shows an excellent example of this. The vine represented is a Rupestris St. George in the spring after the year it was planted. The first year it made an excellent growth, as evidenced by the roots on the lower part. In the spring of the following year, however, the growth, though at first vigorous, soon stopped and the leaves became yellow. On digging up the vine it represented the appearance shown in the figure. The upper part of the vine had grown to twice the thickness of the previous year down to a point about 4 or 5 inches below the surface. Below this point there was no growth at all, and although the roots were still alive they were no larger than the year before. A closer examination revealed the fact that at the point where the change took place the vine had been completely girdled by wire-worms, which had eaten off the bark for about half-an-inch.

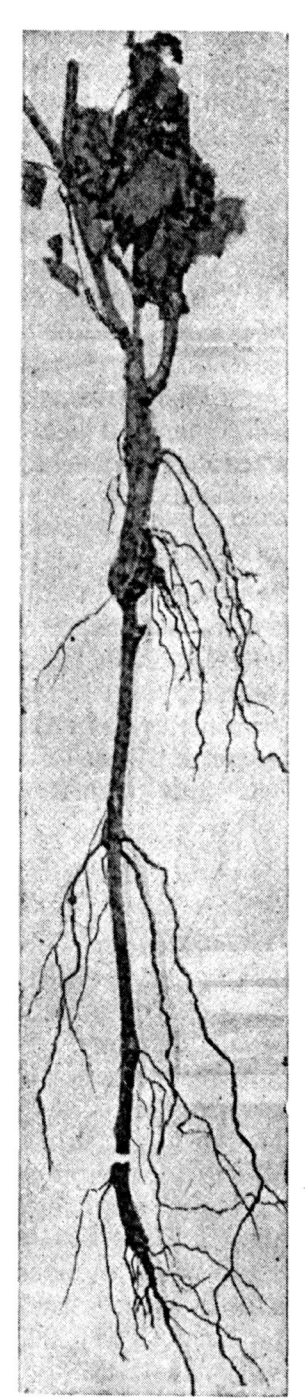

Fig. 181.— Effect of Wire-Worms on Young Vine.

It is unusual for wire-worms to attack such plants as the vine, but the explanation is quickly found. The land in which these Rupestris St. George cuttings were planted had been in grass and hay for several years before, and the roots of grasses being a favorite food for wire-worms they had increased to large numbers. In the spring of the year in which the vines were attacked the land was so thoroughly and carefully cultivated that not a weed was left for the many wire-worms still left in the ground. For this reason they were obliged to attack the only living vegetable substance present. Vines injured as badly as that in the figure died, but the rest were saved by simply digging round each vine and destroying the wire-worms which were congregated near each vine at about the same distance from the surface.

The effect of neglecting to cut the roots which are sent out by the scions is shown in Fig. 182. In the vines shown there the union was good and the top vigorous, but owing to the fact that the roots of the scion were allowed to grow the stock failed to develop. The descending food, which is necessary to the growth of the roots, entered the roots of the scion more easily than it could traverse the irregular and abnormal tissue of the union. Thus there was left a Vinifera on its own roots with the resistant stock starved and killed.

COMPARATIVE EXPERIMENTS IN ROOTING CUTTINGS OF RESISTANT STOCKS.

Rupestris du Lot.—580 cuttings were planted out in the nursery on 18th April, 1899. Most of those cuttings were the thin tips which could not be grafted on account of their small diameter. No attention beyond the ploughing and cultivation given to the vineyard was given them during the growing period, except that they received one irrigation and one hoeing in June. The roots were nine months old when taken from the nursery. The average length of growth of the shoot was 2 feet, usually several were formed on a single plant. The root system was well developed, and from four to six main roots could be counted in most cases on one vine. All the roots were long, strong, and tough, and grew to a depth of 3 to 5 feet; 480 cuttings had made good rooted vines, that is 83 per cent. of the cuttings planted.

Riparia Gloire de Montpellier.—40 cuttings were planted and received the same care as the cuttings of the Rupestris du Lot. The vines showed scanty growth when taken out of the soil. The average length of the shoots was from 1 to 2 feet, but only a few developed on each vine. The root

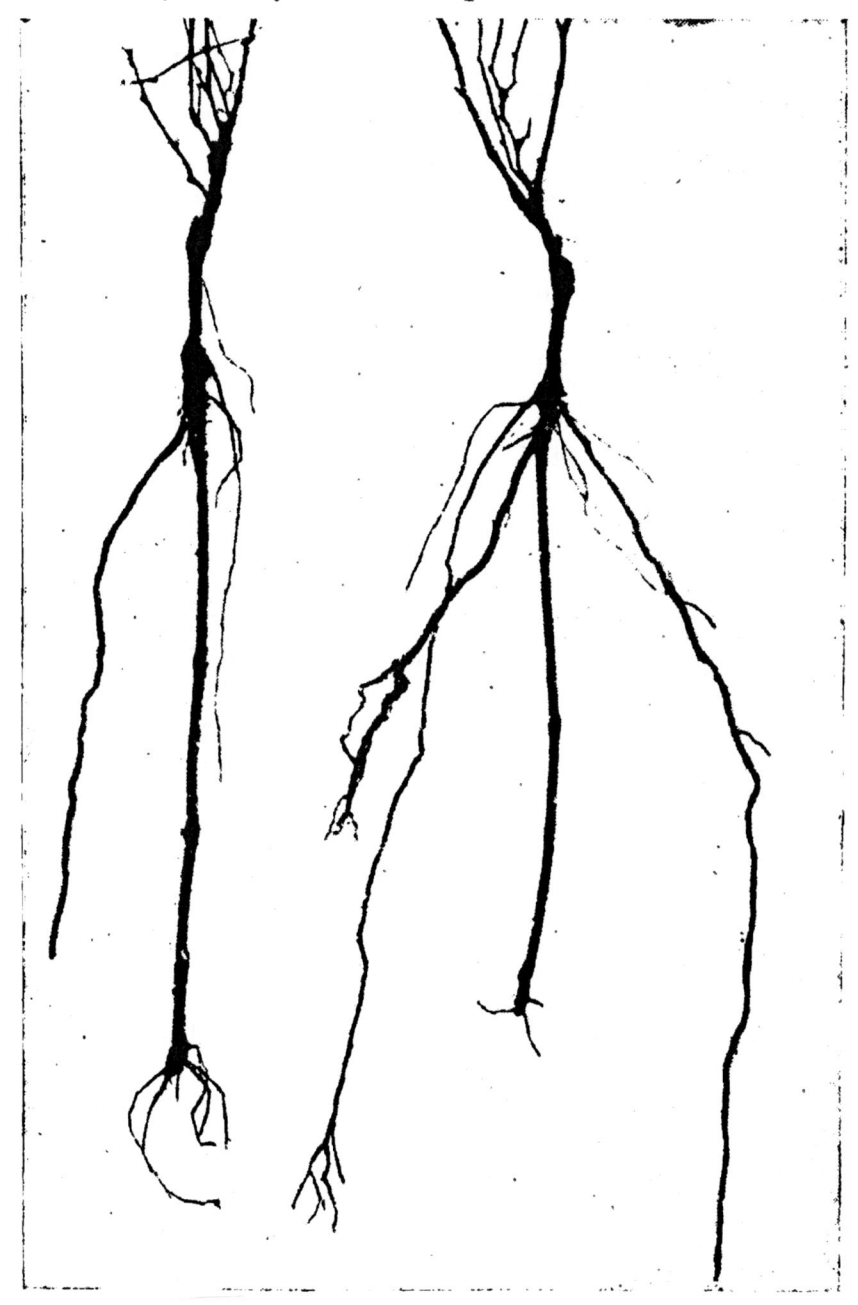

Fig. 182.—Effect of Failing to Cut Off the Roots of the Scion.

system was entirely different from that of the Rupestris St. George. Very few of the main roots went down to the moist regions of the soil; most of the main roots were superficial, growing about 1 foot below the surface, and sending out small rootlets. The roots were not strong, but rather brittle, and broke easily; 32 cuttings out of 40 were well rooted, that is 80 per cent.

Solonis.—45 cuttings were planted in the spring, and were treated like the preceding. The following observations were made on the vines when taken out in the winter:—The shoots were thin and of an average length of 2 feet. The roots were well developed and grew down to the moist depths, although not so straight as the roots of the Rupestris St. George. The small rootlets and root hairs were only formed at the end of roots 3 to 4 feet deep in the soil. The main roots were thicker than those of Rupestris St. George and Riparia Gloire de Montpellier.

The difference in character of the root systems of Rupestris, Riparia, and Solonis is well shown by Fig. 183. These are average specimens of the vines rooted at the St. Helena plot in 1899. The tendency of the Riparia to send out horizontal or even slightly rising roots is illustrated. In extreme cases the roots were found to start toward the surface at an angle of about 45°, and after rising in this way for several inches to become horizontal. About two-thirds of the roots took this horizontal direction, and the remainder went down at various angles, some being nearly vertical.

The cause of the failure of the Riparia in the upper part of the Napa Valley is evidently to be found here. The heat and continual drought of summer penetrates to these horizontal roots, destroy the root hairs, and deprive the vine of water exactly at the time it is most needed. The more deeply penetrating roots are too weak, and too few to supply the amount of water needed by the evaporating leaf surface. This lack of adjustment of the supply of water to the demand is increased when the Riparia is grafted with strong growing Vinifera varieties. This is evidenced by the many grafted vines which die in their second or third year.

The deeply-penetrating roots of the Rupestris shown in the figure explain the resistance of this species to drought. All the roots of this young vine penetrated deeply into the soil in a direction more or less approaching the vertical. As

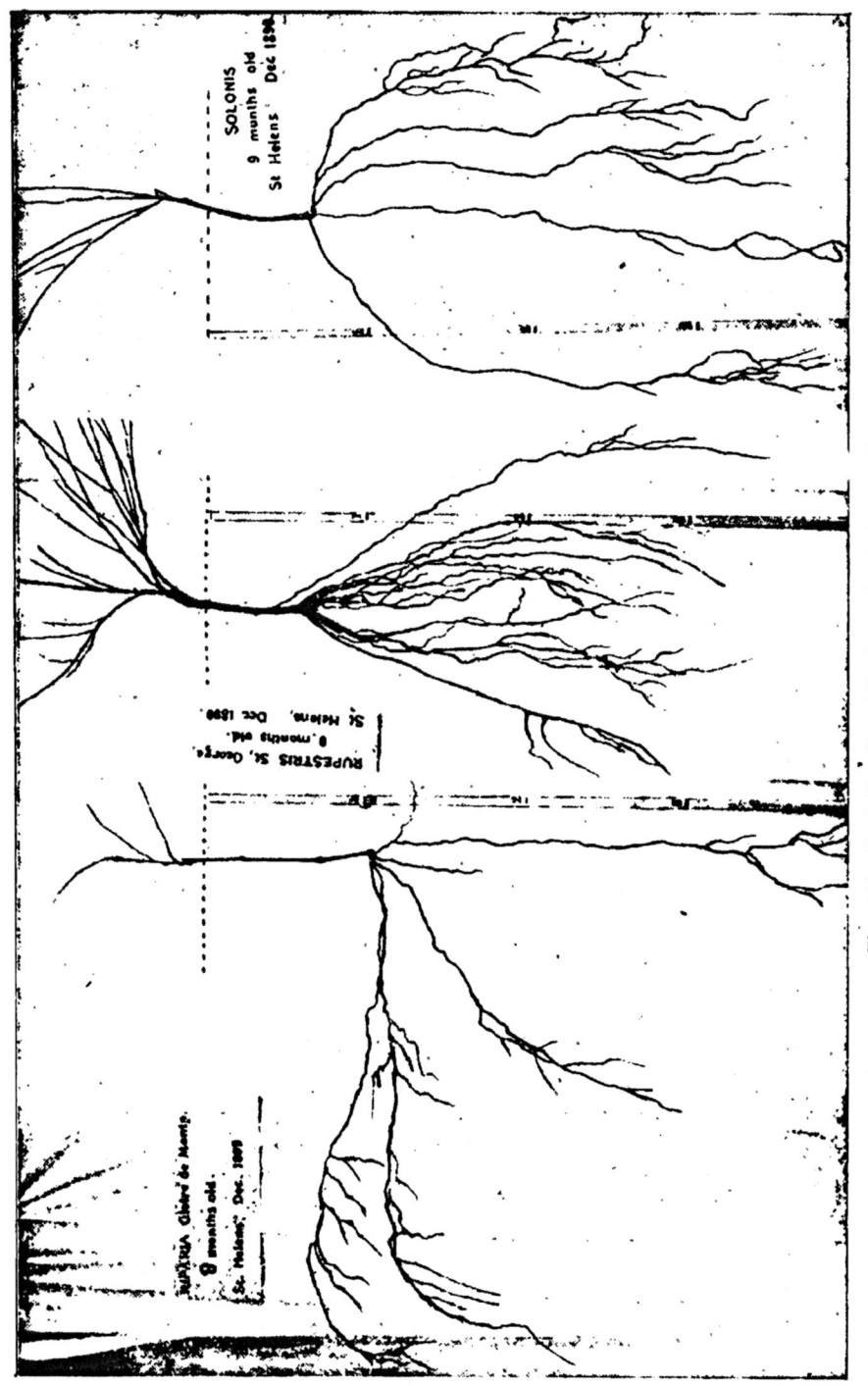

Fig. 183.—Root Growths of Resistant Stock Compared.

the vine grows older, as we have found by the examination of three-year-old Rupestris St. George vines, secondary roots are sent out in a direction more approaching the horizontal. These utilize the upper layers of soil, but as they constitute but a small part of the whole root system and injury to them is not severely felt by the vine.

An injury to the lower roots, however, is more injurious to the Rupestris. This explains the unsuitableness of this species for badly-drained soils, and for soils where the water level is high for a long time in winter and spring, and especially for those irrigated districts where the water level rises during the growing period of spring and summer. The standing water causes the root hairs on the main part of the root system to decay, and deprived thus of its only means of obtaining water the Rupestris dies of drought as truly as does the Riparia when the main part of its rootlets and root hairs are destroyed by the heat and dryness of summer.

The strong sturdy growth of the Rupestris du Lot, as compared with the comparatively slender growth of what seems to be the best of the Riparias, is also well shown by the figures. This makes the Rupestris du Lot particularly valuable as a stock for our heavy-growing varieties of Vinifera. This heavy growth of the grafts on Rupestris du Lot has been found in France to have a tendency to make them bear poorly and "go to wood." This, however, may be considered a good fault, as it is easily counteracted by more generous pruning, by leaving a larger number of buds, and thus by diverting the whole vigour of the vine into a larger number of shoots, decreasing the vigour of each and increasing their fertility. Some grape-growers, especially in the South of France, report enormous crops on vines grafted on Rupestris St. George.

Following are descriptions of the three varieties of resistant stock which at present give the most promise of being adapted to California. The leaves of the three varieties are shown on the title page.

Riparia Gloire de Montpellier.—(Synonyms—Riparia Portalis, Riparia Michel, Riparia Saporta.)—This is one of the most vigorous of all the varieties of Riparia, and is equalled only by the Riparia Grand Glabre and the Scribner Riparia. The stem or trunk is thick; canes spreading, long, with elongated internodes of medium thickness, slightly bent at the nodes (giving the canes a faint zigzag appearance), of a light nut colour, smooth, rather shining, and a little pruinose near the eyes when the wood is well ripened; young shoots of a light purple; leaves large to very large, thick, elongated, somewhat bulging between the main nerves, dark green and shining on the upper surface, lighter green on the under side, with a few stiff hairs on the ribs; the petiolar sinus is open, U-shaped; the upper lobes are well marked by large elongated teeth, the lower barely marked at all; the teeth are sharply pointed and in two series (see figure on title page); the roots are slender and spreading like all varieties of Riparia (see Fig. 183). Resistance to phylloxera, 18.

Rupestris du Lot.—(Synonyms—Rupestris St. George, Rupestris Phénomène, Rupestris Sijas, Rupestris Monticola, Rupestris St. George érigé, Rupestris Lacastelle, Rupestris Colineau, Rupestris Reich, Rupestris Richter.)—This variety is extremely vigorous and produces a very strong thick stem; canes erect (the main laterals spreading), with short internodes and prominent nodes; leaves small, wider than long, with metallic sheen, undulating edges, and relatively thin, those of the laterals often very small and somewhat bronzed at the tips. In hot weather the leaves fold in two at the mid-rib, but less than most varieties of Rupestris. The roots are long and strong, and not so slender as those of other varieties of Rupestris. Resistance to phylloxera, 16.

Solonis.—A vigorous strong grower; canes spreading, with patches of whitish hairs, which become light brownish grey in autumn; leaves of medium size, upper lobes marked by very long teeth, lower lobes lacking; teeth very long acuminate, in two series; petiolar sinus widely open. The leaves are covered with white web-like hairs when young, becoming almost glabrous when old, except on the ribs and petiole; roots strong and intermediate in direction between those of Riparia and Rupestris (see Fig. 183). Resistance to phylloxera, 14.

SUMMARY.

1. Every grape-grower should insure against phylloxera by testing the most promising resistant vines on his own place, and by learning the methods of bench-grafting.

2. It is unsafe to attempt operations on a large scale with cuttings imported from abroad, on account of the danger of injury to such cuttings on the journey.

3. A cutting graft of suitable varieties makes as large and vigorous growth as a simple cutting, so that by the method of bench-grafting no time is lost in establishing a resistant vineyard.

4. Resistant varieties which are difficult to root but easy to graft when old, such as Lenoir, should not be bench-grafted.

5. Care in callusing, planting, and treatment in nursery, and especially in keeping the grafts moist from the time they are made till they are in the callusing bed, will enable even an inexperienced grafter to obtain at least 60 per cent. of good grafted plants.

6. The bluestone should be washed off the outside of the raffia before tying, or it will injure the bark of the graft.

7. Callusing in sand insures more perfect unions and a larger percentage of successful grafts than planting directly in the nursery.

8. The moisture in the callusing bed should not be excessive and the temperature should be relatively warm.

9. The growing grafts should be watched closely, in order to see that the roots of the scions are removed before they become large, and that the raffia is cut before it strangles the graft.

10. The English cleft graft is preferable to the Champin graft, because it gives more perfect unions and can be made with more accuracy and rapidity.

11. Scions of two eyes are preferable to those of one eye, as they give more chances of success.

12. Rupestris St. George seems to be remarkably adapted to California soils (except the heaviest clays) and conditions, and is to be preferred to any variety yet tested here whenever deep penetration of roots is possible and desirable.

13. All the eyes of the Rupestris stock should be cut out deeply and carefully.

14. A vigorous and large growing Vinifera scion promotes an equally vigorous and large growth of Rupestris St. George used as stock.

NUMBER OF VINE SEEDS CONTAINED IN 1 POUND.

Jacquez	...	15,545	Solonis	...	...	8,300
Herbemont	...	18,600	Taylor	...	...	16,000
Cunningham	...	14,545	V. Californica	...	8,910
Wild Riparia		25,820	V. Berlandieri	...	12,000

Summary of the Life History of Phylloxera.

(By R. Dubois.)

The *phylloxera vastatrix* is seen under different forms—some above ground, others under ground. These are—1st, *apterous agamous* (above and under ground); 2nd, *nympha* (under ground); 3rd, *winged agamous* (above ground) and *sexed* (above ground). These different forms proceed from a common origin.

1st. APTEROUS AGAMOUS.

The Apterous agamous forms are hatched from the egg of the *sexed*. They usually appear in the Mediterranean climate in April. They are easily recognised by their rapid movements, and their pale-yellow, rather grey colour, the length of their legs and antennæ, and the rigid hair covering these organs. They crawl on the shoots or travel down on the roots in the soil, according to more or less favorable conditions of the atmosphere.

(*a*) *Gallicole life.*—In the first case the insect punctuates the parenchyma of the young leaves, herbaceous tender shoots, and even tendrils, producing *galls*, in which it fixes itself and constitutes, after three successive moultings, a *laying mother*. It then becomes swollen and more voluminous, laying a large number of eggs (*pseudova*) in the pouch thus formed. These eggs hatch after a very short period. The youngs of this second generation crawl in turn on to the top leaves, forming new galls, or travel down on the roots, as the case may be. The multiplication of this gallicole form may continue until the fall of the leaves if circumstances are favorable.

(*b*) *Radicole life.*—The insects penetrating underground fix themselves on the roots, and may be divided into two groups—those which, like the gallicole, pass after a series of three moultings to the state of *laying mothers*, and those which after five moultings reach the state of *nymphæ*.

1st. *Laying mothers* very similar to those above ground, lay, without being fecundated, from 25 to 30 pseudova, at the rate of two to three for four or five days, after which they die. The *pseudova*, hatched eight to ten days after, give birth to young, which may come out of the ground through the natural crevices of the soil, and, carried by the wind, may fix themselves on other roots. This new generation passes through the same phases as the preceding, and the multiplication continues until the end of October or the beginning of November.

At that time the laying mothers die, the young ones, recently hatched, spend the winter under the roots in a state of complete torpor. They then assume a brown colour, and become very attenuated. In April the hybernating insect continues the series of agamous generations, and this mode of multiplication may last four years at least.

2nd. *The apterous which do not become laying mothers* reach, as we have seen, the state of nympha, after five moultings, in July.

2ND. NYMPHÆ.

The nymphæ have a longer body and a browner colour, and are provided with two winged sheaths of darker colour. After a fortnight the *nymphæ* come out of the ground, and become *winged* after the last moulting.

3RD. WINGED AGAMOUS.

The winged insect resembles a very small fly. It has a long, yellow body, provided with four transparent wings longer than the body and unequal in size, the two upper wings being longer. The winged insect flies, and may be carried by wind to a great distance. It is undoubtedly the principal agent of propagation of the disease to great distances. It stops under the leaves, and lays, without fecundation, from three to six *pseudova*, some being large, others small, from which the sexed are born.

4TH. SEXED.

The *females* are hatched from the large *pseudova* and the *males* from the small. These insects are apterous, without beaks or organ of digestion. The female lays one egg, from which are hatched in the following spring new generations of apterous agamous, which we studied previously.

This egg, which is called *winter egg*, because it remains under the bark of two-year-old wood (just below the spur of the year) during the whole winter without hatching, was proved by V. Mayet as generally found on stumps which have carried galls many years running.

We condense in the following table the biological cycle of phylloxera :—

LIFE HISTORY OF PHYLLOXERA.

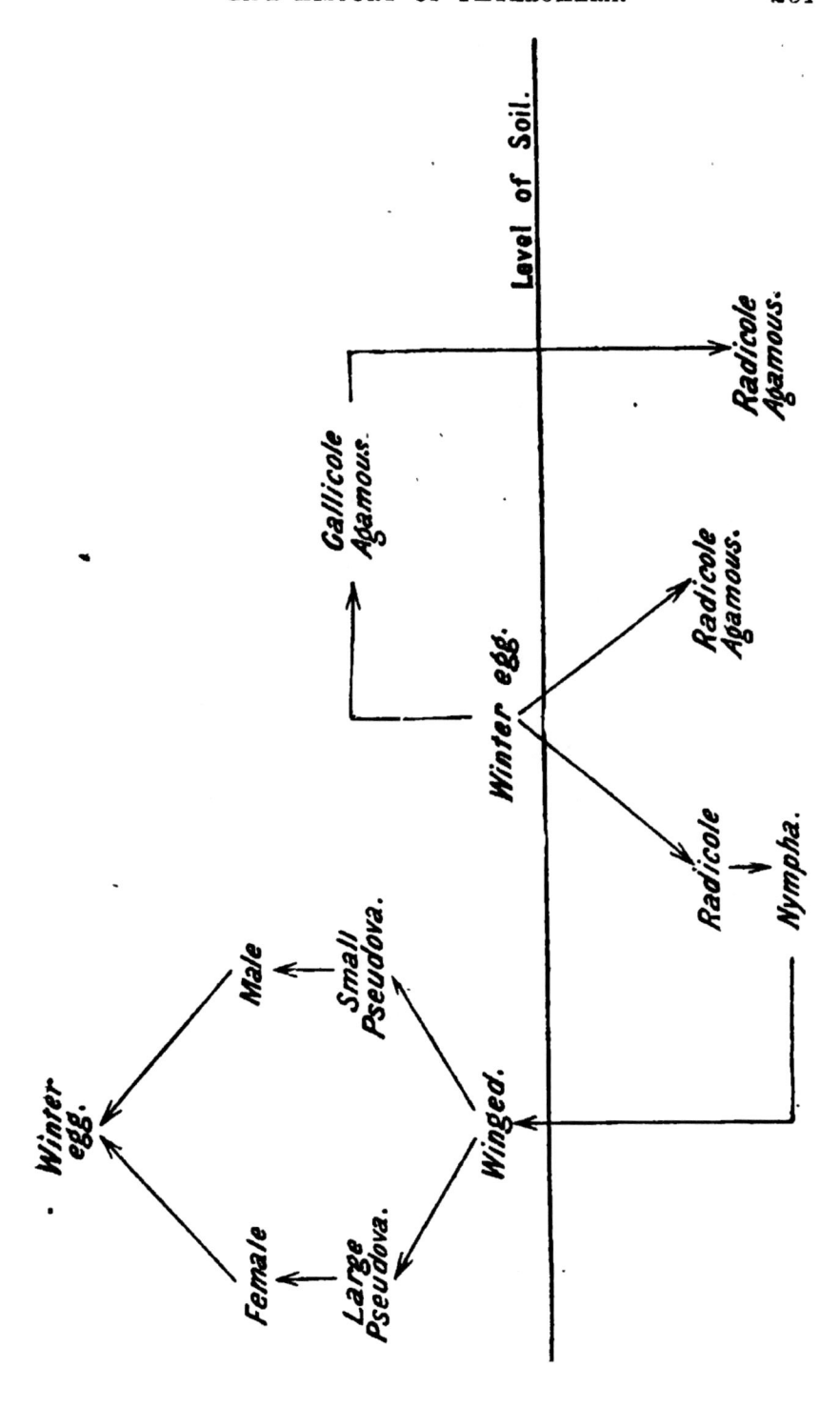

251

GLOSSARY OF THE PRINCIPAL SCIENTIFIC TERMS USED IN THE PRESENT VOLUME.*

ABNORMAL—Contrary to the general rule.
ABORTIVE—An organ or flower is said to be abortive when its development has been arrested at a very early stage.
ACUMINATE, leaf (Bot.)—Ending in a sharp point.
ADAPTABILITY—The quality of being capable of adaptation.
ADAPTATION—When speaking of a plant, that act or process of adapting itself to certain conditions of the surroundings.
ALLUVIAL (Geol.)—Composed of alluvium ; relating to the deposits made by flowing waters, washed away from one place and deposited in another, as alluvial soil.
ALPINE DILUVIUM (Geol.)—A deposit of superficial loam, sand, gravel, stone, &c., caused by former action of flowing waters, or the melting of glacial ice in the Alp ranges, South of France.
AMPELOPSIS (Bot.)—A family of plants closely related to Vitis, commonly called Virginian creepers.
ANALOGOUS—See Analogy.
ANALOGY—That resemblance of structure which depends upon similarity of relations. Such structures are said to be analogous or analogues to each other.
ANASTOMOSIS—Intercommunication between two or more vessels.
ANTHERS (Bot.)—The summits of the stamens of flowers in which the pollen or fertilizing dust is produced.
APEX (Bot.)—The tip, top, point, or summit of a leaf or stem.
ARANEOUS (Bot.)—Cobweblike ; extremely thin and delicate down on vine leaves.
AREOLAR—Filled with interstices or small spaces, as between the fibres composing organs or vessels of plants.
ASYMETRICAL—Having the two sides unlike.
ATAVISM—See Reversion.
ATROPINE—A white crystallizable poison, extracted from different plants, remarkable for its power of dilating the pupil of the eye.
AUTOFECUNDATION—Self-impregnation.
BATHONIAN—Applied to rocks belonging to a certain division of the Jurassic age. The term refers to the age of the rocks alone, and not to their character or composition.
BIFURCATION—A forking or division into two branches.
BINARY HYBRID—Hybrid resulting from the crossing of two cépages only.
BLOOM—When speaking of fruit, the delicate powdery external coating, as on grapes.
BOLTED SULPHUR—Roll sulphur, sifted by means of a bolter, and reduced to a fine powder.
CALCAREOUS—Partaking of the nature of limestone.
CALYX—The outer covering of a flower.
CAMBIUM (Bot.)—A series of formative cells lying outside the wood proper and inside of the inner bark ; the growth of the new wood takes place in the Cambium, which is very soft.

---

* This glossary has been given because several viticulturists have complained that some of the terms used in previous publications were unintelligible to them. (Trans.

CAMBRIAN FORMATION (Geol.)—A series of very ancient palæozoic rocks, between the Laurentian and Silurian, until recently regarded as the oldest fossiliferous rocks. It is named from its occurrence in Cambria, or Wales.

CARBONATE OF LIME—Limestone.

CARBONIC ACID GAS—This term is generally applied to a compound of carbon and oxygen, more correctly called carbon dioxide.

CARBONIFEROUS FORMATION (Geol.)—A series of rocks, including sandstone, shales, limestone, and conglomerates with beds of coal, which make up the strata of the carboniferous age.

CARTILAGINOUS or CARTILAGINEOUS.—Firm and tough, like cartilage.

CELL (Biol.)—One of the minute elementary structures of which the greater part of the various tissues and organs of plants is composed.

CEPAGE (French).—Has no equivalent in English. Any vine when under cultivation.

CHALAZE or CHALAZA (Bot.)—The place on the seed where the outer coats cohere with each other and the nucleus.

CHALAZIC DEPRESSION (Bot.)—Natural depression in a seed formed by the chalaze.

CHLOROSIS (Bot.)—A disease in plants causing the leaves to lose their normal green colour and turn yellow.

CILIA, sing. CILIUM (Bot.)—Small microscopic vibrating appendages found on some vegetable organisms.

COLLOID NATURE—Of the nature of glue or gum.

CONCAVE—Said of the interior of a curved surface.

CONCRETION (Geol.)—Rounded mass or nodule produced by the aggregation of the material round a centre, as, the calcareous concretions common in beds of clay.

CONGLOMERATE (Geol.)—A bed of fragments of rock, or pebbles, cemented together by other material.

CONICALLY—Having the general shape of a geometrical cone, round, and tapering to a point, or gradually decreasing in circumference.

CONVEX—Said of the outside of a curved surface in opposition to concave.

CORALLIAN (Geol.)—A deposit of coralliferous limestone forming a portion of the middle division of the oolite.

CORDIFORM or CORDATE—Having the general shape of a heart, as a cordiform leaf.

COROLLA—The second envelope of a flower usually composed of coloured leaf-like organs (petals) and may be united by their edges in the top part, as in vine flowers.

CORONA OF THE STIGMA—Crown-like appendage at the top of the stigma.

CRETACEOUS FORMATION (Geol.)—The series of strata of various kinds containing beds of chalk, green sand, also called chalk formation.

CRYPTOGAM (Bot.)—Plants belonging to the series or division of flowerless plants, propagated by spores, and generally living as parasites on other plants. A fungus is a cryptogam.

CRYPTOGAMIC DISEASE—An alteration in the state or the function of a plant, caused by a cryptogam such as mildew, black rot, &c.

CUPRIC.—Containing copper.

CUTICLE OF A VINE LEAF—The outermost skin of the leaf.

DEFOLIATION—The falling or shedding of the leaves.

DESICCATION—The state of being dried up or deprived of moisture.

DEVONIAN FORMATION (Geol.)—A series of Palæozoic rocks, including the old red sandstone.

DIAPHRAGM (Bot.)—Partition of wood separating the pith of two internodes in a vine cane.

DILUVIUM—See Alpine Diluvium.

DISCOID—Having a circular structure like the berries of certain vines.

ELONGATED or ELONGATE—Drawn out in length, as an elongated leaf.
EMARGINATE (Bot.)—When speaking of a leaf, means that, in entire leaves, the limb becomes narrow suddenly below the two teeth forming the two lateral lobes.
ENTIRE (Bot.)—When speaking of a leaf, means one consisting of a single piece, having a continuous edge without any lobes.
EOCENE (Geol.)—The earliest of the three divisions of the Tertiary epoch of geologists. Rocks of this age contain shells.
EXCISION—The act of cutting out or cutting off.
EXCORIATED—When speaking of bark, means that detaching in strips.
EXFOLIATING—When speaking of bark, that separating from the trunk and coming off in long pieces.
FECUND—Fruitful; prolific.
FERTILITY—The state of being fruitful or producing offspring.
FIBRO-VASCULAR BUNDLES—Vegetable tissue composed partly of sap tubes.
FILAMENT (Bot.)—The thread-like part of the stamen supporting the anther.
FILIFORM—Having the shape of a thread or filament.
FLORESCENCE (Bot.)—The bursting into flower or blossoming.
FLUTED TRUNK—Trunk with natural grooves situated lengthwise.
FOSSILIFEROUS (Geol.)—Containing fossils.
FRUCTIFEROUS (Bot.)—Bearing or producing fruit.
FRUCTIVITY (Bot.)—The quality of bearing fruit.
FUNGI, sing. FUNGUS (Bot.)—A class of cellular and flowerless plants belonging to the cryptogams.
FUSION OF CHARACTERS—When speaking of a hybrid, means that the characters of both parents are united in the offspring.
GALL, of phylloxera—An excrescence produced on the leaves of American vines by one of the wingless forms of phylloxera.
GARIGUES SOILS—Red, siliceous, dry loam, covering the rock formation of certain hills in the South of France.
GLABROUS—Smooth, having a surface without hairs.
GLAND—An organ which secretes some peculiar product from the sap of plants.
GLAUCOUS—Of a sea-green colour; of a dull green passing into greyish-blue.
GLOBULAR—Having the form of a ball or sphere.
GOFFERED or GAUFFERED—Crimped like the leaves of some vines.
GRANITE—A rock consisting essentially of crystals of felspar and mica in mass of quartz.
GROIES (French)—Applies to certain calcareous soils of the Charante district.
HERBACEOUS—Having the nature, texture, or characteristics of a herb; a shoot in a green state.
HERMAPHRODITE—Possessing the organs of both sexes.
HONEYCOMB STRUCTURE—When speaking of vine leaves, a symmetrically uneven, wrinkly, or goffered surface. See Goffered.
HUMID—Containing sensible moisture; damp; moist.
HUMIDITY—Moisture; dampness; a moderate degree of wetness perceptible to the eye or touch.
HUMIFEROUS—Containing humus.
HUMUS—That portion of the soil formed by the decomposition of animal or vegetable matter. It is a valuable constituent of soil.
HYBERNATE or HIBERNATE—To pass the winter in close quarters, in a torpid or dormant state, as phylloxera.
HYBRID—The offspring of the union of two different species.
HYBRIDIZATION—The act of hybridizing.

GLOSSARY.

HYBRIDIZE—To produce a crossing between two species.
HYPHAE—The long branching filaments of which the mycelium of a fungus is formed.
IMBIBITION—The act of absorbing.
INDENTATION—A notch or recess in the margin of a leaf.
INDENTED—Notched along the margin; cut on the edge into points, like teeth.
INFLORESCENCE—The mode of arrangement of the flowers of plants.
INTERNODE—The space between two nodes or points of the stem from which the leaves properly arise.
INTERSTICES—Spaces between closely set soils or rocks.
INTRINSIC—Real, inherent, not merely apparent or accidental.
INULIN—A substance found dissolved in the sap of the roots of many Composite and other plants. It is intermediate in nature between starch and sugar.
JURASSIC (Geol.)—Of the age of the middle Mesozoic, named from certain rocks in the Jura mountains.
JUXTAPOSITION—Being placed side by side with opposite parts corresponding.
KNIT—United; joined, so as to grow together. Used as a noun, means the parts joined together; the union.
LACUSTRINE DEPOSITS (Geol.)—The deposits which have been accumulated in fresh water areas.
LAMINATED STRATA (Geol.)—Divided into thin layers.
LANCEOLATE LEAF—Rather narrow, tapering to a point at the apex.
LANCINATED—Torn; lacerated.
LANIGEROUS—Bearing woolly hair.
LANUGINOUS—Covered with down.
LENTICLES (Bot.)—Small, oval, or rounded spots upon the stem or branches of a plant. Small lens-shaped glands on the under face of some leaves.
LESION—Change in the texture of a vegetable organ resulting from an injury.
LIBER—The inner bark of plants, lying next to the wood.
LIGNEOUS (Bot.)—Of the nature of, or resembling wood.
LIGNIFICATION (Bot.)—Change in the character of an herbaceous shoot by which it becomes harder or woody.
LIGNIFIED (Bot.)—Converted into wood or into ligneous substance.
LIMB, of a leaf (Bot.)—The flat part of the leaf of any plant.
LITTORAL—Bordering the seashore
LOAM—A soil formed of a mixture of clay and sand with organic matter, to which its fertility is chiefly due.
LOBATED or LOBATE (Bot.)—Having lobes.
LOBE—A rounded projection or division of a leaf.
MARGIN, of a leaf—The outer edge or border.
MARL—A mixed soil, consisting of carbonate of lime, clay, and sand in very variable proportions, and accordingly designated as calcareous, clayey, or sandy.
MEDULLARY RAYS (Bot.)—The rays of cellular tissues seen in a transverse section of exogenous wood, which run from the pith to the bark.
METIS—The offspring of the union of two varieties of the same species.
METIZATION—The act of producing a crossing between two varieties of the same species.
MIOCENE (Geol.)—Middle division of the tertiary.
MORPHOLOGY—The law of form or structure, independent of function.
MUCRO (Bot.)—A minute, abrupt point of a leaf.
MYCELIUM (Bot.)—The white threads or filamentous growth from which a mushroom or fungus is developed; the so-called mushroom spawn.

NITROGEN—A colourless gas composing four-fifths of the atmosphere by volume. It is incapable of supporting life, but forms many important compounds, as ammonia, nitric acid, &c., and is a constituent of all organized living tissues, animal or vegetable.

NODE (Bot.)—The joint of a stem, or the part where the leaf is inserted.

NODOSITIES—Small swellings produced on vine roots by phylloxera.

NODULE—A round mass of irregular shape.

NORMAL—According to an established rule. (Geom.) Perpendicular to a surface or forming a right angle with it.

NUCLEUS (Bot.)—A whole seed, as contained within the seed coats.

NUTRITION—A process or series of processes by which the living organism is maintained in its normal conditions of life and growth

NUTRITIVE MATTERS—Matters having the quality of nourishing.

OBTUSE—Not pointed or acute ; blunt.

OCHEROUS SOILS—Containing an impure earthy ore of iron, or a ferruginous clay. Such soils are usually red or yellow.

OOLITIC—A great series of secondary rocks, so called from the texture of some of its members, which appear to be made up of small egg-like calcareous bodies.

OOSPORE (Bot.)—A special kind of spore resulting from the fertilization of of an oosphere by antherozoids.

OPERCULUM—Any lid-shaped structure in a leaf or flower.

ORBICULAR—Having a spherical form.

OVA, sing. OVUM (Bot.)—Eggs.

OVATE (Bot.)—Having the shape of an egg, that is to say, an oval border at the base.

OVOID (Bot.)—Resembling an egg in shape.

OVULE, of plants—The seed in the earliest condition.

OXFORDIAN (Geol.)—Applied to rocks of a certain age in the Jurassic series.

PARABOLA—A kind of geometrical curve ; one of the conic sections formed by the intersection of the surface of a cone with a plane parallel to one of its sides.

PARASITE (Bot.)—A plant living upon or in another plant.

PARENCHYMA (Bot.)—The soft cellular substance of the tissues of plants, like the pulp of leaves.

PEDICLE or PEDICEL (Bot)—A stalk which supports one flower or fruit. One of the many divisions of a peduncle.

PEDUNCLE (Bot.)—The stem or stalk which supports a cluster of flowers or fruits.

PENTAGONAL LEAF—Having five sides.

PERMEABILITY—The quality or state of being passed through.

PETALS (Bot.)—The leaves of the corolla, a second circle of organs in a flower.

PETIOLAR SINUS—Depression between two adjoining lobes into which the petiole is inserted.

PETIOLE—A leaf stalk ; the stalk connecting the stem with the blade or limb.

PHYSIOLOGICAL—Relating to the science of the functions of living organisms.

PHYSIOLOGY—Study dealing with vegetable or animal life,

PINCHING (Hort.)—Operation consisting in cutting about one inch off the extremity of young shoots a little before or directly after florescence.

PISTIL (Bot.)—The female organs of a flower, which occupy a position in the centre of other floral organs. The pistil is generally divisible into the *ovary*, the *style*, and the *stigma*.

PITH (Bot.)—The soft, spongy substance in the centre of the stem of many plants.

PLANE or PLAIN—A flat, level, smooth, even surface.

PLASTICITY—Retaining any impressed form or shape.
POLLEN (Bot.)—The male element in flowering plants, usually a fine dust produced by the anthers, which by contact with the stigma effects the fecundation of the seeds. This impregnation is brought about by tubes (pollen tubes) which issue from the pollen grains adhering to the stigma and penetrate through the tissues until they reach the ovary.
POLYGAMUS PLANTS—Plants in which some flowers are unisexual and others hermaphrodite.
POURRIDIE (French)—Disease on the roots of vines caused by different fungi.
PROCREATION—Generation or production of young.
PRODUCTIVITY—The quality or state of being productive.
PROTOPLASM—More or less granular material of vegetable and animal cells, the so-called "physical basis of life," the original cell substance.
PROTUBERANCE—A swelling or prominence, such as the protuberance of a node.
PUBESCENT—Covered with fine short hairs, as the leaves of some vines.
PYCNIDIA, sing. PICNIDIUM (Bot.)—One of certain minute sporiferous organs found in certain fungi.
QUATERNARY TUFA (Geol.)—A soft porous stone formed by deposition from water, usually calcareous, belonging to the quaternary age.
RADICEL (Bot.)—A small branch of a root; a rootlet.
RAPHE or RHAPHE (Bot.)—The continuation of the seed stalk along the side of an anatropous seed, forming a ridge or stem.
REVERSION—To return towards some ancestral type or character; atavism.
RIB (Bot.)—The chief nerve or one of the chief nerves of a leaf; also any longitudinal ridge on a stem, as in V. Berlandieri.
ROUNDED LEAF—Having a curved outline without lobes.
RUDIMENTARY—Very imperfectly developed; in an early stage of development.
RUGOSE, leaf—Having the veinlets sunken and the spaces between them elevated.
SCHIST—Any crystalline rock having a foliated structure.
SCHISTOSE SOILS—Are usually metamorphic clays.
SCION—A piece of branch cut for grafting into another.
SEMI—Prefix signifying half, as in semi-erect, semi-climbing habit, &c.
SEPALS—The leaves or segments of the calyx, or outermost envelope of an ordinary flower. They are usually green.
SHOULDERED GRAPES—Those in which the two ramifications of the base are well developed.
SIEVE TUBES (Bot.)—Also called cribriform tubes. Those having here and there places perforated with many holes.
SILICA—Quartz, silicon dioxide.
SILICEOUS NODULES—See Nodule.
SILICEOUS or SILICIOUS SOILS—Those containing silica or quartz.
SILURIAN (Geol.)—A term applied to the earliest of the Palæozoic strata.
SINUS (Pl. SINI or SINUSES)—A depression between adjoining lobes in a leaf.
SPECIES—An ideal group of individuals which are believed to have descended from common ancestors, which agree in essential characters and are capable of indefinitely continued fertile reproduction through the sexes. A species as thus defined differs from a variety or sub-species only in the greater stability of its characters and in the absence of individuals intermediate between the related groups.
SPORANGIA, sing. SPORANGIUM (Bot.)—A spore case in fungi.
SPORE (Bot.)—One of the minute grains in flowerless plants which are analogous to seeds, as serving to reproduce the species.

STAMENS—The male organs of flowering plants, standing in a circle within the petals. They usually consist of a filament and an anther, being the essential part in which the pollen or fecundating dust is formed.

STERILE—Incapable of reproduction; not able to germinate or bear fruit, as a sterile flower, which bears only stamens.

STIGMA—The apical portion of the pistil in flowering plants.

STOCK, grafting—Part which bears the scion in plants.

STOMATA, sing. STOMA (Bot.)—The line of opening of a spore case.

STRATA, sing. STRATUM (Geol.)—Beds of earth or rock of one kind formed by natural causes, and consisting usually of a series of layers.

STRIATED—Marked with striæ, or fine grooves or lines; showing narrow structural bands of lines.

STYLE (Bot.)—The middle portion of the perfect pistil, which rises like a column from the ovary and supports the stigma at its summit.

SUBEREOUS TISSUE (suberous or suberose)—Having a corky texture.

SUBLIMATE SULPHUR—Lemon-yellow powder, called flower of sulphur, obtained by distillation of raw sulphur.

SUB-MEDIUM—Under the average.

SUB-ORBICULAR—Having an elliptic outline.

SUB-RIBS—Secondary ramifications of the ribs of a leaf.

SUB-VEINS—Same meaning as sub-ribs.

SULPHATE OF COPPER—Compound of sulphuric acid and copper, commonly called bluestone.

SULPHATE OF IRON—Compound of sulphuric acid and iron, commonly called green vitriol.

TENDRIL (Bot.)—A slender leafless portion of a plant, by which it becomes attached to a supporting body, after which the tendril usually contracts by coiling spirally. The tendrils of a vine are metamorphosed grapes.

TERNARY HYBRID—Hybrid resulting from the crossing of three cépages.

TERTIARY—The latest geological epoch, immediately preceding the establishment of the present order of things.

TOMETOSE (Bot.)—Covered with matty woolly hairs.

TOMENTUM (Bot.)—The closely matted hair or downy nap covering the leaves or stems of some plants.

TOOTH—Angular or rounded prominence on the margin or edge of a leaf.

TRILOBATE—Having three lobes.

TRITURATED SULPHUR—Ordinary roll sulphur ground into a powder.

TUBEROSITIES—Knob-like prominences developing on vine roots attacked by phylloxera.

TUFA—See quaternary tufa.

UNDULATING LEAF—Rising and falling like waves.

VARIATION—A varied form of a variety.

VARIETY—Differs from a species in that when propagated by seed it will revert to another form. See species.

ZOOSPORE (Bot.)—A spore provided with one or more slender cilia, by the vibration of which it swims in water.

TABLE OF ILLUSTRATIONS.

	Page
Fig. 1.—Leaf of Wild V. Æstivalis (after M. Mazade)	10
Fig. 2.—Seed of V. Æstivalis	10
Fig. 3.—Leaves of Wild Riparia, young and adult (after M. Mazade)	11
Fig. 4.—Seed of Wild Riparia	12
Fig. 5.—Leaves of V. Rupestris, young and adult (after M. Mazade)	13
Fig. 6.—Seed of V. Rupestris	14
Fig. 7.—Seed of V. Berlandieri	14
Fig. 8.—Leaves of V. Berlandieri (after M. Mazade)	15
Fig. 9.—Leaves of V. Monticola (after M. Mazade)	16
Fig. 10.—Seed of V. Labrusca	17
Fig. 11.—Leaf of Jacquez (after M. Mazade)	18
Fig. 12.—Leaf of Herbemont (after M. Mazade)	21
Fig. 13.—Leaf of Cunningham (after M. Mazade)	23
Fig. 14.—Leaves of Riparia Gloire de Montpellier, young and adult (after M. Mazade)	25
Fig. 15.—Leaf of Riparia Grand Glabre (after M. Mazade)	26
Fig. 16.—Leaves of Solonis, young and adult (after M. Mazade)	27
Fig. 17.—Leaves of Clinton (after M. Mazade)	29
Fig. 18.—Leaves of Taylor (after M. Mazade)	31
Fig. 19.—Leaves of Vialla (after M. Mazade)	33
Fig. 20.—Leaves of Rupestris du Lot (after M. Mazade)	36
Fig. 21.—Leaf of Rupestris Martin (after M. Mazade)	38
Fig. 22.—Bernard's Calcimetre	57
Fig. 23.—V. Vinifera grafted on V. Riparia, showing almost normal difference between size of stock and scion	60
Figs. 24, 25, and 26.—Different stages in the opening of a normal vine flower	65
Fig. 27.—Scissors and Forceps used for the removal of Corolla and Stamens	65
Fig. 28.—Gauze Bag used for protecting flowers from contamination	65
Fig. 29.—Gauze Bag kept open with a special wire	65
Figs. 30 and 31.—Mallet Cuttings	73
Fig. 32.—Cutting, with two-years-old wood removed	73
Fig. 33.—Ordinary Cutting	73
Fig. 34.—One-eye Cutting	73
Fig. 35.—Young Plant of average vigour obtained from a one-eye Cutting of V. Vinifera	74
Fig. 36.—A. Vine Resulting from a Short Cutting. B. Vine Resulting from a Long Cutting	75
Fig. 37.—Ordinary Bent Cutting	75
Fig. 38.—Open Trench for plantation of cuttings	79
Fig. 39.—Sand placed at the bottom to promote root growth	79
Fig. 40.—Cuttings placed along the side of the trench	79
Fig. 41.—Soil (T) rammed above the sand	79
Fig. 42.—Mellowed Soil placed above the rammed soil	79
Fig. 43.—Ridge of Sand (s) Covering the Tops of Cuttings	79
Fig. 44.—Ordinary Layering	82

TABLE OF ILLUSTRATIONS.

	Page
Fig. 45.—Complete Burying of the Mother Plant	84
Fig. 46.—Multiple Layering	85
Fig. 47.—Reversed Layering	85
Fig. 48.—Ordinary Cleft Graft (a) Section of Large Stump cut with a chisel. (b) Section of a Small Stump cut with a pruning bill	92
Fig. 49.—Scion used for ordinary Cleft Grafting	92
Fig. 50.—Cleft Graft with Two Scions	93
Fig. 51.—English Cleft Graft	93
Fig. 52.—Whip-tongue Graft with long bevels (a) on Cutting. (b) On Rootling	94
Fig. 53.—Whip-tongue Graft with Short Bevels	95
Fig. 54.—Champin Graft (a) on Cutting (b) on Rootling	96
Fig. 55.—(a) Saddle Graft. (b) Camuset Graft	96
Fig. 56.—Gaillard Graft	97
Fig. 57.—Dauty Graft	98
Fig. 58.—Cadillac Side Cleft Graft	99
Fig. 59.—Forceps used for side cleft grafting	99
Fig. 60.—Knife used for side cleft grafting	99
Fig. 61.—Cutting Graft	100
Fig. 62.—Salgues Graft	100
Fig. 63.—Salgues Graft, knitted	100
Figs. 64 and 65.—Horvàth Graft, preparation of stock	101
Fig. 66.—Horvàth Method, preparation of scion	102
Fig. 67.—Horvàth Graft, finished	103
Figs. 68 and 69.—Herbaceous Graft, preparation of stock	104
Figs. 70, 71, and 72.—Herbaceous Graft, preparation of scion	104
Figs. 73 and 74.—Herbaceous Graft, completed	105
Fig. 75.—Herbaceous Graft (after H. Gœthe)	105
Fig. 76.—Herbaceous Graft, ab scion	106
Fig. 77.—Same after tying, a scion, b ligature, c stock	106
Fig. 78.—Section of Union (after H. Gœthe)	106
Fig. 79.—Grafting Saw	107
Fig. 80.—Mattock	107
Fig. 81.—Grafting Chisel	107
Fig. 82.—Comy's Gauge	108
Fig. 83.—Comy's Arrangement	108
Fig. 84.—Comy's Grafting Knife	109
Fig. 85.—Champin's Grafting Knife	109
Fig. 86.—Kunde's Grafting Knife	109
Fig. 87.—Section of Blade, sharpened on both sides	110
Fig. 88.—Section of Blade, sharpened on one side only	110
Fig. 89.—Castelbou's Grafting Guide	110
Fig. 90.—Richter's Grafting Guide	111
Fig. 91.—Petit's Grafting Machine, used for whip-tongue grafting	111
Fig. 92.—Inclined Socket of Petit's Machine	112
Fig. 93.—Cork Ligature	114
Fig. 94.—Cleft Graft, earthed up	115
Fig. 95.—Triangular Hoe, used for covering grafts with soil	115
Fig. 96.—A Six-year-old Vine, badly grafted, perishing from phylloxera on scion roots	116
Fig. 97.—Old Grafted Vine, showing almost normal difference between size of stock and scion	116
Fig. 98.—Whip-tongue Grafted Cutting	117
Fig. 99.—Arrangement of Cuttings in Nursery Rows	118
Fig. 100.—Straight-edge for placing cuttings in nursery rows	118

TABLE OF ILLUSTRATIONS.

	Page
Fig. 101.—Nursery of grafted cuttings, showing method of planting and banking	119
Fig. 102.—White Mycelium of *Dematophora Necatrix* developed on dead vine	120
Fig. 103.—*Sclerotinia Fuckeliana*	121
Fig. 104.—Arrangement of vines in lines	125
Fig. 105.—Arrangement of vines in squares	126
Fig. 106.—Arrangement of vines in quincunx	126
Fig. 107.—Planting dibble	127
Fig. 108.—Spur pruning	130
Fig. 109.—Spur after pruning	130
Fig. 110.—Longitudinal section of vine cane showing diaphragms	131
Fig. 111.—Gooseberry Bush pruning	132
Fig. 112.—Gooseberry Bush with long rod bent in a circle	132
Fig. 113.—Spalier with rods and spurs	133
Fig. 114.—Cazenave's cordon with rods and spurs	133
Fig. 115.—Chaintre	134
Fig. 116.—Royat Method	135
Fig. 117.—Young vine pruned after Coste-Floret's modification of the Quarante method	136
Fig. 118.—Quarante method modified by Coste-Floret	137
Fig. 119.—Pruning-bill of Provence	138
Fig. 120.—Secateur of Languedoc	138
Fig. 121.—Arrangement of soil after digging	139
Fig. 122.—Arrangements of experiments for ascertaining the relative value of different forms of manure in a given soil	141
Fig. 123.—Arrangement of soil after first ploughing	147
Fig. 124.—Hook used in the Herault	148
Fig. 125.—Different tools used for digging in the Herault (after M. Marès)	148
Fig. 126.—Vineyard plough used in the Aude	149
Fig. 127.—Vernette's vineyard plough	150
Fig. 128.—Renault-Gouin's vineyard plough (elevation)	150
Fig. 129.—Renault-Gouin's vineyard plough (projection)	151
Fig. 130.—Souchu-Pinet's vineyard plough	151
Fig. 131.—Special Harness for vineyard ploughs	151
Fig. 132.—Old Roman foot plough still in use in Bas-Languedoc for vineyard ploughing	152
Fig. 133.—Renault-Gouin's double-furrow vineyard plough	152
Fig. 134.—Portal's Scarifier	153
Fig. 135.—Hoe used for summer dressing	154
Fig. 136.—Shares of Vine Cultivators	154
Fig. 137.—Pilter-Planet's scarifier	154
Fig. 138.—*Broussin* caused by frost	157
Fig. 139.—Hermaphrodite vine flower	161
Fig. 140.—Male flower	161
Fig. 141.—Sterile flowers	161
Figs. 142 and 143.—Flowers rendered sterile through the transformation of the pistil and stamens into rudimentary leaves	162
Fig. 144.—Sulphur box	166
Fig. 145.—Sulphur bellows	166
Fig. 146.—Pensard's sulphuring machine	166
Fig. 147.—Vermorel's torpido sulphuring machine	167
Fig. 148.—Shoot attacked by *anthracnosis* (after H. Marès)	168
Fig. 149.—Berries attacked by *anthracnosis*	168

TABLE OF ILLUSTRATIONS.

	Page
Fig. 150.—Diagram of vine leaf attacked by *Plasmopara*	172
Fig. 151.—Vermorel's Spray-pump (section)	182
Fig. 152.—Vermorel's Torpido-sulphuring machine	184
Fig. 153.—Woman working a Torpido-sulphuring machine	184
Fig. 154.—Brown mycelium filaments of *Dematophora Necatrix* (after P. Viala)	188
Fig. 155.—Transparent, colourless mycelium filaments of *Dematophora Necatrix* (after P. Viala)	189
Fig. 156.—Fructiferous filaments of *Dematophora Necatrix*	190
Fig. 157.—*Dematophora Necatrix a*, mass of white filaments	191
Fig. 158.—Fructifications of *Dematophora Necatrix*	191
Fig. 159.—Extremity of fructiferous filaments of *Dematophora Necatrix*	192
Fig. 160.—Vine root covered with *Agaricus Melleus* (after Millardet)	192
Fig. 161.—Mycelium of *Agaricus Melleus* var. *Subterranea*	193
Fig. 162.—*Agaricus Melleus*	193
Fig. 163.—Bunch of same at foot of a vine	193
Fig. 164.—*Rœsleria hypogæa* on vine root	193
Fig. 165.—Fructifications of *Rœsleria*	193
Fig. 166.—Section of same (after E. Prillieux)	193
Fig. 167.—Section of vine root attacked by *Rœsleria* (after E. Prillieux)	194
Fig. 169.—Centrifugal pump	198
Fig. 170.—Gwyne's centrifugal pump	199
Fig. 171.—Dellon's Rouet	200
Fig. 172.—Pumping station placed in a fixed position	201
Fig. 173.—Movable pumping station	202
Fig. 174.—1. Solonis. 2. Rupestris du Lot. 3. Riparia Gloire de Montpellier	213
Fig. 175.—English cleft graft. A. Proper angle of cut for large cuttings. B. Proper angle of cut for small cuttings. C, D. Proper size and angle of tongues. E, F. Method of uniting and tying graft	222
Fig. 176.—End-to-end and Champin graft	224
Fig. 177.—Callusing bed	226
Fig. 178.—Method of planting in nursery	228
Fig. 179.—An average graft of Zinfandel on Rupestris du Lot. An average graft of Flame Tokay on Rupestris du Lot	239
Fig. 180.—Effect of Black-knot and of failure to cut the raffia	240
Fig. 181.—Effect of wire-worms on young vine	241
Fig. 182.—Effect of failing to cut off the roots of the scion	243
Fig. 183.—Root growths of resistant stocks compared	245
Plate I.—Rupestris × Berlandieri, No. 219	44
Plate II.—Riparia × Berlandieri, No. 33E	47
Plate III.—Berlandieri × Riparia, No. 420A	49
Plate IV.—Riparia × Cordifolia Rupestris, No. 106-8	49
Plate V.—Non-setting of the grape	162

GENERAL INDEX.

	Page
Translator's Introduction	3
Author's Preface	5

PART I.
AMERICAN VINES

A. Choice of Cépages.

	Page
Chapter I.—Description and Study of Species and Cépages...	9
1st.—Description of Species	9
(a) V. Æstivalis	9
(b) V. Riparia	11
(c) V. Rupestris	12
(d) V. Berlandieri	14
(e) V. Monticola	14
(f) V. Labrusca	17
2nd.—Description and aptitudes of cépages	17
(A) Forms derived from V. Æstivalis...	17
Jacquez	17
Herbemont	20
Black-July	21
Cunningham	22
(B) Forms derived from V. Riparia	24
Riparia Gloire de Montpellier	24
Riparia Grand Glabre	25
Solonis	27
Clinton	28
Taylor	30
Vialla	31
Elvira	32
Noah	34
(C) Forms derived from V. Rupestris	35
Rupestris du Lot	35
Rupestris Martin	37
Rupestris Ganzin	37
Rupestris Mission	39
Rupestris of Fortworth	39
Rupestris Metallica	39
Riparia × Rupestris, 3306 and 3309	40
Riparia × Rupestris, 101-14	40
Rupestris, with Taylor habit	40
(D) Forms derived from V. Berlandieri	40
Berlandieri Rességuier, No. 1	41
Berlandieri Rességuier, No. 2	41
Berlandieri Daignère	41
Berlandieri of Augeac	41
Berlandieri Viala	41
Berlandieri Ecole	42

CHAPTER I.—*continued.*
   2nd.—Description and aptitudes of cépages—*continued.*
      (E) Various Hybrids ... 42
         Aramon × Rupestris Ganzin, No. 1 ... 42
         Aramon × Rupestris Ganzin, No. 2 ... 43
         Gamay Couderc ... 43
         Colombeau × Rupestris, No. 1202 ... 43
         Chasselas × Berlandieri, No. 41B ... 44
         Tisserand ... 45
         Alicante-Bouschet × Rupestris, No. 136 ... 45
         Petit-Bouschet × Riparia, No. 142—Ecole ... 46
         Berlandieri × Ripara, No. 33—Ecole ... 47
         Berlandieri × Riparia, No 34—Ecole ... 47
         Seibel's Hybrid, No. 1 ... 48
         Seibel's Hybrid, No. 2 ... 48
         Franc's Hybrid ... 49
         Alicante × Rupestris, No. 20 of Terrars ... 49

CHAPTER II.—CHOICE OF AMERICAN VINES WITH REGARD TO DESTINATION AND SITUATION ... 50
   Use of Direct-producers or Graft-bearers ... 50
      1st.—Resistance to Phylloxera ... 54
      2nd.—Adaptation to Soil ... 55

B. METHODS OF MULTIPLICATION.

CHAPTER III.—METHODS OF PROPAGATION APPLICABLE TO VINES ... 63
   Propagation by Seeds ... 63
      (A) Choice of Cépages ... 64
         Hybridization ... 65
      (B) Selection of seeds ... 66
      (C) Propagation of seeds ... 66
      (D) Sowing ... 67
      (E) Care ... 67
      (F) Lifting ... 67
      (G) Study of utilization of seedlings ... 67

CHAPTER IV.—PROPAGATION BY CUTTINGS ... 70
   1st.—Choice of cuttings, care to be taken in preservation in transit ... 71
      (A) Selection of cuttings ... 71
      (B) Preservation of cuttings ... 71
         Packing ... 71
         Care to be given on arrival ... 72
   2nd.—Best types of cuttings ... 72
      (A) Different systems ... 72
      (B) Length of cuttings ... 73
   3rd.—Means of promoting the root-growth on cuttings ... 75
      (A) Stratification ... 76
      (B) Soaking ... 76
      (C) Barking ... 76
      (D) Watering, &c. ... 76
   4th.—Most favourable time for planting cuttings ... 77
   5th.—Selection of soils for cuttings ... 78
      (A) Planting out ... 78
      (B) Planting in nurseries ... 78
      (C) Establishment of a nursery, and care to be given to it ... 78

	Page
CHAPTER V.—PROPAGATION BY LAYERS	81
1st.—Principal types of layers	81
(A) Ordinary layering	81
(B) Complete burying of the mother plant	83
(C) Multiple layering	84
(D) Reversed layering	85
2nd. Means of promoting rooting of layers	86
3rd. Best time for layering	86
CHAPTER VI.—GRAFTING	87
(A) Grafting operation	88
1st. Age at which stock can bear grafts	89
2nd. Selection of scions	89
(a) Selection of canes	89
(b) Best time to gather canes	90
(c) Preservation of scions	90
(d) Means of ascertaining the vitality of scions	90
3rd. Best time for grafting	91
4th. Different methods used	91
(a) Ordinary cleft graft	92
(b) English cleft graft	93
(c) Whip-tongue graft	94
(d) Side cleft graft	96
(e) Cutting graft	97
(f) Budding	99
(g) Herbaceous grafts	102
5th. Grafting machines and implements	106
(a) Tools used for cleft grafting	106
(b) Tools used for cleft grafting young plants	107
(c) Tools used for whip-tongue grafting	109
6th. Ligatures and waxing	112
7th. Care to be given to grafts	114
(A) Earthing up and protection of grafts	114
(B) Severing roots from the scion and shoots from the stock	115
8th. Condition of application of grafting	115
(A) Grafting cuttings	115

C. ESTABLISHMENT OF A VINEYARD.

	Page
CHAPTER VII.—PREPARATION OF SOIL—	122
1st. Trenching	122
(A) Depth of trenching	122
(B) Mode of execution of trenching	123
(C) Time most suitable for trenching	123
2nd Manuring	124
CHAPTER VIII.—PLANTATION	125
1st. Arrangement of vines	125
(A) Shape of the plantation	125
(B) Distance apart	125
(C) Marking out the land	125
2nd. Grouping the cépages	127
3rd. Planting	127
4th. Care to be given to new vineyards	128

D. Culture.

	Page
Chapter IX.—Cultural Care	129
1st. Pruning	129
(A) Production of fruit-bearing shoots	129
(B) Establishment of vines	131
(C) Height of vines	134
(D) Pruning methods recently recommended in the South of France	135
(a) Royal method	135
(b) Quarante's method	136
(c) Quarante's method modified by Coste-Floret	137
(E) Time most favorable for pruning	137
(F) Pruning tools	138
2nd. Digging	139
3rd. Manuring or fertilizing	140
(A) Manuring	140
Formulæ for chemical manures	144
(B) Means of improvements	145
(C) Time most favorable for manuring	146
(D) Methods of distributing manures	146
(E) Ploughing	146
1st. First ploughing	146
2nd. Scarifying or second dressing	152
Chapter X.—Accidents, Diseases, Parasites	155
1st. Accidents due to unfavorable conditions	155
(A) Frosts	155
(a) Autumn frosts	155
(b) Winter frosts	155
(c) Spring frosts	156
(B) Hail	159
Hail-guards	160
(C) High winds	160
(D) Non-setting	161
1st. Non-setting, resulting from the abnormal constitution of the flowers	161
2nd. Non-setting, resulting from an excess of vegetation	162
3rd. Non-setting, resulting from unfavorable atmospheric conditions	163
(F) Millerandage	163
(G) Scorching	163
(H) Grape-rot	164
2nd. Diseases due to fungi	165
(A) Oidium	165
(B) Anthracnosis	168
1st. Preventive treatment	168
2nd. Curative treatment	169
(C) Mildew	170
Aspect of mildewed vines	170
Cépages most liable to mildew	171
Mycelium	173
Fructiferous filaments	173
Summer spore (conidia)	174
Winter spores (ovæ)	174

GENERAL INDEX.

Page

Chapter X.—*continued.*

  2nd.—Diseases due to fungi—Mildew—*continued.*

Most favorable conditions for the development of mildew	175
Means recommended to combat mildew	177
(a) Use of cépages resisting mildew	177
(b) Use of copper salts	177
(a) Liquid matters	178
1st.—Bordeaux mixture	178
2nd.—Blue water	179
3rd.—Ammonia solution of copper	179
4th.—Mixture of dauphinée	180
5th.—Verdet gris	181
6th.—Lucrate of copper	181
Mode of application of cupric compounds	181
(b) Pulverized solid matters	183
1st.—Mixture of sulphur and sulphate of copper	183
2nd.—Sulpho-steatite of copper	183
3rd.—Skawinski powders	183
(D) Black-rot	185
Means of combating the disease	186
(E) Coniothyrium diplodiella or white-rot	187
(F) Pourridié	189
3rd.—Maladies	194
Chlorosis	194

PART II.

SUBMERSION OF VINEYARDS.

Chapter I.—Conditions Necessary to the Success of Submersion.

1st.—Water	196
(A) Quantity of water	196
(B) Quality of water	196
2nd.—Soil	197
(A) Permeability	197
(B) The contour of the land	197
3rd.—Adaptation of cépages to submersion	197

Chapter II.—Establishment of Submersion Plant.

1st.—Sources of water supply	198
(A) Channels	198
(B) Raising water by mechanical means	198
(C) Stopping drainage pipes	200
2nd.—Formation of submersion basins, or bed-work system	200
(A) Shape of beds	200
(B) Size of beds	203
(C) Banks	203

Chapter III.

	Page
1st.—Most favorable time for submerging vineyards	205
2nd.—Duration of submersion	205
(A) Influence of climate	205
(B) Influence of soil	206
(C) Influence of season	206
3rd.—Age at which vines can be submerged	206
4th.—Periodicity of submersion	207

Chapter IV.—Planting and Cultivation.

1st.—Planting	208
2nd.—Cultivation	208
(A) Pruning	208
(B) Manures	208
(C) Ploughing	209

PART III.

PLANTING IN SAND.

Chapter I.—Selection of Soil and Cépages.—Planting.—Culture.

1st.—Selection of soil	210
(A) Indemnity	210
(B) Conditions favorable to the success of vines	211
2nd.—Selection of cépages	211
3rd.—Planting	211
(A) Preparation of soil	211
(B) Planting in sand	212
4th—Cultural care	212
(A) Manuring	212
(B) Summer Ploughing	212

APPENDIX.

Bench-Grafting Resistant Vines, by F. T. Bioletti and A. M. dal Piaz.—Bulletin No. 127, University of California, 1900	213
The work of the experiment station	215
Adaptability of various varieties of vinifera to various resistant stocks	217
Grafting	220
Preparation of cuttings for grafting	220
Methods of grafting	221
English-cleft or whip graft	222
Champin graft	223
Binding grafts	225
Methods of aiding callusing	225
1st—Callusing in sand	226
2nd—Callusing in straw or moss	226

Bench-Grafting Resistant Vines—*continued.*	Page
Planting grafts in the nursery	227
Planting immediately after grafting	227
Planting the grafts after previous callusing	228
Removal of scion roots and suckers from the stock	229
Condition when scion and suckers were cut	230
Condition when raffia was cut	232
Condition when grafts were removed from nursery	232
The experiment with two-eye and one-eye scions	237
The difference between previously callusing the grafts	237
The influence of scions of different varieties	238
The effects of failing to cut the raffia	240
The effects of neglecting to cut the roots	242
Comparative experiments in rooting cuttings of resistant stocks	
Rupestris du Lot	242
Riparia Gloire de Montpellier	242
Solonis	244
Summary	247
Number of vine seeds contained in one pound	248
Summary of the life history of phylloxera	249
Glossary of the principal scientific terms used in the present volume	252
Table of Illustrations	259
General Index	263

By Authority: Robt. S. Brain, Government Printer, Melbourne.

PUBLICATIONS

RELATING TO

VITICULTURE AND WINE-MAKING.

BY

RAYMOND DUBOIS

AND

W. PERCY WILKINSON.

Wine-making in Hot Climates. By L. Roos. 273 pp., 61 illustrations, 5 plates. 1900. Cloth-bound, 2s.

First Steps in Ampelography. By Marcel Mazade. 95 pp., 43 illustrations. 1900. Cloth-bound, 1s.

Trenching and Sub-soiling for American Vines. 171 pp., 110 illustrations, 10 plates. 1901. Cloth-bound, 2s.

New methods of Grafting and Budding as applied to Reconstitution with American Vines. 72 pp., 89 illustrations. 1901. Cloth-bound, 1s.

American Vines: Their Adaptation, Culture, Grafting, and Propagation. By P. Viala and L. Ravaz. 297 pp., 150 illustrations, 10 coloured plates. 1901. Cloth-bound, 3s. 6d.

Studies on Wine-sterilizing Machines. By U. Gayon. 103 pp., 45 illustrations, 2 coloured plates. Cloth-bound, 2s.

PLATE

RUPESTRIS × BERLANDIERI No. 219.

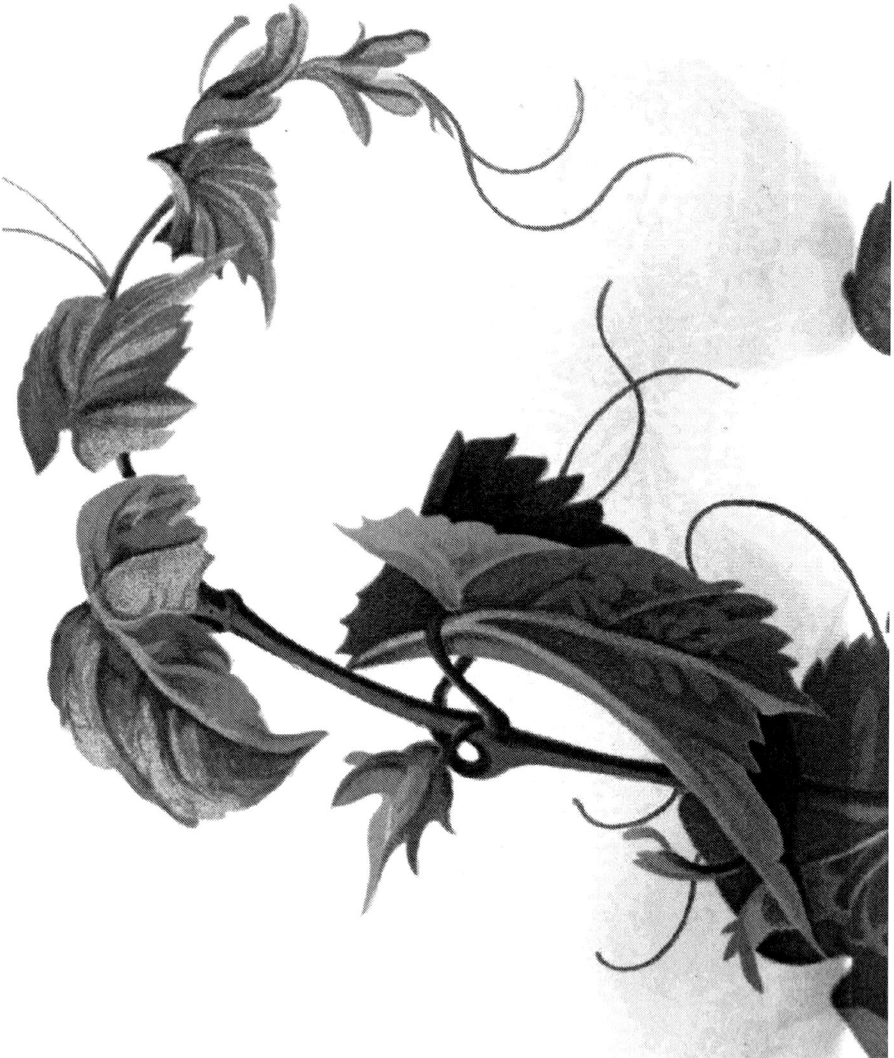

RIPARIA x BERLANDIERI No. 33 E.

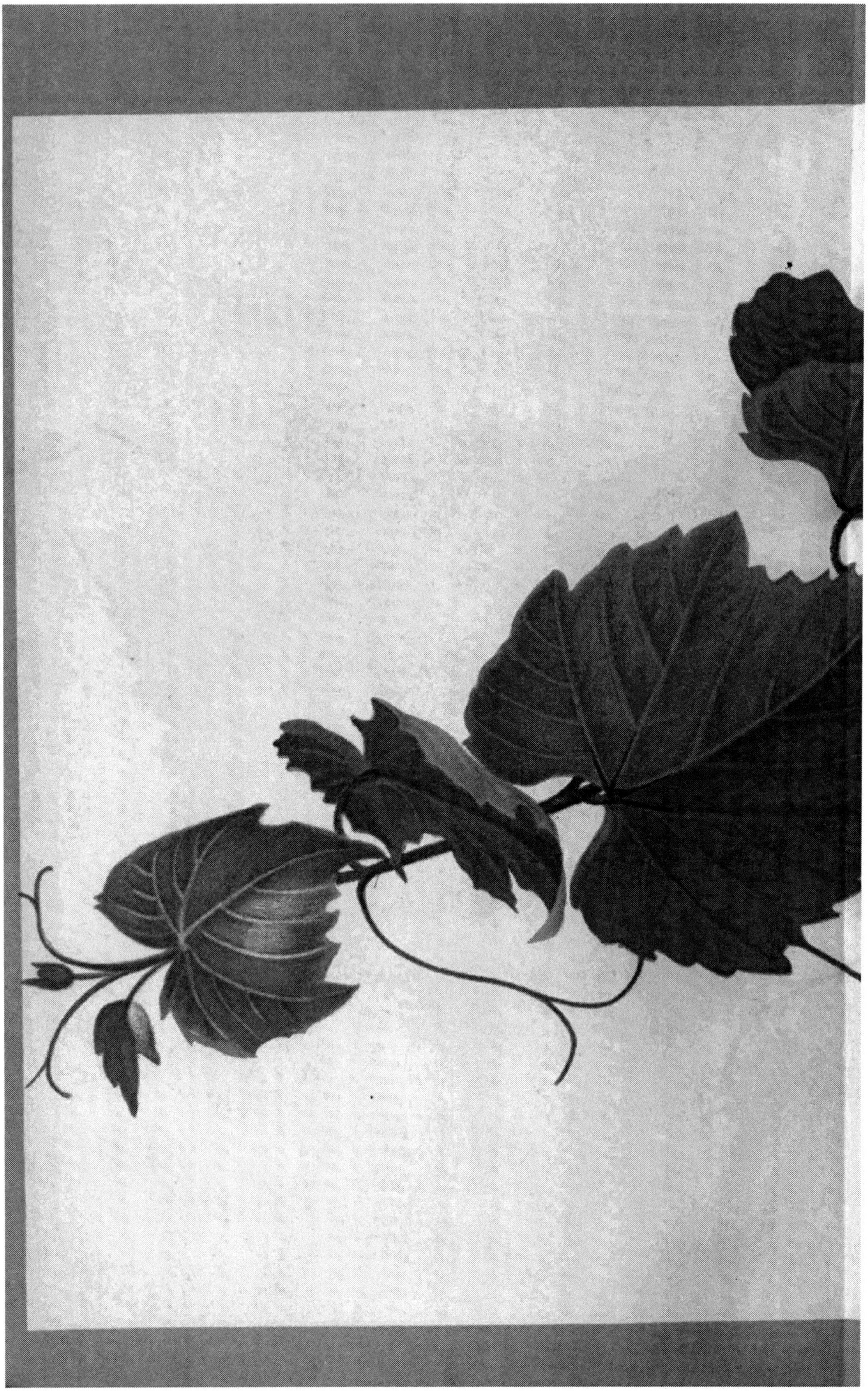

BERLANDIERI × RIPARIA No. 420-A

PLATE IV.

RIPARIA x CORDIFOLIA-RUPESTRIS No 106.8

NON-SETTING OF THE GRAPES.

THIS BOOK IS DUE ON THE LAST DATE STAMPED BELOW

AN INITIAL FINE OF 25 CENTS WILL BE ASSESSED FOR FAILURE TO RETURN THIS BOOK ON THE DATE DUE. THE PENALTY WILL INCREASE TO 50 CENTS ON THE FOURTH DAY AND TO $1.00 ON THE SEVENTH DAY OVERDUE.

JUL 14 1933

FEB 10 1941 M

REC'D LD
FEB 15 '65 -4 PM

LD 21–50m-1,'83

Lightning Source UK Ltd.
Milton Keynes UK
173506UK00004B/24/P